State Child Care

of related interest

Child Welfare Services
Developments in Law,
Policy, Practice and Research
Edited by Malcolm Hill and Jane Aldgate
ISBN 1 85302 316 7 pb

Children's Homes Revisited
David Berridge and Isabelle Brodie
ISBN 1 85302 565 8 pb

Young People Leaving Care
Life After the Children Act 1989
Bob Broad
ISBN 1 85302 412 0 pb

**Understanding and Supporting Children
with Emotional and Behavioural Difficulties**
Edited by Paul Cooper
ISBN 1 85302 662 2 pb
ISBN 1 85302 665 4 hb

Social Work with Children and Families
Getting into Practice
Ian Butler and Gwenda Roberts
ISBN 1 85302 365 5 pb

Lesbian and Gay Fostering and Adoption
Extraordinary Yet Ordinary
Edited by Stephen Hicks and Janet McDermott
ISBN 1 85302 600 X pb

Effective Ways of Working with Children and their Families
Edited by Malcolm Hill
ISBN 1 85302 619 0 pb

Homeless Children
Problems and Needs
Edited by Panos Vostanis and Stuart Cumella
ISBN 1 85302 595 X pb

Traveller Children
A Voice for Themselves
Cathy Kiddle
ISBN 1 85302 684 0 pb

State Child Care

Looking after Children?

*Carol Hayden, Jim Goddard, Sarah Gorin
and Niki Van Der Spek*

Jessica Kingsley Publishers
London and Philadelphia

The right of Carol Hayden, Jim Goddard, Sarah Gorin and Niki Van Der Spek to be identified as authors of this work has been asserted by them in accordance with the Copyright, Designs and Patents Act 1988.

First published in the United Kingdom in 1999 by
Jessica Kingsley Publishers Ltd,
116 Pentonville Road, London
N1 9JB, England
and
325 Chestnut Street,
Philadelphia, PA 19106, USA.

www.jkp.com

Library of Congress Cataloging in Publication Data
A CIP catalog record for this book is available from the Library of Congress

British Library Catalogue in Publication Data
A CIP catalogue record for this book is available from the British Library

ISBN 1 85302 670 0 pb

Printed and Bound in Great Britain by
Athenaeum Press, Gateshead, Tyne and Wear

Contents

ACRONYMS AND ABBREVIATIONS 7

INTRODUCTION 9

1 A Brief History of State Child Care 15
Childhood and child care before 1834 15
State child care after the 1834 Poor Law Amendment Act 17
Children in the welfare state: 1945–1989 21
Responding to Colwell: the 1975 Children Act 25
The 1989 Children Act 27
Enduring themes in child welfare 29

2 Contemporary Issues and Concerns 31
Themes and issues in the 1989 Children Act 31
Child care: themes and issues 35

3 Coming Into Care – Family Placement
and Residential Care 51
Choice and availability of placements 54
Multiple placements and placement breakdown 56
Research findings 58
Discussion 69
Conclusions and implications 72

4 Developments in Foster Care 73
Professionalising foster care 75
Life inside foster families 77
Research findings 78
Discussion 87
Conclusions and implications 90

5 Managing the Behaviour of Looked After Children 91
Emotional and behavioural difficulties 93
Research findings 96

Discussion 103
Conclusions and implications 107

6 The Education of Looked After Children 111
Attendance and exclusion 114
Expectations and achievement 116
Education and the looked after experience 118
Post-sixteen education 119
Research findings 119
Discussion 129
Conclusions and implications 131

7 Leaving Care 133
Inter-agency cooperation and coordination 135
Youth transitions 136
Research findings 137
Discussion 152
Conclusions and implications 153

8 Training, Support and Service Quality 155
Training 157
Support 158
Service quality 160
Research findings 162
Discussion 171
Conclusions and implications 173

9 Involving Young People in Decision-Making 175
Research findings 177
Discussion 186
Conclusions and implications 187

10 Conclusion 191
Looking after children? 192
Moving forward? New Labour, social policy and
looked after children 204
Wider changes in state child care 209

APPENDIX: OUTLINES OF THE FOUR RESEARCH PROJECTS 213
REFERENCES 223
SUBJECT INDEX 234
AUTHOR INDEX 238

Acronyms and abbreviations

ABAA	Association of British Adoption Agencies
ABH	Actual Bodily Harm
ADHD	Attention Deficit Hyperactivity Disorder
ADSS	Association of Directors of Social Services
BAAF	British Agencies for Adoption and Fostering
BASW	British Association of Social Workers
CCETSW	Central Council For the Education and Training of Social Workers
CHE	Community Home with Education
CQSW	Certificate of Qualification in Social Work
CSO	Central Statistical Office
CSS	Certificate in Social Services
DfE	Department for Education
DfEE	Department for Education and Employment
DHSS	Department of Health and Social Security
DipSW	Diploma in Social Work
DoH	Department of Health
DSS	Department of Social Security
EBD	Emotional and Behavioural Difficulties
EOTAS	Education Other Than At School
FE	Further Education
FLSW	Family Link Social Worker
FPSW	Family Placement Social Worker
GCSE	General Certificate of Secondary Education
GNVQ	General National Vocational Qualification
HAS	Health Advisory Service
HHTS	Home and Hospital Teaching Service
LBCH	Locally Based Children's Home
LEC	Local Enterprise Company
MLD	Moderate Learning Difficulties
NAYPIC	National Association of Young People In Care
NCB	National Children's Bureau
NFCA	National Foster Care Association
NFER	National Foundation for Educational Research
NHS	National Health Service
NSPCC	National Society for the Prevention of Cruelty to Children

NVQ	National Vocational Qualification
OFSTED	Office for Standards in Education
PRU	Pupil Referral Unit
RCCI	Residential Child Care Initiative
SLD	Severe Learning Difficulties
SRU	Social Research Unit
SSD	Social Service Department
SSI	Social Services Inspectorate
SSRIU	Social Services Research and Information Unit
SVQ	Scottish Vocational Qualification
TEC	Training and Enterprise Council
TQM	Total Quality Management

Introduction

At the time of writing, state child care in England and Wales is undergoing one of its regular periods of significant change. It is a good time to be looking both backward and forward in this field. Looking backward, we can come to terms with developments in practice during the past decade. Looking forward, we can examine how the lessons of past practice can best be applied in the context of the changes that are currently taking place.

There are several factors that have prompted this period of change, but three are especially significant. The first of these is the election in May 1997 of a Labour government. Having been out of office for eighteen years, 'New' Labour has been highly active in demonstrating its reformist credentials in certain areas of state activity (even while accepting the broad economic philosophy and, initially, spending priorities of the previous Conservative administration). While this radicalism has been most evident in the field of constitutional reform, there are echoes of it in the field of state child care. One reason for this is the crucial location of looked after young people – and especially of care leavers – within Labour's discourse on 'social exclusion'. The second factor prompting this period of reform is that the spate of child care system abuse cases that were emerging as the 1989 Children Act was being implemented (see Kirkwood 1993; Levy and Kahan 1991) proved to be merely the first wave of a series of such cases. While these have mainly occurred within residential care, the potential for abuse to occur within foster care has been increasingly recognised and has prompted continued official concern regarding the general quality of child care services (SSI 1998b; Utting 1997). The third major reason for reform is more arbitrary and relates to a confluence of circumstances that includes those above. The field of child care appears to generate major revisiting (legislative or otherwise) every five to ten years. The 1989 Act has suffered from the same inevitable fate as its predecessors: over time, its virtues have become accepted or taken for granted while its defects have become more apparent. Continued poor performance in such fields as education and leaving care in particular (DoH 1998b, p.41; SSI 1997) have fuelled a developing sense that the policies stemming from the Children Act are in need of revision, up-dating and development. In the last few years, official sources and academic research have increasingly pointed to shortcomings and defects in the existing policy framework.

In the context of these developments, this book seeks to assess the current state of provision for looked after children in England and Wales. (A child is described as 'looked after' when s/he is in local authority care or is being provided with accommodation by the local authority (Children Act 1989, s. 22.1). This definition therefore includes those with a 'care order' living at home, fostered or in residential care, or remanded or detained. The broadness of this definition, and the consequent variety of the experiences that it encompasses, must be borne in mind, despite the fact that in this analysis we focus on the experiences of those in foster and residential care.)

The book assesses provision partly by drawing together the findings of four different but complementary research projects on the conduct of state child care. Three of the projects were commissioned or part-funded by social services departments and one project was funded by a Training and Enterprise Council (TEC). The studies examine the services provided by five local authorities in England (three County Councils and two unitary authorities). The book therefore presents a research-based overview of the state child care system in practice after the long settling-in period that followed the introduction in late 1991 of the main provisions of the 1989 Children Act. It examines in depth some of the main forms and issues of modern state child care. These include foster care, residential care, education in care and policy and practice with regard to leaving care. It incorporates the views of a wide range of actors in this field, including care managers, residential workers, foster carers, the children of foster carers, looked after children and care leavers. The book finishes by outlining and reviewing the current policy reform agenda – particularly the government's Quality Protects initiative (DoH 1998a; 1998b) and the *Modernising Social Services* White Paper (DoH 1998d) – in the light of both our own research findings and those of others. More specific details of the findings from the research projects mentioned above are to be found within Chapters 3 to 9 of the book. The methodology and content of each study is also summarised in the Appendix. However, we provide a brief summary of the research projects here in order that readers can gain some sense of the issues and areas that we focus on in subsequent chapters.

The study by Carol Hayden examined the current context of children's residential care in respect of issues of care and control in three local authorities. The fieldwork for the research was carried out in 1996–1997. In particular, the research focused on reports of violent and aggressive incidents and the use of physical restraint in over thirty residential units in those authorities. However, it also moved on from these events to examine how individuals came to be looked after and the life events which may have contributed to their behaviour. It investigates staff experiences of working in the residential environment as well as user views in a small number of case studies. Case studies of individuals who experienced particularly problematic periods whilst in residential care are used to illustrate the complexity of needs which some children bring to the residential environment.

The study by Dee Lynes and Jim Goddard was an analysis of the user view of child care services provided by one county local authority, conducted while the authors were active in running a local in-care group. It is based on the detailed questionnaire responses of 186 young people with substantial experience of being looked after in either foster or residential care: 121 young people, aged between ten and eighteen years, who answered a detailed questionnaire on their lives in care; and 65 young people who had left care between 1988 and 1994 and who responded to a questionnaire about their leaving care experiences. The two questionnaires were distributed and returned during the summer of 1994.

The study by Sarah Gorin was of family placement in two unitary authorities and one county authority, with fieldwork undertaken during 1996–1998. The research was conducted in two stages, the first being a postal questionnaire returned by 376 foster carers. The questionnaire examined a broad range of issues. These issues included: the recruitment of carers; the motivation to foster; and the payment, support and training of carers. The questionnaire also sought information on the behaviour patterns of fostered children and the challenges that these can sometimes present to carers. A short questionnaire was also sent to the birth children of those who foster (over 250 responses) in order to investigate their thoughts and feelings with regard to having a foster child in their home. The second stage of the research used a case study approach to examine in more depth how a random sample of ten placements were made and to follow through what happened in these placements over a six month follow-up period. This provided an opportunity to study the dynamics of a small number of foster families and raised issues concerning the use of specialist fostering schemes and the future of the fostering system.

The study by Niki Van Der Spek examined the post-sixteen educational participation and performance of looked after children. It was conducted over two school years (September 1995 to August 1997) and examined the post-compulsory education and training of care leavers in one county. Taking into account the well-known disadvantages attendant upon membership of such a group, it followed the experiences of a cohort of 143 care leavers by means of a range of research methods. These methods included the analysis of policy documents, surveys of care managers and social work staff and interviews with young people while they were in the process of managing the transition from care.

However, in spite of the wide range of the above studies, there are some omissions with regard to young people looked after by the state. These are necessitated by both the length of this book and by the priorities of the authors' research. We do not, for example, consider in any depth the special issues and provision relating to young people with learning or physical disabilities. Nor do we examine the special provisions made for juvenile offenders in state child care facilities outside of local authority children's homes. Provision made by the voluntary sector, important though it is, raises some separate issues that are also not specifically addressed here. Specialist therapeutic provision is not referred to in any depth in our studies. That said, what we do have to say relates to the majority of looked after young people in England and Wales.

Broadly speaking, the book examines state child care in three separate but related ways. First, it outlines the historical and policy context within which we locate our analysis. Second, it considers what research evidence (both our own and that of others) tells us about some significant features of state child care. Finally, it outlines some of the things that need to be done to construct a modern, responsive and high-quality child care system and relates this to the contemporary policy agenda. What follows is a more detailed summary of our approach.

The aim of the opening two chapters is, first, to provide a historical context for our empirical analysis and, second, to provide a policy context for the direction of that analysis. In Chapter 1 we follow a brief and thematic account of the historical development of state child care provision before 1945 with a more detailed account of the period since 1945. Key policy developments are analysed in the context of the changing practices and philosophies of this latter period, including the development of a children's rights perspective as an important theme and the often crisis-driven nature of policy change. The chapter ends by considering the background to, and the guiding principles of, the 1989 Children Act. The second chapter focuses on the general themes and issues that have been debated within the child care field since the implementation of the main provisions of the 1989 Act. As well as seeking to provide an up-to-date summary of debates in this field, it sets out a framework by which later chapters in the book seek to test out the level of achievement of the 1989 Act and establish an agenda for future development.

The subsequent seven chapters (Chapters 3–9) provide an account of the practice of state child care that draws on all four of the research projects mentioned earlier. Chapter 3 discusses the availability of placements and the issue of choice in relation to different forms of care. It focuses on the ability or otherwise of local authorities to match children's needs to the foster and residential placements available. It also raises concerns about multiple placements and placement breakdown. Chapter 4 focuses exclusively on foster care, the main form of substitute care in England and Wales. As well as exploring some of the everyday realities of life within foster families, the chapter examines the increasing professionalisation of the fostering service, a development implicitly encouraged by the 1989 Act. The chapter brings to the debate concerning professionalisation a consideration of the expectations and abilities of foster carers and the differing perspectives of foster carers, their families and foster children. Chapter 5 explores the issues raised by the need to balance care and control within both residential and foster care settings. It considers this particularly in relation to those children who present emotional or behavioural difficulties or mental health problems. Chapter 6 considers an issue of growing concern in both the literature on child care and at an official, governmental level: that of the education of looked after children. It considers the experience of school whilst being looked after, expectations and achievements, school exclusion and post-sixteen education. Chapter 7 (written jointly with Dee Lynes) examines the experience of leaving care and reconsiders current debates in the leaving care field. One particular point of emphasis will be the 1989 Children Act powers, specifically Section 24 powers, with regard to those leaving care. Chapter 8 considers the levels of support and training provided for both residential and foster carers in the context of quality debates in child care services. It also examines the meaning of 'quality' through considering young people's perceptions of what constitutes 'good' and 'bad' care from their carers and social workers. Chapter 9 (written jointly with Dee Lynes) assesses the reality of involvement by young people in the processes that affect them while they are looked after. It does so in light of the policy emphasis put on this by the 1989 Act and in subsequent regulations and guidance. It considers such involvement through examining basic decision-making, consultations and the review process.

Finally, Chapter 10 seeks to build upon the general understanding of good practice and recommended future policy in this field. It brings together the lessons that can be drawn from the evidence provided in previous chapters. Much of the chapter also looks to the future, examining the current Labour government's policy agenda and proposals in this field, particularly the Quality Protects initiative. It aims to contribute constructively to contemporary discussions on the best way forward for improving practice with regard to looked after children and young people.

To finish these introductory comments, a word about terminology. The allegedly stigmatising and overly paternalistic concept of being 'in care' was officially replaced with the 1989 Act (Hill and Tisdall 1997, p.219). This introduced the concept of being 'looked after', which implied a more partnership-based, fluid form of service provision. However, at an informal level language naturally changes less swiftly. Researchers working with those looked after, or involved in promoting the views of those looked after, recognise this and either continued to use a combination of terms, such as Fletcher's 'looked after in care' (Fletcher 1993) or acknowledged that there is little effective substitute for the concept of being 'in care' for the purpose of developing user groups and user initiatives (First Key 1997). Accordingly, our use of the term varies during the chapters which follow. In discussions where the views of young people in the care system are prominent, it is often more natural to use their own terminology of being 'in care' than to impose a professional lexicon. However, on most other occasions the official, professional and academic language of being 'looked after' predominates.

Acknowledgement

Thanks are due to Nick Frost of the School of Continuing Education at the University of Leeds for his helpful comments on most of the manuscript. Any remaining errors or defects in the text remain, of course, the sole responsibility of the authors.

CHAPTER I

A Brief History of State Child Care

The history of childhood is intimately connected to the history of social policy. The development of child welfare law, in particular, is in part a reflection of changing social attitudes toward childhood through history. Accordingly, this chapter is concerned to present the broader welfare policy canvas upon which developments in child care policy take place. While the latter cannot be simply read off against the former, tracing the development of child care services requires an appreciation of the concurrent changes taking place in the wider field of welfare provision.

State involvement in the care of children in England and Wales has a rich and varied history that is centuries old. Knowledge of this history is essential to a balanced understanding of current practice. Accordingly, this first chapter begins by considering the development of state child care policy prior to the 1834 Poor Law. It then moves on to examine the period between 1834 and the end of the second world war and ends its historical account by considering the post-war period up to the 1989 Children Act. Finally, key relevant themes and issues are highlighted for consideration in later chapters.

Childhood and child care before 1834

Aries (1962) suggests that we need to adopt fundamentally different conceptual lenses when viewing the topic of childhood historically. He denies the existence of a separate social space that can be defined as 'childhood' prior to the medieval period and locates the development of the concept in the sixteenth and seventeenth centuries among the professional and property-owning classes. Although Aries' blanket denial of the concept of 'childhood' in the earlier period has been criticised as too sweeping (Brandon, Schofield and Trinder 1998, p.11), it is at least clear that whatever conceptions of childhood did exist were different from modern conceptions in some important respects. The increased importance of knowledge, associated with the Reformation and the Enlightenment, is important here since it extended the time required for education, at least among the children of more affluent classes. Simplifying greatly, it is nonetheless true to say that this requirement for education – in its widest sense – was gradually filtered down to middle and working class children by increasing economic development and, especially, by the industrial revolution.

Frost and Stein (citing Heywood 1978) add to Aries' more general analysis the claim that orphaned and illegitimate children were well served by the ethos of feudal society. This form of society provided, within a system of social obligation much wider than that of the nuclear family, mechanisms for the placement and boarding of such children even while still evoking moral taboos and stigma with regard to their origins (Frost and Stein 1989).

For our purposes, social policy for children begins, effectively, in the sixteenth century with this 'boarding out' system of apprenticing Poor Law children (usually orphans or deserted children) to whoever would take them. The Elizabethan Poor Law Act of 1601 (largely re-enacting a similar measure of 1597) was a general measure, attempting to deal with various forms of rural poverty (Jones 1994, p.2). Included within its remit for helping the old and the infirm, the sick and the unemployed, were its provisions relating to children. The emphasis on putting orphans (and also those children whose parents were perceived as being unable to maintain them) to work reflected a wider concern with increasing problems of vagrancy and destitution in Elizabethan society. It also reflected a developing rationale regarding the social benefits of morally educating the children of the poor (Pinchbeck and Hewitt 1969, pp.91–105).

Being geared towards the needs of a predominantly rural society at a time when transport and communication links were poor, there was a certain logicality to the implementation of the Act being left to local parishes. It became rather less logical, however, as society became more industrialised and the inevitable inconsistencies produced by local discretion became more apparent and problematic. A further difficulty was its positive disincentive to labour mobility, with relief only being available from one's own locality while the chance of work was often far away in the booming towns of the industrial north.

State child care after the 1834 Poor Law Amendment Act

Hendrick (1994), adopting a similar position to that of Aries, claims that there was no universal or accepted concept of childhood in England in 1800. Class and regional differences, among others, militated against the development of such a shared understanding. However, the nineteenth century was nothing if not a century of change. Perceptions of childhood – indeed, that there could be a definable sense of 'childhood' – had altered radically by 1914. The influences of Romanticism, evangelical Christianity, industrialisation and the growth of the professional middle classes throughout the nineteenth century were central to explaining this change. The change was given legislative embodiment in the 1908 Children Act. Later in the twentieth century, the influence of psychoanalysis and of educational and clinical psychology were to alter perceptions still further. Sharing Hendrick's analysis, Davin (1990) further points out that obvious class differences in perceptions of appropriate childhood behaviour (as exhibited in the views of reformers such as Lord Shaftesbury, Henry Mayhew and Mary Carpenter) lead one to question the extent to which Victorian philanthropy was about compassion rather than social control. This insight that mixed motives of fear, necessity and altruism all play their part in child care reform is, of course, as valid to contemporary policy analysis as it is to the Victorian period. The child care system can be viewed throughout its history as exhibiting such tensions between care and control, with some arguing for the critical role of class and other social divisions for explaining child care policy (see Frost, Mills and Stein 1999, pp.32–34).

Mixed motives were also a feature of the 1834 Poor Law Amendment Act. This led to a partial shift to 'indoor' industrial training in buildings separate from workhouses, but was not dissimilar in its wider social objectives to the 1601 legislation. However, as Jones (1994) notes, the original utilitarian logic of Bentham and of Edwin Chadwick did not demand the cruelties inflicted by the Poor Law Commissioners in the name of the principle of 'less eligibility'. Ensuring that those in the workhouse were in a condition worse than those outside did not necessitate the separation of children over the age of seven from their mothers, nor the limitation of education to such children on grounds of cost. That said, in some cases the 1834 legislation represented an improvement on the often arbitrary system of parish provision that had preceded it. Also, there were those connected with the Poor Law Commission – such as Assistant Commissioner Kay – who argued quite openly for greater eligibility in the field of education (rather than less), and at least equal eligibility, with regard to maintenance, for children in workhouses (Pinchbeck and Hewitt 1973, pp.499–505).

The Victorian era as a whole was one of increasing activism in the field of child welfare, as in so many other areas of social reform. Just as the 1834 Act was the springboard for much of the wider discontent that eventually fed into Chartism (Jones 1994, pp.20–24) so, in child welfare, social protest was growing. Key figures such as Shaftesbury, the Tory social reformer, helped to mobilise a frequently evangelical Christian social conscience in the direction of social reform. By the 1870s, a concept of the 'child' was indeed emerging and the introduction of compulsory schooling aided the development of a sense of universal childhood experience. Not surprisingly, given the above context, this emerging definition was based on 'middle-class patriarchal and domestic ideals' (Hendrick 1994, p.37).

In some areas, however, Victorian reforming zeal was manifest in a rigorous and not noticeably child-centred approach. Large, closed institutions were popular as a way of seeking to discipline the poor in general. Foucault (1979) reminds us that this process, in the field of penal matters, was related to a shift from concern with external discipline (public punishment of the body as a deterrent and an example) to internal discipline (a focus on changing the mental states of offenders). We should see the shift from 'outdoor' to 'indoor' relief of the poor in the same light. Industrial Schools, set up under the Industrial Schools Act of 1861, were one aspect of this. These schools sought to equip young people for the world of work and so ensure that they avoided future pauperism. Young people could be sent to Industrial Schools for begging, wandering or being in the company of known thieves.

However, large institutions for children came into disrepute later in the century for their non-family atmosphere and inherent rigidities. While institutional care continued to apply to the majority in public care, the Education Act of 1870 encouraged a shift back towards a boarding-out approach of one kind or another. Nonetheless, Hendrick (1994) estimates that between 1900 and 1914, 70,000–80,000 children were in various forms of residential care under the Poor Law, while only about 10,000 were boarded out (p.76).

Another of the less salubrious aspects of Victorian reform was the use of emigration to give children a 'fresh start'. Children had been sent to the colonies since the early seventeenth century (Pinchbeck and Hewitt 1969, pp.105–107). However, it began on a large scale in the 1860s and was in part evangelical in motivation. Dr Barnardo's were particularly active in this field and children were sent to Canada, South Africa, Australia and New Zealand. Redding (1989) estimates that between 1870 and 1967 at least 150,000 children were dispatched in this way. As well as the desire to provide children with salvation (from the corrupting effects of urban life), other motives were involved, such as finance (the one-off cost of emigration compared with the year-on-year cost of support) and empire building (repopulation of the colonies with Anglo-Saxon stock) (Hendrick 1994; Redding 1989).

Child protection: state intervention in the private world of the family

The nineteenth century also saw a growing concern not just with the problems of orphaned or abandoned children but also with the problem of child abuse. Ironically, the liberal ideology which discouraged intervention by the state in 'private' matters provided very strong justification for interference in the hitherto private world of the family. J.S. Mill, the great apostle of liberalism, expresses this most forcefully in his unequivocal endorsement of state protection (whether by police or social workers) of both women and children from the abuse of power and the neglect of duty (such as to educate offspring) within families:

> It is in the case of children that misapplied notions of liberty are a real obstacle to the fulfilment by the State of its duties. One would almost think that a man's children were supposed to be literally, and not metaphorically, a part of himself, so jealous is opinion of the smallest interference of law with his absolute and exclusive control over them; more jealous than of almost any interference with his own freedom of action: so much less do the generality of mankind value liberty than power. (Mill 1972, pp.159–160)

In essence, the core justification of state powers to intervene in family child care lies in this recognition of children as individuals with interests separate from those of their parents.

Child abuse was highlighted as a specific issue, in the latter part of the nineteenth century, by the medical profession. The British Medical Association was particularly active in the growing criticism of the practice of 'baby farming' (the permanent farming out to others, for a fee or a one-off payment, of new-born children). Charles Dickens had given a wonderfully ironic comment on the practice, through the character of 'Mrs Mann', as early as 1838 (reprinted 1992, pp.22–26). Revelations of the barbarities associated with this often callous form of 'substitute care' led to the Infant Life Protection Acts of 1872 and 1897. Change was prompted, initially, by one of those periodic scandals that pepper the history of child care legislation. In this instance it was the 'Waters case' of 1872, in which the bodies of sixteen dead babies were found in Brixton, formerly in the care of a local 'baby farmer' (Owen 1989, pp.369–370). A further scandal in 1896 prompted a strengthening amendment the following year.

Voluntary and state activism

Other indications of the growing public concern with child welfare during the Victorian period included the foundation of various voluntary child care organisations, such as Dr Barnardo's (1870), National Children's Home (1869), the Church of England Waifs and Strays Society (1881), the Catholic Children's Society (1887) and the NSPCC (1884). Examining the histories of these societies, however, suggests an element of competition to 'protect the faith' as much as of philanthropy. Interest in the subject was also reflected in the passage of the Prevention of Cruelty to Children Act of 1889 (strength- ened in 1904) and the Children Act of 1908. This latter Act was a significant consolidating measure and introduced a landmark development in the field of juvenile justice in the creation of the juvenile court, with the focus on treat- ment and rehabilitation rather than punishment. The Act can be regarded as significant in other respects too, such as in the abolition of imprisonment for children and young people. As a half-way house, before this issue was con- clusively dealt with by the Children and Young Persons Act 1933, the Act loosened the distinction between Industrial Schools (previously just for the 'neglected') and Reformatories (for young offenders). The use of both, and transfers between, was permitted for 'appropriate' juvenile offenders (Stewart 1995). The 1908 Act also increased measures against child cruelty and neglect.

At the start of the twentieth century, this increasing social concern for children and fears of the disorderly lower classes had been augmented by a focus on racial purity, national efficiency and the needs of the Empire. Fortunately, this also provided further motivation for intervening positively in the child care field. As well as the 1908 Act, the wider social reforms of the 1906–1914 Liberal government were important as part of a focus on general child welfare. The introduction of school meals (1906) and school medical inspections (1907) signified a growing concern with state responsibilities in relation to children. Walvin (1972) goes so far as to suggest that:

By 1914 it was clear beyond doubt that children had rights of their own, which were independent even of their own parents and which the state would try to safeguard for them. In this, the child of 1914 was recognisably more akin to the modern child than to the early Victorian child. (Walvin 1972, p.198)

Psychoanalytic and psychological approaches to child care

During the inter-war years, there was increased interest in the emotional adjustment of children from deprived or abusive backgrounds. This was reflected in the increasing numbers of child guidance clinics and promoted by the work of psychologists such as John Bowlby and Cyril Burt. One can trace a longer history of child psychiatry, but it was not really until this period that its influence was noticeable (Hersov 1986; von Gontard 1988). The first child guidance institution in the United Kingdom, the East London Child Guidance Clinic, was established in 1927. Prior to this, it was only in the latter half of the nineteenth century that children with mental illness had begun to be treated separately from adults. However, the development of large-scale Poor Law institutions had at least aided these developments by providing 'laboratories' for scientists and doctors.

Psychoanalysis did not begin to have an impact on these developments until well into the twentieth century, popularised by such controversial figures as Havelock Ellis. It was not, in fact, until after the 1939–1945 war that child psychiatry became well established and began to have significant influence in shaping policy in a more individualist, therapeutic direction. From then onwards, one predictable outcome of a more psychoanalytic or psychological approach was an increasing blurring of the boundaries between the children who were viewed as 'depraved' and those who were viewed as 'deprived'. The former implies a strong element of choice in the performance of individual anti-social acts, while the latter points the finger of blame (and likewise the hand of redemption) at the social environment.

Children in the welfare state: 1945–1989

The immediate post-war years were a period when children were viewed very much as a positive asset – to be cherished, supported and provided for as the nation looked forward optimistically to recovery from war (Fox Harding 1997). After the hiatus of the interwar years and following the second world war, there was a flurry of activity in relation to child welfare. The Labour Party was as active in this field as in the rest of its efforts to establish a welfare

state. Much of the history of this crucial period is already widely known.
There are a number of important landmarks: the O'Neill case, the subsequent
Monckton Inquiry, the Curtis Committee and the legislative culmination of
concern in the form of the 1948 Children Act.

The Curtis Committee and the Children Act 1948

Part of the background to this post-war activity was the concern generated
by the experience of evacuation during the war. The evacuation process had
revealed to many middle-class families the extent of social deprivation experienced by a large number of children (Philpot 1994). It has also been argued
that the experience of looking after other people's children in shared adversity had a profound effect on adult understanding of and empathy for
children (Gardner and Cunningham 1997). There was a further, more practical, issue generated by the question of what to do about those children who
were unable to return to their homes after the war due to family bereavement
or other war-related factors. Poor Law workhouses and Public Assistance
homes were no longer acceptable to public and establishment opinion. Establishment concern led to the setting up of the Curtis Committee in 1945. One
month later, on 9 January 1945, there occurred the death of Denis O'Neill at
the hands of his foster parents. His death at the age of 13, weighing four
stone and after eight months of increasingly brutal treatment, led to a major
public outcry and was to prove one of the defining moments in post-war
consciousness in the child care field (O'Neill 1981; Philpot 1994). The
subsequent Monckton inquiry into the case found that social work training
and the supervision of foster carers was inadequate and that there had been a
general lack of service coordination.

    While the Curtis Report reflected the atmosphere created by the O'Neill
case and the war-time experience, it ranged more widely in its review of
general service provision. The Report refers to the O'Neill case in several
places, most obviously when 'boarding out' regulations and inspections are
discussed (Home Department 1946). Yet, notwithstanding the case, the
report comes out in favour of the expansion of 'boarding out' (still, then,
applying only to a small minority of those in care) as a general improvement
on the conditions prevailing in institutions (Home Department 1946,
Recommendation 21). The Report's conclusions were based on a very wide
survey, undertaken by the members of the committee themselves, of the
range of services provided in England and Wales.

The Children Act of 1948 closely followed the recommendations of both Curtis and its Scottish counterpart, the Clyde Report (Holman 1996). There were five key features of this legislation: first, it led to the setting up of local authority children's departments in order to coordinate child care work; second, there was an emphasis on the restoration of the child to its natural family where feasible; third, a high priority was given to fostering; fourth, there was an increased focus on inspections; finally, there was a focus on safeguarding the child's interests and on the integration of children with the rest of society (encapsulated in section 12 of the Act).

Delinquency and deprivation – blurring the boundaries

During the early post-war period, 'delinquent' increasingly became the accepted term for children who were earlier referred to as 'depraved'. We have already noted the growing influence of child psychology and psychiatry during this period. It is no surprise, therefore, to find this approach increasingly reflected in subsequent policy documents. The 1960 Ingleby Report, for example, focused on the need to intervene in families to forestall later delinquency rather than merely prevent abuse. Likewise, the 1964 Labour Party report, *Crime – A Challenge to Us All*, which strongly influenced subsequent government policy, exhibits a psychological approach to the issues of juvenile justice. The Ingleby Report responded to a brief it had already been given to look at child care provision and juvenile justice matters in tandem. Its solution, of promoting preventive services aimed at forestalling delinquency, fitted in with a wider ethos of preventive work with families in the home and elsewhere in order to forestall entrance into the care system. Such ideas were reflected in the subsequent Children and Young Persons Act of 1963 (Fox Harding 1997). The Act, following Ingleby's lead, gave local authorities increased powers to intervene in the family home.

Throughout the 1960s, social democratic approaches to child care policy were in the ascendant. It was reflected in two influential Fabian pamphlets of the time (Donnison, Jay and Stewart 1962; Donnison and Stewart 1958), which stressed the responsibility of government for dealing with child care problems. These pamphlets did, however, focus on skill deficits and other forms of social deprivation rather than on psychological factors. The same broad analysis, emphasising the influence of various forms of deprivation, is evident in the high water mark of the progressive approach to juveniles, the 1969 Children and Young Persons Act. The most significant – and contentious – feature of this Act was the replacement of the specific sentencing powers of magistrates with the power to issue a Care Order, placing a child in the care of a local authority, who were then to provide the most appropriate (that is, beneficial for the child) placement. In a direct, practical, sense this was an attempt to funnel young offenders away from the juvenile justice system and into the child care system. The debate on the wisdom of this approach continued throughout the subsequent decade (Goldson 1997). What was certainly true was that perceptions of the care system began to change as the nature of its clientele changed. No longer was it an avenue for public sympathy for 'neglected' children. As child care, particularly residential care, began to house relatively older children (fostering, adoption and preventive work catering for most of the others) and more of those who had been in trouble with the law, the nature of the stigma attaching to those in care changed. Children in care (particularly residential care) began to be seen as young criminals being given an easy ride by the courts rather than as those most deserving of public sympathy.

Other milestones from this period included the Seebohm Report of 1968 and the recommendation for generic social service departments, which effectively disbanded specific children's departments. This was enacted through the Local Authority Social Services Act of 1970. Along with the unification of social work training and the development of qualified professionals, through the establishment of the Central Council for the Education and Training of Social Workers (CCETSW) and the British Association of Social Workers (BASW) in the same period, it represented a more complex treatment of children's issues in the context of families (Daniel and Ivatts 1998, p.203; Jones 1994, pp.172–175). The 1960s and early 1970s was, generally, a period of sustained optimism in the field of child care, as it was in the field of local and central government welfare services more generally. The growth of interest in child care, in particular, prompted the development of such bodies as the National Children's Bureau (originally the National Bureau for Cooperation in Child care) in 1963, designed to act as a 'clearing house' for ideas, research and best practice within the growing statutory, voluntary and academic sectors (Cooper 1993).

The 1970s was also the era of 'permanency', a shift away from the philosophy of prevention and of return to families of the 1963 Act. Keeping children for longer in care in the hope of reuniting them with their families was coming to be seen as deleterious and a new focus on finding a more 'permanent' placement in adoption or long-term fostering was developing (Daniel and Ivatts 1998, p.203). Given that the numbers of children in care had been steadily rising, from just over 55,000 children in England and Wales in 1949 to a peak of over 100,000 in the late 1970s (Daniel and Ivatts 1998, p.208), it was clear that prevention and reintegration were not proving particularly successful. One further factor encouraging the development of 'permanency' was the Maria Colwell Inquiry.

Responding to Colwell: the 1975 Children Act

A renewed focus on social services intervention in families was partly a response to abuse cases, particularly the widely publicised death of Maria Colwell in 1973. Colwell had been killed at the age of six by her stepfather, after having been returned from the home of her aunt, who was acting as foster carer, to the home of her mother. She had been with her aunt for five years before being returned at the request of her mother and with the support of the local authority. The latter were keen to support the reintegration of the family. Maria had made it clear that she had no wish to return to her family and was noted to be increasingly depressed. In the last nine months of her life, thirty complaints were received by the local social services department, referring to neglect, weight loss and physical injuries (Parton 1985).

The next major legal development was the 1975 Children Act. In response to the Colwell enquiry, the 1975 Act strengthened long-term fostering, allowed account to be taken of the child's wishes and allowed application for legal custody by foster parents and others. It reversed the focus on the birth family as always being the preferred option. The Act also gave local authorities the key coordinating role in adoptions following the 1972 Houghton Report. There was a shift in focus towards the welfare of the child rather than the interests of parents. Local authorities were given greater powers to intervene. The Act also required the appointment of Guardians *Ad Litem* to act exclusively on behalf of the child in certain cases.

The 'rediscovery' of child abuse

Part of the atmosphere that helped to undermine faith in families during the 1970s was the 'rediscovery' of child abuse. This theme fed into debates about the proper means for the protection of children. This rediscovery had begun with an American Medical Association article on the 'battered baby syndrome' in 1962. In the UK, the NSPCC and the medical profession picked up on the issue in the late 1960s and early 1970s (NSPCC 1976). There followed the establishment of child abuse care committees in local authorities. DHSS circulars between 1974 and 1976 encouraged this focus on child abuse, mainly through the establishment of child abuse registers and Area Review Committees. In 1977, a House of Commons report on *Violence to Children* estimated that possibly 40,000 children were the victims of abuse. The report called for more support for parents, such as an increase in provision of under-fives facilities, child-minders and playgroups, and also for more social work and police training in this field (House of Commons 1977). The high profile of child abuse as an issue continued throughout the 1970s. Between 1973 and 1981, there were 27 inquiries into the deaths or serious abuse of children by carers. In almost all of these cases, health and/ or social service professionals were already involved in the case at the time that the abuse occurred.

Rights, scandals and enquiries

Alongside the focus on abuse, there developed from the late 1970s a focus on a more rights-based approach rather than a simple emphasis on welfare. The crucial sets of rights were children's rights and parents' rights. Organisations such as the Children's Legal Centre, the National Children's Bureau and the Family Rights Group all sought to use legal solutions on behalf of those involved in care disputes (Hendrick 1994). In the field of children's rights in particular, there was renewed optimism and activism following the United Nations 'International Year of the Child' in 1979, although an increased focus on children's rights had been developing in such fields as education for many years prior to this (Franklin and Franklin 1996). This must be seen, of course, against a wider background of declining confidence in welfare and other professionals during this period. This rights-based approach was endorsed by a House of Commons Social Services Committee Report in 1984, which advocated more supervision of professional discretion and greater focus on the rights of clients (House of Commons 1984).

Although abuse scandals continued to feature in newspaper headlines in the 1980s, the lessons were much more mixed. Cases such as those of Jasmine Beckford and Kimberley Carlisle offered the usual lesson of insufficient intervention. The publication of the Beckford Inquiry report in 1985 illustrated this most starkly. Jasmine Beckford had died at the age of four at the hands of her stepfather. He had a previous suspended sentence for injuring Jasmine and her sister in 1981 and Brent social services, the locally responsible department, were strongly criticised for failure to intervene sufficiently. The subsequent increased focus on child protection saw a major rise in the numbers of children entering care due to abuse and also in the numbers on child protection registers.

However, providing an opposite lesson was the Cleveland case. This arose in 1987 when 121 children were taken into care in Cleveland following child abuse investigations that used controversial paediatric techniques. The subsequent inquiry was critical of the paediatricians involved. The general consensus from this inquiry (and also later cases such as that in the Orkneys) was that there had been too much intervention rather than too little, needlessly disrupting many families. The 1989 Children Act partly reflected the fears raised by Cleveland. It stressed parental responsibility and support for children and families in a partnership with social services.

The 1989 Children Act

The 1989 Children Act was the culmination of many of the developments that we have been discussing. Furthermore, research in the 1970s and 1980s highlighted increasing dissatisfaction with legislation and professional practice. The growth of the Family Rights Group, as well as official reviews by professional bodies and parliamentarians, added to the pressure for change. As a wide-ranging measure, it sought to bring together several streams of thought and practice. It remains, at present, the primary legislation for work in relation to children in the United Kingdom. Current child care policy and practice in relation to the work of local authority social services departments and others is based almost exclusively (adoption being an exception) on the 1989 Act, with its main provisions having come into force in October 1991. Since then, there have been some changes made to the operation of the Act. For example, the Family Law Act of 1996 (which combines and updates divorce and domestic violence legislation) attached exclusion powers to Emergency Protection Orders, permitting the exclusion of alleged abusers from a home rather than the removal of the child (Ryan 1999, p.89). However, rather than focus on legislative detail, we finish this chapter by outlining key principles and issues arising out of the legislation. Further details of the legislation, which particularly relate to the operation of the Act in practice in relation to looked after children, will be provided in Chapter 2.

The 1989 Act was designed to bring together and simplify all relevant legislation relating to children in one piece of legislation. For that reason, it covered such issues as pre-school day-care, local authority provision for children, child protection, children involved in divorce or custody proceedings and the care of children in independent schools (DoH 1989). In relation to local authorities, the focus of the Act was on providing services for children 'in need' for one reason or another. There are three major principles which underpin the Act. The first key principle, familiar by now from previous legislation but here in a stronger form, was the primary importance of the welfare of the child, or the 'paramountcy principle', that:

> The overwhelming purpose of the Act is to promote and safeguard the welfare of children. That purpose is seen at its clearest in the opening provision of the Act. It tells all courts to treat the welfare of the child as the paramount consideration when reaching any decision about his upbringing (or, incidentally, the administration or application of his property). The word 'paramount' repeats the previous legislation. It emphasises that no change is intended from the current position. Thus, whilst the courts are to take into account all the relevant surrounding circumstances, including, for example, the wishes of parents, at the end of the day they must do what is best for the child. (DoH 1989, pp.3–4)

Second, there was the view that minimal delay in expediting proceedings was important. Delays in decision-making, whether for legal or administrative reasons, were seen as inevitably disadvantageous for children unless good reasons could be found to justify them. Finally, the Act held that intervention is only justified if it is better than the alternative:

> These necessarily potent powers, if misdirected, may themselves cause harm to a child by enabling the state to intervene in his or his family's life when it should not. Accordingly, the Act seeks to target the powers on cases where the circumstances are such that on balance the bringing of proceedings is likely to be in the best interests of children. (DoH 1989, p.6)

The 1989 Act's comprehensiveness is reflected in the fact that it repealed many previous Acts and parts of Acts. However, there are two important contextual points to note about the origins of the Act. The first of these is that in some respects it largely codified 'best practice', establishing in statute many practices (for example, consultation of children in care) that a large number of local authorities had already adopted. Second, it proceeded on the basis of bipartisan support and considerable professional backing. It was a consensual measure, because of the diverse benefits it offered to many groups and shades of opinion. Packman and Jordan (1991) note that the Act is very un-Thatcherite in tone. Winter and Connolly, who strongly argue that the Act's particular interpretation of children's rights is Thatcherite in its focus on rights against the state rather than against the family, concede that it represents a positive move in the discussion of children's rights more generally (Winter and Connolly 1996). Moreover, the Act lacks much of the focus on privatisation and voluntary care that was a feature of community care legislation. Instead, it focuses on a strong package of services for children 'in need'. As suggested, the Act also reflects the scandals and debates of the 1970s and 1980s: Maria Colwell, Jasmine Beckford, Kimberly Carlisle, Cleveland. It responded to both Cleveland and to a growing body of opinion by focusing on the need for professionals to work in partnership with parents and children. This emphasis on partnership was not made explicit in the Act but was a central feature of subsequent guidance (Ryan 1999, pp.4–5).

Enduring themes in child welfare

In this brief historical overview, we have traced the evolution of some of the enduring themes that continue to dominate contemporary discussion of state child care. Three of these themes are particularly important:

1. The tension between family-based and institutional care. Each has its merits but each also has its ideological as well as its practical defenders.

2. The tension for social services departments between intervening too early or too late in child protection cases. Either approach can be, and has been, heavily criticised by politicians and the media.

3. The perception in some quarters of important links between childhood deprivation, delinquency and later criminality.

The tendency to conflate issues to do with deprivation and issues to do with delinquency and criminality has understandable theoretical and empirical origins, but has had major deleterious effects on the modern child care system. The associations between these issues exemplify well the tensions between care and control in social policy debates about children and their families. However, it was not until the post-war crime wave really got under way in the mid-1950s that concern with crime, especially juvenile crime, began to mount (Morris 1989). This latter issue can be seen as enduring and one which continues to perplex government and provoke public debate about child care services, as we will see in later chapters.

What we have sought to do in this chapter is to explain the background to current debates about child care. What will become evident in subsequent chapters is the extent to which many of the issues considered in this historical account remain with us. Newsome (1992), in particular, detects strong continuities that stretch back over at least two centuries. These include the problems of leaving care and the relatively low levels of staff support and training. In the midst of a period of reform, it is important to recognise that:

> many issues are not new, but firmly rooted in the historical development of institutions. Many of the social attitudes and personal motives which existed in the past are far from dead issues, though most practitioners are unlikely to be conscious of the fact. (Newsome 1992, p.155)

CHAPTER 2

Contemporary Issues and Concerns

We saw in the previous chapter that a number of separate developments converged in the Children Act 1989. One can see reflected in its pages, and in those of the various volumes of regulations and guidance which followed, many of the historical debates that we have already examined being replayed within a contemporary context. In this chapter, after outlining the point to which the Act brought us, we seek to explore the developments that have taken place since its implementation in October 1991. This provides a thematic background to the more specific examinations of particular issues of policy and practice provided by subsequent chapters.

Themes and issues in the 1989 Children Act

As Fox Harding (1997) has noted, many of the divergent themes in the Act are contradictory when pushed to extremes. She analyses four perspectives on child care that can each be perceived in the Act: a laissez-faire approach; a state paternalist approach; a parental rights approach; and a children's rights approach. Within the Act, an attempt at balance is made. The 'laissez-faire' approach is encapsulated in the principle that intervention must not take place unless it is better than the alternative. There is also support for the parental rights lobby in the greater rights to contact and in the rights of parents to challenge local authority decisions in the courts and to be consulted when changes are made to care arrangements. This addresses some of the concerns raised by the Cleveland case. In contrast, state paternalism is given greater scope through the allowance that 'likely' significant harm – not just that which has already occurred – is grounds for a care or supervision order (Children Act 1989, s. 31 (2)). Also, the focus on the paramount importance of the child's welfare is consistent with a paternalist perspective.

From the children's rights perspective, it is worth noting that in the relationship between local authorities and young people in care, the focus is very much put on consultation. This comes across in section 22 of the Act. With regard to those children in the care of the local authority, section 22 explicitly lists 'the child' as the first person to be consulted 'as far as is reasonably practicable' before any decision with regard to the child is made (s. 22 (4)). Also, there is specific instruction in section 26 (3) for local authorities to provide consultation procedures for young people and for others. In this sense, the Act is in line with the general thrust of a number of official and semi-official reports issued around this time. The Howe Inquiry, for example, in reviewing a wide range of residential care, called for a 'code of rights' for all residents (Howe 1992, pp.123–124). With regard to the Act, it was pressure from the child care rights group Voice of the Child in Care, and others, that led to complaints procedures being mandated by the Act.

Such a measure as the 1989 Act was bound to have many supporters but also to leave the door open to future conflicts and disputes. Positively, it was welcomed by those working with children with disabilities for incorporating such children within the remit of the Act (with all of the implications that this held for consultation and children's rights). More negatively, the Act has been accused of creating a more legalistic, less flexible system. By default, its emphasis on paperwork and on written agreements has surely contributed, for good or ill, to the professionalisation of foster care (as discussed in Chapter 4). Further important changes brought about by the Act in relation to looked after children are reflected in the concepts of 'accommodation' and of 'significant harm' as well as the notion of a 'welfare checklist' which courts must take into consideration when deciding a child's future.

Providing accommodation

Providing accommodation for children in need replaced the system prior to the Children Act of 'voluntary care' or 'reception into care'. The provision of accommodation was seen as one of the main support services that a local authority should provide for children in need and their families. An essential characteristic of the concept of 'accommodation' is that it should be seen as voluntary in nature. Accommodation should be based upon continuing parental agreement and partnership between the parents and the local authority. Clearly, the Act intended that parents should retain control over the use of accommodation by their power to veto it in the first instance or to remove the child without notice (Kent, Pierson and Thornton 1990).

As Frost *et al.* point out (1999, pp.70–71), this structures the population of looked after children into two groups: those accommodated by agreement under section 20 and those subject to care orders under section 31. The recasting of 'voluntary care' into 'accommodation' was, ironically, intended to ensure that such care remained genuinely voluntary through ensuring that parents and young people retained their rights in such circumstances. Packman and Hall, in a return to the site of earlier (pre-Children Act) research on this subject, sought to test out the working of section 20 in the years immediately following the 1989 Act and found mixed results. The increased use of accommodation as a form of respite care was seen as positive and there appeared to be a genuine move away from legal and towards negotiated solutions to problems. On the other hand, parents and children often had problems in accessing such help due to a gate-keeping, 'last resort' mentality persisting amongst professionals. Also, the genuine voluntariness of agreements among all parties to it and problems for parents and children in being genuine partners in the planning process remained difficult areas in many cases (Packman and Hall 1998, pp.257–270).

'Significant harm' and compulsory state intervention

Before the 1989 Children Act, there were many ways in which a child could come into care, each with different grounds. These routes were dependent upon which proceedings the care order emerged from. For looked after children who were not voluntarily 'accommodated', the Act formulated a new threshold for compulsory state intervention, through the concept of 'significant harm' (Children Act 1989, s. 31). The Act defines harm as 'ill-treatment or the impairment of health or development' (s. 31 (9)). 'Ill-treatment' includes sexual abuse and forms of ill-treatment which are not physical and significant harm with regard to health or development is established by comparison with that which could reasonably be expected of a similar child (s. 31 (10)).

Even where significant harm – or, importantly, the *likelihood* of significant harm – is established, a care or supervision order will not necessarily follow. In deciding what to do next, the court will focus on the chief principle of the welfare of the child. In order to aid its decision in this regard, it will have regard to several factors listed in section 1 (3) of the Act and collectively known as the 'welfare checklist'.

The welfare checklist

The following factors must be taken into consideration when courts decide a child's future:

1. the ascertainable wishes and feelings of the child concerned (considered in the light of his age and understanding)

2. his physical, emotional and educational needs

3. the likely effect on him of any change in his circumstances

4. his age, sex, background and any characteristics of his which the court considers relevant

5. any harm which he has suffered or is at risk of suffering

6. how capable each of his parents, and any other person in relation to whom the court considers the question to be relevant, is of meeting his needs

7. the range of powers available to the court under this Act in the proceedings in question. (Children Act 1989, s. 1 (3))

There is an interaction between these sorts of consideration – why young people enter the care system – and what happens to them subsequently. This is especially so when being looked after comes as a result of child abuse. Professional culture and organisational structures have a subtle impact upon the prioritisation of resources. *Child Protection: Messages from Research* (Dartington SRU 1995, p.54) notes that there is often overlap between services which cover *child protection* work, *family support* and *child welfare* for those living away from home. Whilst some overlap is inevitable, and indeed necessary in the interests of an effective child care system, the research studies concerned questioned the balance between child protection and other areas and suggested that too much of the work undertaken comes within the category of child protection. The experience of 'drift' by a significant minority of young people who are looked after (SSI 1998b), whilst linked to a variety of factors, is also arguably a response to some extent to a perception that the immediate risk to the child or young person has been reduced by placement. However, findings from the SSI report indicate that only a few SSDs were able to base placement decisions on an assessment of need which clearly considered safety and risk and that decision-making tended to be crisis led rather than adequately planned. Child protection routes to becoming looked after also have a subsequent impact upon the quality of assessment, with findings that assessment practice is more structured and coherent where there had been court proceedings or child protection investigations (SSI 1998b, p.34). Delays in the allocation of social workers were also less likely in child protection cases, which had the highest level of priority. The report argued that children looked after away from home should have the same priority for allocation to a social worker as those at risk in the community. Following the publication of *Messages From Research* there has been a more general recognition that the emphasis in many areas of child care service delivery has been dominated by incident-led Section 47 enquiries rather than the provision of Section 17 services for children and families (including for those looked after away from home).

As noted in Chapter 1, the 1989 Act remains the primary legislation for work in relation to children in England and Wales. Broadly, its approach remains dominant with regard to looked after children. However, the election of a Labour government in May 1997 has led to a flurry of policy activity. These include two Select Committee reports, a government inspectors' report on planning and decision-making, the creation of an all-party Parliamentary Group for Children and Young People In and Leaving Care, the publication of the government's Quality Protects central monitoring and inspection proposals (DoH 1998b) and a consultation paper on 'Supporting the Family' (Ministerial Group on the Family 1998). These are already developing legislative implications (DoH 1998d), which will be discussed more fully in Chapter 10. The Crime and Disorder Act 1998 has also introduced a number of measures which will have an impact on families, including parenting orders, child safety orders, local child curfews and final warnings.

Putting the Act in context, we now consider some of the key themes and issues which underpin or are dealt with in subsequent chapters. As well as considering the impact of the Act in these areas, we also consider subsequent and contemporary developments.

Child care: themes and issues

The changing pattern of provision – foster and residential care

The trend towards foster care and away from residential care is well illustrated by official figures. This general reduction in residential care for children is part of a trend which can be found in other European Union countries and in the United States (Berridge and Brodie 1998). By March 1998, 66 per cent of children looked after were in foster care, with only 12

Table 2.1 Changes in the number and main types of placement provided for looked after children in England, 31 March 1981 – 31 March 1998 (thousands)

Placement Type	1981	1982	1983	1984	1985	1986	1987	1988	1989	1990	1991	1992	1993	1994	1995	1996	1997	1998
All children	92.3	88.7	82.2	74.8	69.0	66.7	65.8	64.4	62.1	60.5	59.8	54.4	52.0	49.3	49	50.8	51.6	53.7
Foster placements	35.7	36.9	36.5	36.1	34.8	34.9	35.0	34.9	34.2	34.5	34.8	31.3	32.5	31.2	32.1	33.1	33.4	35.2
Children's homes	29.7	26.3	22.0	28.2	16.1	14.8	14.5	13.3	12.0	11.5	10.6	8.7	7.2	7.4	7.3	6.8	6.5	6.5

(DoH 1988; 1994; 1998f)

per cent in 'community homes' (DoH 1998e, p.60). The rest of the looked after population were in a variety of settings, including placement with parents and for adoption. This has taken place within the context of a fall in the total number of children looked after by local authorities in recent decades, a reduction accelerated by the implementation of the Children Act. Overall, the number of children looked after or in the care of local authorities in England, Wales and Northern Ireland fell by 42 per cent between 1981 and 1995. The proportion of these children living with foster carers increased, however, from about two-fifths to over two-thirds in the same time period. This means there were approximately the same number of children in foster care in 1995 as there were in 1981. However, the number of children in local authority children's homes has declined rapidly: between 1986 and 1996, numbers placed in children's homes fell from approximately 15,000 to 7,000. Changes in the percentage of those looked after in local authority residential and foster care can be seen in Table 2.1. Since this focuses on those in foster and residential care, it leaves out figures for those who are looked after but who are living at home or in lodgings or schools.

One explanation for the decline in the use of residential care lies in its relative cost. The costs of the two main types of placement for looked after children have been estimated at an average of £51,500 per residential placement and £8125 per foster placement. However, foster placement costs are difficult to calculate accurately and do not include the full costs of social work time (Berridge 1997; CIPFA 1996; CSO 1997).

Policy and practice emerging from the Children Act has reduced admissions to care, as intended. However, the use of foster care, as we have seen, has remained high and has increased in recent years, both in real numbers and, especially, by comparison with residential care. Despite the wider use of foster care, there have been criticisms of the fostering service. The main criticisms have been linked to service organisation and quality. Recent reports have shown a lack of strategic planning for children, inadequate care plans and assessments and a severe shortage of carers, particularly for older children, sibling groups, within certain localities and for children with emotional and behavioural difficulties (EBD) (DoH/SSI 1995b, 1996; Waterhouse 1997). Many local authorities have had difficulties recruiting new foster carers and as a result have been struggling to match children's needs to the abilities and experience of foster carers. Foster families may be providing care for children outside of their approval range, with potentially serious implications both for the foster child and the foster family. The increasing use of foster care as the preferred form of accommodation for most looked after children means that carers are often expected to look after children with a wide range of needs, such as children who have been sexually abused, children permanently excluded from school and children with significant emotional and behavioural difficulties.

These increased expectations of foster carers apply not only with regard to the characteristics of the children they look after. The 1989 Children Act also requires that foster carers play a more involved role in drawing up foster care agreements, appearing in court, and attending a range of reviews, conferences and relevant meetings. The 1989 Act has had a particular impact through its emphasis on maintaining family links. The use of contact orders may involve elaborate and detailed arrangements for children to be kept in touch with their birth families while in care, and foster carers are often asked to facilitate visits. The implicit expectation of the Children Act is that foster carers should become more professional (Ryan 1999, p.51). However, while foster carers receive a maintenance allowance – sometimes in line with National Foster Care Association guidelines, sometimes not (see Chapter 4) – they often receive relatively little support and training (see Chapter 8).

Availability and choice of placement

The decline in the availability of residential placements is not without its problems. Many children like residential care, finding it less restrictive and less likely to produce conflicts of loyalty with their birth family (Kahan 1995; Utting 1997). More generally, there has long been dispute in this area about the relative benefits of foster and residential care, with some believing that the closest substitute to a real family is desirable, others seeing an important place for residential provision. Colton (1988), for example, concluded that foster care is more child-oriented than residential care along the dimensions of everyday care, the child's community contacts, physical amenities and the sanctions applied. Berridge (1994), in a review of the foster versus residential debate, sees the use of both types of placement as complementary and as serving different functions. The wider, and perhaps more significant, issue is the extent to which a shift to foster care has undermined choice and limited the opportunity for young people to find solutions that meet their needs. Both the Utting Report and the 1997/98 SSI report comment on the negative effect on choice of the decline in the number of children's homes (SSI 1998a; Utting 1997). The SSI report is explicit on this point:

Many children looked after are accommodated in the only available placement, rather than one which meets their particular needs. Many local authorities have closed children's homes, without investing in foster care services to meet the needs of very demanding young people. Some have no children's residential care provision of their own and yet have made no contractual arrangements with independent providers to meet their needs. (SSI 1998a, p.12)

This problem of finding appropriate placements has been especially acute with regard to young people from racial or ethnic minorities. The Children Act reflected a growing suspicion of transracial adoption or fostering through its stipulation in section 22 that ethnic or racial origins should be taken into account in local authority decision-making. However, having regard to a child's 'religious persuasion, racial origin and cultural and linguistic background' (Children Act 1989, s. 22 (5) (c)) has frequently come up against the barrier of finding appropriate carers.

Race and ethnicity

With regard to race and ethnicity more generally, data is patchy. Rowe and Lambert (1973) reported that social workers identified racial background as one of the main obstacles to finding long-term placements for some children. In particular, black children were disproportionately represented amongst children who wait to be placed. The 1980s saw an attack from organisations representing racial and ethnic minorities of what were seen as the 'colour blind' practices of social services departments (Cliffe with Berridge 1991). There is no national data on the ethnic composition of looked after children, although some local authorities and voluntary organisations have collected and monitored data in this respect (Kahan 1995). The recent DoH (1998c) overview of messages from research concludes that 'it is likely that about one in ten children looked after are from a minority ethnic background' and that 'children from minority ethnic groups are slightly less likely to be fostered and slightly more likely to experience movement between residential and foster settings' (p.13). Kahan (1995) notes that: 'Black children appear(ed) to enter residential care at a younger age than other ethnic groups, but remained for shorter periods' (p.14).

Our own research did not focus on this subject, so it features only briefly in subsequent chapters. In Gorin's research, 1.4 per cent of carers were from an ethnic minority background in authorities where 1.9 per cent of the population were from such a background. In Hayden's research, one of the

31 residential units had a black unit manager. None of the case studies of either Hayden or Gorin were from an ethnic or racial minority. In Lynes' and Goddard's survey, four of the 121 in care respondents identified themselves as non-white (specifically, of a mixed ethnic or racial background). None of their questionnaires raised any issues related to this or otherwise indicated any relevant concerns.

Abuse within the care system

Residential care has, claim some, been in a state of 'crisis' since the early 1990s (Berridge and Brodie 1996). References to 'crises' in foster care most often relate to lack of available placements, whereas references to 'crises' in residential care usually relate to allegations of abuse of children and young people. Although it is well known that children and young people are abused in both types of setting (Utting 1997), inquiries and reviews (including Utting) focus most upon residential care.

Kendrick (1998) notes that there is no absolute definition of abuse, which creates major problems in the identification and response to abuse in both services. Citing Gil (1982), Kendrick identifies three broad categories of abuse which are known to occur within residential and foster care: physical and sexual abuse; programme abuse; and system abuse. Physical and sexual abuse has been a feature of such high profile scandals as Leicestershire, Clwyd, Merseyside and Cheshire (de Cruz 1998). Kendrick, quoting Morris, Wheatley and Lees (1994), suggests that there is evidence that physical abuse from foster carers is a more significant problem for children than that which occurs within residential care.

Programme abuse, on the other hand, includes over-medication, inappropriate isolation, mechanical restraint and disciplinary techniques. Many of the well known enquiries have also uncovered this type of abuse alongside abuse from individuals. For example, 'pindown', in Staffordshire, involved the social isolation of children in barely furnished rooms, with no education, for long periods (sometimes weeks). At Ty Mawr there was inadequate supervision, adolescents 'out of control', and alleged staff brutality. In Leicestershire, Frank Beck, the Officer in Charge in various homes from 1973 to 1986, turned out to be a serial sex abuser, not discovered despite various complaints from young people. Beck also operated a form of 'regression therapy' in cooperation with other staff (Kirkwood 1993).

System abuse as a concept relates to the way that the state child care system operates: by allowing drift in care, through multiple placements and disruption, through insufficient attention to the ordinary requirements for security and stability and proper and effective access to health and education services. Although this type of abuse may be the most difficult to define, acknowledge and remedy, as a concept it underpins many of the more general critiques of the way in which the child care system currently operates for looked after children.

Recent debate about the safety of looked after children whilst they are in care has been dominated by the Utting Report (1997), which was commissioned by the previous Conservative government. It examined both foster and residential child care provision in light of the various scandals that emerged in residential child care in the early 1990s and the changing nature of foster care. It called for greater inspection and regulation of residential and foster care and questioned the reduction in residential provision. Choice, it claimed, has been restricted by this. Developments since Utting, and the current government's response to Utting (DoH 1998j), are discussed in the final chapter.

Care and control

Reaching an appropriate balance between care and control is central to the task of looking after any child. What makes this issue more pertinent in relation to looked after children is that their everyday care and control is devolved away from their parents and onto others sanctioned by the state – foster carers and residential workers in the main. A common issue for carers looking after children who have received inconsistent and sometimes abusive parenting is that of providing realistic boundaries and behavioural expectations. The issues of appropriate behaviour in different contexts and the understanding of the needs expressed through behaviour as well as responses to it are strongly debated by a range of professionals (Blau and Gullotta 1996). We can only hope to touch upon the complexity of these issues here and elsewhere in the book. Most observers would agree that difficult to manage behaviour, whether it is of the 'acting out' variety or is more internalised, is common amongst the population of looked after children (Packman and Hall 1996). When children have been hurt, psychologically or physically, they may react in anti-social or self-destructive ways which can have long-term consequences for their lives (Cleaver 1997). For example, behaviour perceived as aggressive, disruptive or anti-social lies behind most school exclusions, with all of the associated disadvantages which may follow (Hayden 1997b). Some of these behaviours can lead to the intervention of the police if carried out in the community. Misuse of alcohol and other drugs can also, clearly, have a significant impact on the physical and mental health of young people. Whilst these issues can affect many young people at some point in their lives, looked after children are more vulnerable to getting into some of these difficulties than the rest of their peer group (Sinclair, Garnett and Berridge 1995).

Implicit in all forms of caring for children is a concern for their health. In comparison with physical health, the mental health of children in care has received more attention. As we noted in Chapter 1, psychoanalytic and psychological approaches to child care became more common after the second world war and studies of children in care played a key role in the development of various theoretical models put forward to explain the origins of childhood psychopathology (Kahan 1989). The interrelationship between stressful experiences and certain types of ill health, both mental and physical, is acknowledged, as are the different levels of resilience to adversity found in individuals (Jackson and Martin 1998; Rutter 1997). Available evidence suggests that looked after children appear to suffer an excess of minor infections (Kahan 1989). Children with recurrent physical illnesses such as infections of the ears and chest have been found to be more likely than is usual to have developmental and behavioural problems as well (Bax, Hart and Jenkins 1983, quoted in Kahan 1989). Research focusing upon the physical and emotional health and educational development of looked after children has been fairly minimal until recent years. Incomplete evidence is available about children's health, although several studies have found health to be insufficiently prioritised (Bamford and Wolkind 1988; Butler and Payne 1997; Mather, Humphrey and Robson 1997).

Knowledge about an individual's health is important in detecting any adverse changes which may require investigation or treatment. However, the division in responsibility for health care between social worker and either residential worker or foster carer can compound issues of both knowledge and also responsibility (Butler and Payne 1997; Parker *et al.* 1991). Serious undiagnosed medical conditions continue to be found at adoption medicals carried out on children who have spent many years in the care system (Mather *et al.* 1997). Yet, as in so many areas in relation to looked after children, there are plenty of statutory regulations but these appear not to be adhered to in practice. For example, national data shows a take-up of only about 25 per cent for the statutory medical for looked after children (Cleaver 1996). Mather *et al.* (1997) argue that the focus on the statutory medical has been unhelpful and appears to be undertaken more for the benefit of social services departments and the medical profession than addressing the health needs of the child. Professionals emphasise physical examination, advice on smoking, drinking, drugs and sexual health, and reporting to social services. Teenagers in their study wanted to avoid the physical examinations and wished for advice on skin and hair care, eating disorders, stress and self-esteem, with complete confidentiality. In talking to young people themselves, Mather *et al.* found that young people talked overwhelmingly about depression, isolation and the lack of a trusted adult with whom they could discuss personal health matters. Unresolved issues to do with loss, bereavement and separation were common.

Education

Many of the issues outlined in the previous section also have a bearing upon the experience of looked after children in the education system. The poor educational participation and performance of looked after children and young people has been recognised since the late 1980s (Fletcher-Campbell and Hall 1990; Jackson 1987; SSI/OFSTED 1995; Utting 1997). Furthermore, research into the outcomes for children who have left the care system has consistently produced findings which show that they remain educationally disadvantaged and that this, in turn, leads to disadvantage in other areas of their lives (Biehal *et al.* 1995; DoH/SSI 1997; SSI/OFSTED 1995; Utting 1997).

The long-term outcomes of research projects, both local and national, on the education of statutory school age children (Fletcher-Campbell and Hall 1990; Heath, Colton and Aldgate 1994), have confirmed the poor educational attainment of this group, and highlighted some of the barriers to educational access experienced by 'looked after' children. Possible causal relationships between early experience and later educational performance were identified. However, also highlighted was the *in loco parentis* role of local authorities and their duty to ensure that a child's performance is not adversely affected by factors that are within their control.

Young people 'looked after' increasingly deviate from the trend towards greater participation in full-time education post-sixteen. Whilst precise figures are difficult to establish owing to a lack of effective national monitoring strategies, it was estimated at various points during the early 1990s that:

- 75 per cent leave school with no qualifications (Biehal *et al.* 1992)

- fewer than 20 per cent continue in full time-education after sixteen (Broad 1994)

- between 50 per cent and 80 per cent of 16–24-year-old care leavers are unemployed (Biehal, Clayden and Stein 1994)

- there is a high level of non-attendance and exclusion from school – 25 per cent of this group are not in regular attendance at school. (SSI/OFSTED 1995)

The SSI/OFSTED report (1995) also confirmed the existence of many administrative barriers to educational access and made recommendations on good practice, concluding that:

> The care and education systems in general are failing to promote the educational achievements of children who are 'looked after'. The standards which children achieve are too low and often the modest progress they make in primary schools is lost as they proceed through the system. Despite the clear identification of this problem in several research studies and by committees of enquiry, little has been done in practice to boost achievement. (SSI/OFSTED 1995, p.49)

The SSI/OFSTED report pays little attention to the role or importance of careers guidance for this group, it meriting only one four-line paragraph (SSI/OFSTED 1995, p.43) in which it points out that the substantial number of children who did not attend school regularly in Key Stage Four (the last two years of compulsory schooling) missed out not only on academic opportunities but also on programmes that might have helped them to prepare for adult and working life. The DfE publication *Pupils with Problems* (1994) does seek to address some of these issues of effective working partnerships, setting out legal provisions and responsibilities as well as advice to those in contact with looked after children on a daily basis – particularly class teachers and social services department staff. However, neither the SSI/OFSTED report on looked after children nor the DfE circular 13/94 directly addressed educational provision or participation beyond the age of compulsory schooling. Of course, one possible explanation for the non-issue of post-sixteen education in these official sources is the traditionally low numbers of looked after young people taking up higher and further education within each local authority (invariably less than twenty individuals and seldom even into double figures), together with a possible lack of appreciation of the changing patterns of transition for young people in the general population and their implications for looked after young people (Jesson and Gray 1990; Sime, Pattie and Gray 1990). The issues of post-sixteen educational participation and access to careers advice are addressed specifically in Chapters 6 and 7.

Leaving care

There are obvious links between poor educational outcomes and some of the problems associated with leaving care. However, there are also a number of other issues, particularly the young age at which most young people leave care and the amount of discretion that local authorities have traditionally had in providing help up to the age of 21, which compound educational and other disadvantages suffered by this group. The very high levels of unemployment, homelessness and other social problems afflicting care leavers are widely known (Hazelhurst and Tijani 1998; Stein and Carey 1986; Stone 1990; West 1995, 1996). Statistics relating to the experience of leaving care, although they sometimes vary depending on the author, are uniformly depressing. Since this became a major research area in the mid-1980s, research reports have consistently demonstrated that young people leaving care are amongst the most disadvantaged and vulnerable of their age group. Leaving care is so well-researched an area partly because leaving care provision continues to be so poor. Again, accurate figures are difficult to come by. However, the current government's policy in this field (see Chapter 10) is proceeding on the basis of the best available estimates. These are that:

- An estimated 30 per cent of children looked after have statements of special education need, as against 2–3 per cent of children generally. (DoH 1998d, p.57)

- In some local authorities, as many as 75 per cent of young people leave care with no educational qualifications. (DoH 1998d, p.57)

- Seventeen per cent of young women leaving care are pregnant or already mothers. (Utting 1997)

- Twenty-three per cent of adult prisoners and 38 per cent of young prisoners have been in care at some time in their lives. (Utting 1997, p.91)

- Thirty per cent of young single homeless people have been in care. (Utting 1997, p.91)

Some young people will of course have entered care in the first instance because they were already experiencing significant difficulties or disadvantages. Also, it is worth bearing in mind that while these figures are indeed depressing and compare poorly with the general population of young people, they mark out major differences of degree rather than kind. Young care leavers suffer a high degree of multiple disadvantage, which often has extreme consequences, but they are not experiencing things known only to those who have been in care. Many of the 70 per cent of young homeless people who do not have a care background will have experienced difficulties that might, in other circumstances, have led to them entering the care system.

Most of the literature on leaving care identifies the same factors as responsible for the problems of care leavers. The majority of these follow logically from the above list of problems. The most frequently cited are: the early age of 'independence'; the relative lack of educational qualifications and, consequently, of employment opportunities; frequent moves while looked after, which have both educational and social consequences; the lack of leaving care preparation with respect to key skills such as budgeting; the lack of post-care support; insufficient leaving care grants; the relative lack of family and personal support systems.

User views

In subsequent chapters, the authors draw on research projects that examine the child care system from a number of different perspectives and in a number of different areas. We consider, in various ways, the perspectives of managers, of field and residential social workers, of foster carers and their children and of young people in care and care leavers. This is important, since it helps us to avoid the danger of being guided too closely by professional or élite-led agendas. More recently, several developments have added impetus to the focus on consulting users and those at the grass roots of policy. The first of these was the series of care-system child abuse scandals that emerged in the late 1980s and early 1990s, referred to earlier in the chapter. Much of the investigation into these scandals emphasised – either explicitly or implicitly – the importance of the user's voice in preventing such tragedies. In the case of the Howe inquiry, this was explicit (Howe 1992, paras 5.16–5.18), whereas the 'pindown' report focused on the importance of proper complaints procedures (Levy and Kahan 1991, para. 23.34). Since these reports, the emergence of further abuse patterns in children's homes in Cheshire and North Wales serve to illustrate how important this issue remains. Regardless of what other procedures are put in place, it is clear that one of the best ways of preventing the abuse of looked after children is to find methods of ensuring that the concerns of looked after children and of whistle-blowing staff and carers can gain routine access to inspection and monitoring systems.

Literature on leaving care has often consulted users, since this is the clearest way of understanding the problems of such young people (e.g. Smith 1998; Stein and Carey 1986). Some of the research in this field has gone further and included the perspectives of care leavers in designing research projects and deciding issues to be addressed. Such studies include West's work with care leavers in the production of *You're On Your Own: Young People's Research on Leaving Care* (West 1995; see also 1996), Saunders and Broad on *The Health Needs of Young People Leaving Care* (Saunders and Broad 1997; see also 1998) and Stone's research for the Royal Philanthropic Society, involving user groups in the evaluation of projects (Stone 1990). Other studies involving care leavers as participants have been more locally based, such as Lynes and Goddard's use of care leavers in the design and piloting of their questionnaires (Lynes and Goddard 1995) and research conducted by care leavers into local provision in Hull (RAPP 1998). The importance of this approach also appears to be increasingly recognised at an official level, with official reviews and inspections having involved structured meetings with young people (Utting 1997, p.76) and user assessors (SSI 1997, pp.6–8).

Service quality

Two further developments encouraged greater willingness to listen not just to children in care and care leavers but also to grass roots practitioners such as foster carers. These have been the increased emphasis on children's rights and the spread of the managerial doctrines of Total Quality Management (TQM) within the public sector. The former has arguably been a more public issue in the USA, where it has enthusiastic advocates. However, a focus on children's rights has certainly become more prominent in the United Kingdom during the 1990s (and is discussed in more depth in Chapters 1 and 9). Second, TQM, as a doctrine focusing on the constant pursuit of quality in the provision of goods and services, spread from the private into the public sector during the 1980s. Although now waning in influence, part of the legacy of the TQM approach in the public sector has been a greater focus than has traditionally been the case on the views and wishes of service users (Moore and Kelly 1996; Wilding 1994). This can take several forms, and Wilding cites the particularly appropriate example of the inclusion of care leavers in Department of Health inspection teams investigating children's homes in the early 1990s (Wilding 1994, p.63). Part of the goal here is to counteract the dominance of professional ideologies in defining quality services. Other methods of achieving the same goal include the involvement of service users on advisory committees, in the development of complaints procedures, on user councils and as lay assessors at complaints hearings (Wilding 1994, p.66). That said, despite the emphasis of the TQM approach on the importance of consumer views, there has been relatively little attempt to operationalise this at a practical level in the child care field. Certainly something more is needed than the approach of Knapp, Baines and Gerrard (1990), who attempt to measure performance in the reduced use of foster care without any reference to the views of the children and young people involved, let alone foster carers or social workers. Such approaches can lead to a misleading focus on performance indicators that have been designed to serve the needs and purposes of local authorities, government, professionals or managers – but not necessarily the recipients at the sharp end of policy decisions. As Wilding points out:

> Users must be involved in the development, planning and management of services. Unless they are there to help operationalise the definition of Quality, then managerial and professional ideologies will take over. (Wilding 1994, p.66)

Information and outcomes: 'looking after children'

Finally, with regard to assessing service quality, some mention should be made here of the use of Assessment and Action Records for looked after children. Although these were not a significant feature of our own research, and are therefore discussed relatively briefly in Chapter 8, they have come to occupy an increasingly important place in the routine work of seeking to monitor progress across a range of indicators for looked after children and young people. They are 'becoming a central aspect of the care planning process' (Frost et al. 1999, p.58). The progress of this initiative is also worth discussing because it is particularly illustrative of the trends in thinking that have led us to the explosion of target and standard-setting that is 'Quality Protects'.

The initial motivation for the 'looking after children' approach lies in the TQM focus on effectiveness and accountability that we have already discussed. In the late 1980s and early 1990s this focus was reflected in an increasing research concern with measuring 'outcomes'. There were two particularly important publications on this subject at the time of the implementation of the Children Act. The DoH publication *Patterns and Outcomes in Child Placement* highlighted a number of issues, which were later to become familiar, around the relative neglect of health care and education and the ongoing problems of care leavers (DoH 1991c). More importantly, however, its central conclusion was the lack of hard evidence on outcomes and the need for extensive information-gathering in order that decisions might be based on objective assessments rather than assumptions, personal philosophies and feelings (DoH 1991c, pp.77–78). The second important publication on this theme, but taking it forward in a more practical way, was the DoH-sponsored report on *Assessing Outcomes in Child Care* (Ward *et al.* 1991). This advocated a system of ongoing assessment along 'seven key developmental dimensions: health, education, identity, family and social relationships, social presentation, emotional and behavioural development and self-care skills' (Ward 1996, p.243). It was a paper-bound system designed to be used in foster and residential care by carers and field social workers in consultation with parents and young people (see Appendix 2 of Ward *et al.* 1991 for a copy of the original forms). Extensive evaluation of the original system led to considerable amendment and revision (Ward 1995; 1996).

The system has not been without its problems. Frost *et al.* (1999, p.58) note that the forms themselves are daunting. Berridge and Brodie (1998, pp.36–37) recorded their own attempt to use the system on a six-monthly basis as a failure (though they ascribe this in part to the attempt being a pilot). There have also been problems of discontinuity when young people move and with carers not always being meticulous, accurate or responsive (House of Commons 1998b, p.xxii; Ward 1996). However, the system has also been seen as enhancing the professionalism of foster carers and embodying the principles of accountability and partnership in the Children Act. Accordingly, it has both spread – with the House of Commons Health Select Committee reporting the claim that by autumn of 1997, 92 per cent of local authorities were using the system (House of Commons 1998b, p.xxii) – and been welcomed by a wide range of academic commentators and official bodies (e.g. Berridge 1997, p.23; House of Commons 1998b, pp.xxii–xxiii;

SSI 1998b, pp.19, 35). It now features in the *Modernising Social Services* White Paper as a commitment to 'improvements in assessment and decision-making through further development and implementation of the assessment and planning tool "Looking After Children"' (DoH 1998d, p.56). Much of Quality Protects can be seen as a transferral of the 'Looking After Children' approach from the individualistic, child-focused level of monitoring onto the broad canvas of local authority and public policy.

In the chapters which follow, the themes and topics outlined in this chapter are taken forward and developed through the detailed consideration of research findings that are relevant to these issues. Some of these themes and issues are also returned to in the final chapter.

CHAPTER 3

Coming into Care – Family Placement and Residential Care

In this chapter, we first consider the main literature on placement in foster and residential care before considering our own findings within the context that literature provides. The most obvious point to be drawn from that literature is that children who come into care are drawn overwhelmingly from families with multiple disadvantages. They are more likely than other children to come from a single parent household, to live in poor quality housing with a low family income and to have a larger than average number of siblings. When all of the factors contributing to a situation of material disadvantage are combined, the chances are one in ten that a child will enter the care system, in comparison with 1 in 7000 for a white child living with two parents, in an owner-occupied household supported by paid employment, with three or fewer siblings (Bebbington and Miles 1989). Material deprivation is thus most often the background from which children come into care. However, for this to happen there have to be additional factors, most commonly the mental illness of a parent, domestic violence, physical and/or sexual abuse of the child (Osborn and Sinclair 1987). The family is likely to have become isolated or alienated from friends and relatives, who might otherwise have stepped in to care for the children (Jackson 1998a). However, studies have also shown that around half of all looked after children return home within six months of being taken into care (Bullock, Little and Millham 1993) and more recent work suggests that as many as two-thirds of children return to their families within six months (Jackson 1998a). It follows that children who remain looked after for longer periods are likely to be those from the most troubled and divided families. Of course there are exceptions; parents still fall ill and die, they may not have an extended family network, they may be overwhelmed by a series of unpredictable catastrophes. However, in general children within the care system are most unlikely to come from 'ordinary' working class families; that is those who simply lack material resources (Jackson 1998a).

In seeking to explain the links between particular family circumstances and entry into care, there is a great deal to consider beyond the broad categories of risk factors. Bebbington and Miles (1989) conclude that 'although children who are admitted to care for different reasons come from very similar backgrounds, the dynamics of the situation that creates their problems may be very different' (p.365). For example, Rutter (1985) has found that it is not marital breakdown *per se* that causes behaviour problems among children, but the extent of the child's previous exposure to family discord. Quine and Pahl (1986) report evidence that a child with disabilities, including behavioural difficulties, is a major cause of marital tension and family breakdown. Children in poor social circumstances are also more likely to receive professional attention and surveillance and thus some difficulties will be uncovered which may not come to light in families with better material circumstances (Bebbington and Miles 1989).

As noted in the previous chapter, the lack of available foster carers for all looked after children has particular consequences for children from minority ethnic backgrounds. The importance for children of being placed with foster carers or in a children's home where there is at least one adult of the same ethnic origin has subsequently received much media coverage. Guidance on the Children Act from the Department of Health (DoH 1991a) states that each case should be considered individually, but placing children with carers of the same ethnic origin is viewed as most likely to meet their needs. However, a national study found that authorities in England, particularly county authorities, had serious shortages of foster carers from ethnic minority backgrounds (Waterhouse 1997). Earlier research conducted during the 1980s showed that children from minority ethnic backgrounds were seldom placed with carers of the same ethnic origin (Cliffe with Berridge 1991) and a survey conducted in the mid-1990s still found that 41 per cent of Local Authorities said they felt unable to meet the needs of black children requiring foster care (ADSS 1997).

The reasons for children entering care have shifted considerably over the years. Bebbington and Miles (1989) compare their own survey in 1987 with that of Packman (1968) in 1962 and note that a far higher proportion of children admitted in 1987 were in care because of their behaviour, including offending behaviour, in comparison with 1962 (19% in 1987 in comparison with 4% in 1962). There had been a major reduction in the proportion of children coming into care because of the ill health of their parents between the two surveys (19% in 1987 and 56% in 1962). Bebbington and Miles (1989) concluded that entry into care in 1987 was even more associated with 'deprived' families than in 1962. Utting (1991) notes that very few children come into care because they are abandoned, compared with earlier in the century. A greater proportion have been neglected or abused. Utting concluded that coming into care is more often associated with a constellation of issues relating to relationship breakdown in families, particularly with adolescents. Berridge and Brodie (1998) in comparing reasons for admissions to residential care in the early 1980s and mid-1990s in the same local authorities confirm this latter view. They found an increase in the proportion of children coming into care who had been abused (61% in the mid-1990s, compared with 44% in the early 1980s). More generally, they outline a range of stress factors which they view as responsible for individuals' admissions to care in the local authorities that they studied. Of relevance in relation to discussion of care and control in Chapter 5 is Berridge and Brodie's finding that two-thirds of the residents in their study had previously presented serious behavioural problems at home, in school or in the community. Department of Health figures show that there has been an increase in the proportion of children starting to be looked after under care orders during the 1990s (from 8% of all new placements in 1994, to 15% in 1998). Consequently, there has been a decrease in children coming into care under voluntary agreements in the same time period (from 79% of all new placements in 1994, to 69% in 1998) (DoH 1998a).

'Coming into care' is likely to be a stressful time for children, their birth families, their carers and the social workers managing this process. We have relatively little published evidence of this *process* as a lived event by all parties, perhaps partly because it is such a sensitive and difficult period in many cases. Utting (1997) makes brief reference to the bewilderment, displacement and loss that young people report feeling at the point of entry to care and warns that at this time children are particularly vulnerable to the negative influence of predatory adults or delinquent peers. Utting also notes the lack of control in the situation from the point of view of the child – lack of choice of who one lives with, type of placement, location, school, social worker and so on. Sadly, the upheaval and displacement associated with the process is likely to be repeated a number of times because of placement breakdowns. Placement breakdown has been the subject of research for some time and there is concern about the multiple placements experienced by some children. The Quality Protects initiative specifically identifies reduction in the number of changes in main carer for children looked after as one of its sub-objectives. The proportion of children who experience three or more placements in a year is reported to be as high as one-third in some local authorities (DoH 1998b).

Choice and availability of placements

Increasingly, published work which includes any reference to the process of 'coming into care' highlights the difficulties created by a lack of choice with regard to placements. One of the conclusions to the review into the safeguards for children living away from home (Utting 1997) was that choice of placements was a fundamental safeguard. A principal recommendation of the Utting review was that local authorities should 'secure sufficient provision of residential and foster care to allow a realistic choice of placement for each child' (p.8). This recommendation contrasts sharply with the findings of a number of investigations and research reports in recent years. Indeed, the SSI concluded that there had been 'no choice in the majority of cases' (quoted in Utting 1997, p.40) and that this meant that children's needs were not being met. A study in Scotland which examined the placements of 201 children found that, on average, social workers across three regions would have preferred a different placement in 44 per cent of cases (Kendrick 1995). This figure was higher on average for residential care (55%) than for foster care (35%), although there were regional differences. In the case of foster placements, the majority of social workers wanted a different foster or community placement, not a residential placement. In the case of residential placements, although it might have been expected that social workers would have preferred a foster placement, this was only the case for a third of the placements. One of the most important factors for social workers in both types of placement was the proximity to the child's home. Foster placements tended to be closer to the child's home than residential placements. Choice of placement was also found to be poor in the Waterhouse study of foster care. Predictably, the situation was worse for older children. For children under ten years, 19 per cent of authorities said they were almost always able to offer a placement choice, whilst only 3 per cent said the same for children over ten years (Waterhouse 1997). The lack of choice of placements is not new and since the 1980s research has been warning that children are being placed where there is a vacancy, rather than somewhere which is matched to their needs and the ability of the placement to meet these needs.

J. Kelly (1995) highlights the disparity between the guidance to volume four of the Children Act with regard to admissions to care and the practice found as an inspector of children's services. Guidance makes plain that admissions to children's homes should take careful account of the suitability of the home, its current staff and residents and the needs of the child to be placed. For example, it is stated in the guidance that it would be inappropriate to place a sexually abused child in a home accommodating children who are themselves abusers (DoH 1991a). Kelly goes on to illustrate instances where exactly that situation has arisen. Indeed, an instance is described in which an abused child and an abuser were sharing a bedroom in one children's home. Kelly found staff were often not in receipt of the relevant information about children in such situations and were usually 'blissfully unaware' of the relevant Children Act guidance. Parallel issues are clearly also in evidence in foster placements. One of the most widely known examples of recent years concerns a case in Essex involving the placement of a fifteen-year-old boy in a foster family with four children aged twelve years and under at the time. The boy placed was the son of a convicted paedophile. While the family knew this, they claimed that they were not told that the boy had gone on to abuse. During his stay in this family, the boy abused all of the children, who went on to have psychiatric counselling. The High Court ruled, in this case, that the local authority had a duty of care to give the foster family as much information as any 'reasonable' social worker would provide. The Appeal Court cleared the way for the children to pursue a claim of negligence against the council, even though their parents' claim for compensation for the trauma that they suffered was blocked (Inman 1998a).

The reduction in places in residential care and the failure to recruit and retain sufficient foster carers are the main reasons why there is little or no choice of placement in many cases. Yet even with choice of placement the capacity of residential staff and foster carers to address the complex needs of some looked after children may be restricted. It is important in this context to note that resources released by closing residential homes have generally not been redirected into foster care. Indeed, the closure of facilities does not necessarily release substantive new resources if the unit costs of remaining services go up. Warwickshire famously took the decision to close the last of its children's homes in 1986. Research evaluating the impact of this decision found that there was a reduction in both the choice and number of placements available to children (Cliffe with Berridge 1991). It was concluded that the consequences of the closure of children's homes were that children's needs were less likely to be met and that the effects on foster carers, who were under pressure to care for more difficult children, were likely to be damaging. The closure of local authority residential homes in Warwickshire also led to an increased use of non-county placements.

When recognising the importance of choice, one must also consider what children say they want and also what they tell us about their experiences in both settings. Kahan (1995) and Utting (1997) both remind us that some children do not want placement in a family and might positively choose residential care or some combination of residential care, own home, foster care and residential school. On the other hand young people told the Utting review that foster care was experienced as safer than residential care, with regard to the unwanted attentions and influences of other children. However, for others foster care was said to be worse than living in a residential home, if they found none of the benefits of living in a family and lost the benefits of communal living.

Multiple placements and placement breakdown

Some looked after children experience numerous episodes of care and a minority of them experience multiple placements. These changes are sometimes preceded by the breakdown of an existing placement, which affects a significant proportion of looked after children (Utting 1997). Cliffe with Berridge (1991) found a higher rate of multiple placements in Warwickshire after all their children's homes were closed; a third of the cohort in their study had three or more placements in a fifteen-month period, almost double the rate found in other studies. However, Kendrick (1995) found a similar proportion (29%) of individuals with three or more placements in a twelve-month study in Scotland. A Barnardo's study, also in Scotland, found that each child coming to the attention of their projects had already moved on average of 3.73 times. Within the Barnardo's study, thirty-one children had moved more than five times before coming to a Barnardo's project and one child had moved forty times (Sone 1997). A DoH/SSI report (1996) into foster care found that 12 per cent of children had moved more than three times. The shortage of placements is connected to multiple placements and placement breakdown in that a child's first placement is often an emergency placement and may not match the child's needs. Children are often then moved on too quickly to allow for planning the move adequately and to an appropriate placement (Sone 1997).

Clearly there are definitional problems and even the term 'placement breakdown' is not used by some practitioners, who prefer to use terms like 'premature ending'. Certainly there may be important differences between what amounts to a 'breakdown' and the acknowledgement that a placement is not meeting a child's needs and therefore moving them to another more appropriate placement in a planned way. However, we must not lose sight of how and why placements end, particularly in relation to whether that placement was one that initially appeared to meet the child's needs, or was used because there was no other placement available. Taking into account the definitional problems, Parker (1988) estimated that about 20 per cent of foster placements are likely to break down in any particular year and that 75 per cent of these children are likely then to be admitted into residential care. Several studies have shown that foster placements often break down over a long period of time, rather than as a result of one particular incident, although a specific event may mark the end of a placement (Aldgate and Hawley 1986a, 1986b; Berridge and Cleaver 1987). Researchers have compiled lists of general factors as the result of outcome studies which indicate when placements are most likely to survive. Triseliotis (1989) has separated these factors into child related factors, foster placement related factors, birth parent related factors and agency related factors. Child related factors are, for example, those relating to the behaviour and age of the child. Foster placement related factors include the age of foster carers, the number and age of their children if they have any, their relationships with birth parents, the support and training they have received and the way they deal with difficult behaviour. Factors relating to birth parents include the consistency with which they visit children and agency related factors are, for example, matching of placements and level of support provided. The results of such studies can be used to inform practice about the placement of children, for example outcome studies indicate that placements are most likely to survive if there is not another child close in age already living in the household. Research on looked after children shows that there is a flow of children between residential and foster care and that these two sectors are inter-dependent. For example Parker (1988) found that 79 per cent of children in foster care had previously been in residential care and Berridge (1985) found that 35 per cent of children in residential care were being prepared for a foster placement. Parker (1988) concludes that: 'seen from the child's viewpoint residential care and foster care are often sequential episodes in a string of different placements' (p.73). In their follow-up study on residential care, Berridge and Brodie (1998) raise the issue of inappropriate placements (whether certain young people were placed in the right setting in relation to other residents and the home's statement of purpose). They note the varied ability of unit managers to resist placements which they feel are inappropriate.

Research findings

In what follows, we develop the previous discussion by considering the research findings of Gorin (1997) on family placement and Hayden (1997a) on residential care in the same three local authorities (see Appendix, sections 3 and 1 respectively). We focus on evidence within those studies on the following two areas:

- the ability to plan placements
- case studies of how children came into residential and foster care.

The ability to plan placements

RESIDENTIAL CARE

Most of the residential units in our authorities were locally based children's homes. In some areas there was little or no specialist short-stay emergency provision, so that local homes had to cater for a mixture of emergencies, short-stay and long-stay residents. Residential staff were asked whether, in general, admissions to their unit were planned. Fewer than four in ten staff reported that this was the case, with three in ten unit managers describing admissions as 'generally unplanned'. The ability to plan placements was said to be related, in some cases, to care and control issues, as we shall see in Chapter 5. Staff often focused upon the mix and needs of a resident group when explaining why they thought a placement was inappropriate, as the following quote from a unit manager illustrates:

> I feel that if the young people's placements were planned we would be less likely to get into physical restraint. Certainly the last two [individuals restrained] in this unit were with young people whose needs were not being appropriately met in the unit, mainly due to the mix of youngsters at

the time. However, due to resources there was nowhere else for them to be accommodated.

Care and control issues and, specifically, the use of physical restraint, surfaced frequently in discussions of why care staff thought certain individuals were inappropriately placed (partly because of the focus of the research project; see Appendix, section 1). In certain cases young people and staff could be left in difficult situations for extended periods of time. This did a great deal of damage to staff morale and clearly did not meet the young persons' needs. A residential worker describes an incident of this kind in the following way:

> The level of restraint required for the particular male young person in our unit should not have occurred, as he was not in the best place for the level of care he needed. He knew this, but despite all our efforts and his requests to be moved, nothing happened for nearly two years. The staff felt as though everyone was 'passing the buck' and in the end I feel the young person felt he had nothing to lose by putting himself into restraint situations, and maybe it was the only way he was going to get the help he needed.

This young man went on to be cared for separately from other young people within a secure unit before attempts were made to reintegrate him into group living. This was not successful and he subsequently moved on to specialist foster carers out of county and from there to a regional secure unit. This was one of the most challenging cases found during the period of monitoring. Several staff felt very strongly that he had been allowed to drift in the system, increasing the damage to himself and those around him. Because of emergency admissions and unplanned placements, many staff felt that there was little stability for other residents or staff in the homes where they worked; this situation compounded an already difficult situation:

> Due to the nature of the work, situations can change very quickly – that is the number of children, level of aggression and violence, other issues such as staffing, pressures of shifts and lack of sleep [and so on] can also affect working ... Sometimes it has to be crisis management and goodwill of staff is often expected and demanded. Staff [are] still expected to work long hours with no breaks and very little sleep, with the possibility of violence and aggression, being kept awake all night and no staff to take over. This obviously affects the care of young people and quality of the work that staff are able to do.

Although residential staff often described a system which felt overstretched and crisis-driven, it is important to acknowledge that particular placements could have a disproportionate effect on staff perceptions about both planning and their ability to care for young people appropriately. Nonetheless, the common view held by residential staff was that despite the efforts and views of staff and statements of purpose in particular units, service managers both could and would override them when they needed a placement. This was seen as a major source of difficulties:

> Staff work in a caring and consistently professional manner and as a team to implement care plans for individuals. Problems arise when the department as a whole doesn't recognise our statement of purpose and function, e.g. inappropriate admissions, admissions directed by the service manager, directed against our stated purpose and function.

In certain cases, such admissions could lead to major damage to the fabric of units, including the closure of one unit due to damage during the period of research, staff attacked and hurt, as well as damage to other residents. Despite the relatively small number of children who could be described as extremely difficult to contain in certain placements, the number of residential homes, and proportion of their residents and staff affected, could be significant (again, see Chapter 5).

Although the above picture may seem bleak, it was also reported by nearly four in ten staff that placements were generally planned and two-thirds of staff reported that they felt their residential unit provided a positive experience for young people who needed to spend time outside of a family environment. Many staff were able to look beyond the placements which did not work, because of the inability to plan or provide appropriate care for complex needs, to placements which were more positive for all concerned.

FOSTER CARE

In the case of foster placements, the ability to plan a placement for a child was shown to be very difficult, not least because there are often very few, if any, available carers. Family placement teams had a difficult job in trying to find carers when children needed placing and this could result in children staying in unsatisfactory circumstances or not being given a choice of placement.

Social workers were aware of the pressure that family placement teams were under and felt that pressure was often displaced from the child's social worker onto the family placement social worker and then in turn onto the foster carer to take a child that they may not otherwise be prepared for. Almost half (46%) of all carers were found to have cared for children outside their own approval range. This proportion was much higher for emergency care, short-term care and project care. Long-term carers were more likely to care for children within their approval range, indicating a better matching of individuals and placements. However, the outcomes of caring for children outside approval ranges were not always negative; some families reported that they found they preferred a different age group from that for which they were approved or simply enjoyed looking after particular children. On the other hand, more than four in ten carers reported negative experiences. One example was:

> [We had] one eight-year-old girl for eight months respite! ... [she] was very disruptive [and] made my daughter's life hell, eventually [we] had to move her on for my daughter's sake. Present nine-year-old is special needs ... [the] children get very frustrated especially [my] seven-year-old son as she gives him no space; he has learnt to cut himself off from the endless noise.

Families frequently commented on the particular placements that could cause stress and be very hectic and hard work for the whole family. There were sometimes practical difficulties, such as overcrowding in the home or the inability to transport all the family together by car. Carers said that they could feel under pressure to keep children longer than was originally planned, or than they wanted to, one carer noting that: '...Children often arrive on a Friday or Sunday night. Social Services often leave them with me until I complain.'

Carers also reported that they often did not receive enough information on children before they arrived. Half of all carers said that they did not receive enough information, this proportion rising to 60 per cent for emergency carers and almost two-thirds (65%) for carers with a combination approval and for short-term carers. While carers understood that in emergencies it was often difficult to provide information, many also felt that they had been deliberately left without important information, either because it was not felt necessary for carers to know certain details or because social workers were concerned that carers would not take the child if they were made aware of the full details of the case. Comments made by carers indicated the difficulties and potential dangers that this could cause, for example:

> We had a really bad time with a little girl who suffered with asthma, no inhaler or medicine [was] given, also a food allergy that no one told us about. [She was] sick every night for two weeks. If any information had been given this wouldn't have happened.

More extreme cases included carers not being told of actual bodily harm (ABH) charges that a child had to face and a history of arson.

The children's social workers felt very strongly about the lack of placement choice for children, particularly as it meant that it was simply not possible to match needs to placements. For example, a social worker in our study said:

> In an ideal world we would match children's needs to what a foster carer can offer, but it's not like that ... You can't make choices with foster carers, there just aren't enough ... Sometimes you feel you take the child away from one set of problems and give them another.

There was little doubt in most social workers' minds that the restrictions on accessing the type of placement which would best meet a child's needs were largely financial in origin. In several cases, children were living in foster placements when everyone involved agreed that a place in a residential EBD school would be far more beneficial for that particular child. Social workers believed that given a bit more emotional and financial support there would also be a much larger bank of foster carers. In the words of one social worker, which are fairly representative:

> Everything is a funding battle – if we had more money we could use it more creatively ... money is the overriding force in looking after children. Arguments to service managers are resource led ... plans are geared by money and not what is best for the child.

The social workers were working within a very difficult and pressurised environment and even when placements were not emergencies the ability to plan them was minimal because of the lack of foster carers available. The lack of carers meant that children were often placed without any choice of placement and it was often a case of luck whether the placement met the child's wider needs. Foster carers were also being placed in compromising positions with regard to the children that they took and the level of information that they were provided with.

Case studies of how children came into residential and foster care

The two research projects (Gorin 1997; Hayden 1997a) had a different emphasis with regard to the nature of the in-depth case studies that they each conducted. The young people in residential care were individuals perceived to be behaviourally most challenging over a three month period of monitoring. Thus these young people studies may be assumed to be more likely to represent the more challenging end of the behavioural spectrum when investigating how children came to be in care or in a particular placement. The young people in foster placements, on the other hand, were chosen randomly; they were the first ten placements from a representative range of family placement teams in the authorities in a two month period. We will now explore the circumstances in which these particular children came into care and the extent to which it was possible to plan their placements.

RESIDENTIAL CARE

There were eleven children in the case studies in nine different residential units within the authorities. None of the case studies were of new cases for the SSD. In three cases the SSD had been involved with the whole family since the child had been born. In all but one case the SSD had been involved with the family for between five and ten years. In four cases, the young people had only experienced residential care, two had severe learning difficulties, one was a young carer and the other a victim of long-term neglect in a family well known to social services. In only one of the cases was reception into full-time residential care preceded by respite care. Overall, the precipitating circumstances behind admission into care involved neglect and concerns about parenting in four cases, a serious breakdown in family relationships in four cases, parents unable to cope with the behaviour associated with severe learning disabilities in two cases, and bereavement and mental health problems for the surviving parent in one case. There had been no contact between the young person and birth parents for over a year in two cases. Allegations about sexual abuse of the young person were a factor in seven cases, although this was not always a precipitating reason for entry to care. Relationship difficulties between birth parents was the norm (10 in 11 cases) and violence was a very definite factor in four cases. Single parents and reconstituted households were more common (7 of the 11 case studies) than both birth parents living together.

Table 3.1 Residential case studies – placement and care issues

Name (age in brackets)	Placement issues				Selected needs indicators		
	Placement at start of research/ time in placement	Entry to this placement	Number of previous placements	Change over 6-month period. Plans beyond this time, if different	Education	Mental health problems	Suspected sexual abuse
Alice (12)*	LBCH (4 years)	Planned	3 (1FC; 2CH)	Grand-parents	Mainstream F/T exclusions	YP	Yes
Bradley (14)	LBCH (<6 months)	Emergency	——	Foster care	Mainstream F/T exclusions	YP Parent	Yes
Diane (14)	LBCH (2½ years)	Placement breakdown	C15 (FC and CH)	Temp. Move to another LBCH	Special school (MLD)	YP	Yes
Helen (15)	SLD Unit (9 years, incl. respite)	Planned	——	Plan to close unit – future uncertain	Special school (SLD), F/T exclusion	YP	Yes
John (15)	LBCH (18 months)	Placement breakdown	C10 (FC and CH)	Secure unit -> O-O-C	No school (EBD/ MLD) excluded permanently	——	——
Kelly (16)	LBCH (<6 months)	Emergency	17 (6FC; 11 supported lodgings)	Secure unit -> O-O-C	Left school, previously excluded permanently	YP Sibling	Yes
Mark (15)	LBCH (1 year)	Emergency	——	Plan to return home	Special school (EBD), previous permanent exclusion	——	——
Melanie (15)	LBCH (<3 months)	Placement breakdown	6 (3FC; 3CH)	Independent then supported in hostel	No school, excluded permanently	YP	——
Peter (16)	LBCH (<3 months)	Placement breakdown	6 (3FC; 3CH)	Independent	No school (EBD), excluded permanently	YP Parent	Yes
Tracey (14)	LBCH (<3 months)	Placement breakdown	5 (1FC; 4CH)	O-O-C -> Home with support	Special school (EBD) P/T attender, previous permanent exclusion	YP Parent	Yes
Trevor (12)	Respite Care Unit, SLD (3 weeks)	Emergency	——	Flat with 2 agency staff, within LBCH	Special school (SLD) F/T exclusions	YP	——

*Age during 1996 in brackets

Key:

CH	Children's Home
EBD	Emotional and Behavioural Difficulties
FC	Foster Care
F/T	Fixed-Term (exclusion)
LBCH	Locally Based Children's Home
MLD	Moderate Learning Difficulties
O-O-C	Out of County (placement)
P/T	Part-Time (attender)
SEN	Special Educational Needs
SLD	Severe Learning Difficulties
YP	Young Person

Seven of the eleven case studies conducted involved young people who had three or more placements in residential or foster care, had been known to social services for several years and had spent at least a full year in residential care. Placement breakdowns characterise their care histories. All but one of the placements were described as an emergency or came about as a result of another placement not working. Thus these young people came into care in especially stressful circumstances. Some of the key issues with these young people are summarised in Table 3.1.

What is notable is the range of needs that these children had and the difficulty that locally based children's homes had in meeting these needs. One young woman already had two out-of-area placements which had not worked out (one because the place had closed some months after her admission) and three others went on to such placements in the months following the fieldwork in the study. Two key service needs stood out as inadequately met in these cases: access to appropriate education, and mental health/psychological services. These problems seemed insurmountable at the time of placement out of area, although there was also evidence that these needs were not always easily or well met in more specialist placements.

FOSTER CARE

There were thirteen children in the foster care case studies, which accounted for a total of ten placements (siblings are identified in Table 3.2 with the same letter after their first names). These placements were taken from six family placement teams in both city and rural locations within the authorities. The children were aged between two and fifteen years. There were a wide variety of care histories. However, all of the families had been previously known to the SSDs for a considerable amount of time. Two of the mothers had been in care themselves. Out of the ten placements, seven children came from families with single mothers and the remaining three had step-fathers or the mother's boyfriend living with the family. All the parents either could not cope with their children, did not want to (in four of the placements) or were unable to protect them adequately. In the case of several of the children it was not that their mothers did not want to provide care, but they did not seem to be able, or know how to protect themselves and their children from male partners who presented a danger to the family. The parents were all facing a multitude of stresses themselves including: being a single parent; being unemployed; having a low income; lacking a close supportive network of family or friends; living in poor housing; having experienced some form of abuse themselves; having several children under ten; drug and alcohol related problems; and mental health problems. Indeed there were concerns from social workers about parents' mental health in all but two of the placements (again, see Table 3.2).

For two children this was their first experience of a full-time placement. Half of the placements were unplanned, two were due to other foster placements breaking down and three were planned. As was indicated earlier, there was no choice of placement for any of the children. In those cases where the placements were said to be 'planned', the children moved into the foster family within a short space of time and there was little evidence of much preparation for anyone involved, although children had at least met their new carers prior to moving in. In two of the three cases where the placement had been planned, carers still complained about the lack of up-to-date information about the children. All except one of the children had experienced emotional abuse, neglect, physical abuse or sexual abuse and the majority had experienced a combination of types of abuse. Educational difficulties were common amongst these children and young people. Of the ten school-age children, six had a statement of special educational need and one had a full-time special needs assistant assigned solely to him. Half of the children had experienced an exclusion from school, either temporary, permanent or both and one young person had a list of exclusions including exclusion from a school for children with emotional and behavioural difficulties. All five of the children who were twelve or over had been involved with the police. Two of these children had been charged with actual bodily harm and one, aged twelve, was suspected of being involved in serious arson attacks and burglaries.

Table 3.2 Foster care case studies – placement and care issues

Name (age in brackets)	Placement issues				Selected needs indicators		
	Placement at start of research	Entry to this placement	Number of previous placements	Change over 6-month period. Plans beyond this time, if different	Education	Mental health problems	Suspected sexual abuse
Angela B (5)	Foster care	Unplanned	1 (FC)	New foster placement. Plan to look for adoptive parents	Mainstream school	Parent	Yes
David (14)	Foster care	Planned	1 (CH)	Move to CH. CH can't cope with him and closing shortly. Plan to look for foster carers	No school, excluded permanently (SEN)	Parent	——
Heidi A (10) *	Foster care	Unplanned	2 (2 FC)	Same foster carers. Plan to look for long-term care	Mainstream school F/T exclusion	Child Parent	——
Jamie C (7)	Foster care	Planned	1 (FC)	Went to aunt's, then to new foster placement	Full-time special needs assistant	Parent	Yes
Julie (14)	Project care	Placement breakdown	1 (1 FC)	Same project carer	Special school (MLD)	Parent YP	Yes
Justin C (2)	Foster care	Planned	1 (FC)	Went to aunt's then home	Not school age	Parent	——
Justine B (7)	Foster care	Unplanned	1 (FC)	New foster placement. Plan to look for adoptive parents	Mainstream school (SEN)	Parent	Yes
Linton (4)	Foster care	Unplanned	(0)	Same foster carer	Not school age	Parent	——
Lisa (12)	Project care	Unplanned	1 (FC)	Same project carers part of week, rest of week at home. Trying to find EBD school	Out of school (SEN), excluded permanently	YP	Yes
Roger (12)	Project care	Placement breakdown	2 (FC)	Back home	No school, excluded permanently (SEN)	Parent	Yes
Sarah (6)	Project care	Unplanned	(0)	Same foster carer, due to move to adoptive parents shortly	Mainstream school	Parent Child	——
Terry (15)	Project care	Planned	5 (3 CH; 2 FC)	Same project carers	Special school (EBD), several exclusions	YP	——
Tom A (3)	Foster care	Unplanned	1 (FC)	Same foster carers. Plan to look for adoptive parents	Not school age	Child Parent	——

* Age during 1998 in brackets

Key:

CH	Children's Home
EBD	Emotional and Behavioural Difficulties
FC	Foster Care
F/T	Fixed-Term (exclusion)
LBCH	Locally Based Children's Home
MLD	Moderate Learning Difficulties
O-O-C	Out of County (placement)
P/T	Part-Time (attender)
SEN	Special Educational Needs
SLD	Severe Learning Difficulties
YP	Young Person

Many of the children in the case studies had been in what were reported to be inappropriate placements previously, or were currently living in unsuitable circumstances. The factors which made the children's placements inappropriate were not related to the carer's ability or willingness to meet essential care needs, but with contextual factors such as the number of children or mix of children already living in the foster home, the child needing to be placed with siblings or the carer about to go on holiday at the time of placement. Placements were difficult to find for all the children and although some of the children were placed with carers that they already knew, this was usually a case of luck rather than judgement. In the cases of both teenage boys, they had been waiting in residential care for over two months for a foster placement.

Discussion

The research reported upon in this chapter confirms and adds to the findings of the Utting (1997) review and the concerns expressed by the ADSS (1997) and Warren (1997a) reports in respect of the availability of placements, the ability of placements to meet children's needs, the mix of children in particular placements and problems of placement breakdown. It presents a worrying picture in relation to the ability of these local authorities to plan placements, either in residential or foster care. The impact of what were described as 'inappropriate' placements in residential care could affect the morale of whole staff teams as well as the well-being of other residents. A similar situation was found in family placement, with the added difficulty of inadequate information about a child being passed on to more than half of the foster carers. There were clearly child protection issues for other residents in the placement of particular individuals within the residential setting. Sinclair and Gibbs (1996) report attempted bullying and unwelcome sexual advances (singly or together) in around half of their sample of young people in residential care and the significance of this problem is confirmed by the Utting review. Equally there is the issue of whether placements, particularly foster placements and especially private agencies (foster and small residential homes), are properly vetted and monitored.

Although the residential case studies were deliberately drawn to represent some of the cases viewed as more problematic within the residential sector and the foster placements were simply new placements in foster care in a particular time period, there are some obvious similarities in the issues illustrated. First, unplanned placements were more common than planned placements. Second, there was virtually no opportunity to match the needs of the child or young person to the placements available. Third, the majority of the children and young people had experienced previous placements. Fourth, it was common for children to have special educational needs, to have experienced exclusion from school, to have mental health problems and for there to be suspected sexual abuse of the child. The main difference between the two sets of case studies was in the ages of the children and young people placed, with eight of the children in the foster placements being under twelve years of age and all of the residential placements being twelve years of age and over (a finding similar to that noted in the Utting review).

Certain young people were spending long periods of time in residential care, when the primary purpose of the home was not long-stay provision. These individuals were constantly witnessing other children and young people moving on to foster placements or back to their birth family. Similarly, there were long-term residents in respite care units for children with severe learning difficulties. A child with severe learning difficulties and severe challenging behaviour was moved out of an emergency placement at a respite care unit (which, incidently, had caused disruption to other planned respite care) on to a self-contained flat in a locally based children's home (LBCH) with two full-time carers around the clock. Children and parents could be waiting weeks or months after the parents were told that they would be provided with a foster placement. Five foster placements in our study were made with project carers, rather than with mainstream foster carers. Four of the children placed with project carers clearly did have a high level of need and were all twelve years old or over. However, one child of six with no major behavioural problems was placed with a project carer and one teenage boy with major behavioural problems was placed with mainstream carers, in both cases because there was no other placement available at that time. All of the placements that broke down were with mainstream carers. However, the number of the case studies is not large enough to be able to draw firm conclusions from this and it is worth noting that all the foster carers had provided successful placements in the past. The majority of the young people in the case studies of residential care had not moved out to live with their birth parents or relatives after a six month period, although most were in regular contact. There were plans to return two young people home as soon as possible, although there were real concerns about the ability of the parents to cope in each case. Ironically, one young woman was returned home with substantial support during the period of monitoring, but this was because her out-of-area placement had closed and there were no other alternatives at the time. There were plans to place a further two young people in out-of-area specialist foster placements and this happened in both cases within a year of the start of the case studies. Two young people spent periods of time living independently in supported lodgings during the year in which they became sixteen, both needing substantial support from social services and with very little help from their birth families. Neither of these young people had a school place, although one of them attended a further education college briefly before giving up formal education.

The foster placements were also followed up after a period of six months and in this time four of the ten placements (involving six children) had ended. One child returned home as had been planned and three placements ended prematurely. Two of the three placements which had been planned broke down. This was, however, possibly to do with an initial inability to choose suitable placements to meet children's needs in the first place. In one case, the foster carers had previously only looked after children with special needs; they were told that the placement of two sisters would only be for a week. The children were moved on after six months because of tensions between the foster children and the carers' own daughter, who was of a similar age. The other two placements broke down largely because of the behaviour of the children.

The remaining six foster placements reported mixed results with the children. Three placements had experienced near breakdowns because of difficult to manage behaviour from the children. In these cases the behaviour was extreme: one child took an overdose; another had Attention Deficit Hyperactivity Disorder (ADHD) and displayed overtly sexualised behaviour towards men; the third, a young child, smeared faeces over himself and the house. However, this did not mean that these placements were not beneficial for the children in some respects. For example, the foster carer looking after the girl who took an overdose remained committed to her throughout her difficulties and this was reported, by the social worker, to be of tremendous support to her. Several of the placements were considered (by the social workers and foster carers) to have been very beneficial for children in terms of increasing their self-esteem and providing them with a secure, consistent environment. The best example of positive outcomes involved a teenage boy who had experienced multiple previous placements and was placed with project carers. The support he had received was illustrated by his subsequent lack of involvement with the police and a much improved school attendance record. Other children were said to have become more integrated with their peers and less prone to problems such as enuresis (bed-wetting).

Conclusions and implications

The research findings presented in this chapter underline the recommend- ations of the Utting review in relation to the continuing need for residential care and room within the service in order to match needs to placements. The interdependence of residential and foster care is illustrated by the case studies in that children entering residential care had often experienced foster care and some of the children in the foster placements had been in residential care previously. The relationship between residential care, foster care and family support is also apparent. Children and young people entering the care system were all previously known to the social services departments, their needs for support had not been met and a crisis or major difficulty precipitated the children's entry into care. This latter point is important because although better family support systems may be able to predict and avert certain crises, they will not always manage to do so. That is, emergencies need to be planned and provided for. Some children do not return to birth families quickly for a variety of complex reasons. These children need stability in their placements and a recognition that they are likely to be in a placement for an extended period. This placement may be a residential unit in some cases. Thus a better differentiation in, and adherence to, statements of purpose within residential care is required. This is central to ensuring that residential workers can develop consistent and positive working patterns and that young people within residential homes can live in safe and stable environments. Also required is a better connection to, and relationship with, family placement and family support systems. A more positive use of and connection between the sectors is required in order to improve plans for matching needs to services. However, central to the placement of most looked after children is the future development of foster care – the subject of the following chapter.

CHAPTER 4

Developments in Foster Care

As noted in Chapter 2, local authorities have increasingly favoured the use of foster rather than residential care. However, relatively little research evidence exists on the comparative outcomes for children and young people in foster and residential care. Berridge's research review suggests that once the differing population characteristics are controlled for, outcomes are broadly similar (Berridge 1997, pp.23–24). There remain, however, many significant areas of difference between the two types of care. Some of these will be discussed in both this and the following chapter.

Fostering has come under increasing pressure in recent years as it attempts to place children with a wider range of needs, without a sufficient number or range of foster carers. At the same time, national standards for foster care have been developed, alongside uneven developments in the payment, support and training of carers. Indeed there is increasing recognition that the 'professionalisation' of foster care may be necessary in order to achieve the required standards, as well as to recruit and retain carers. This chapter considers the future of the fostering service in the light of these developments and our own research evidence.

The reduction in the use of residential care and in numbers of children entering the care system has meant that young people in foster care have 'more complex needs than previously' (Utting 1997, p.30). In other words, those children entering foster families are likely to be older, more challenging and more vulnerable than in previous years (Warren 1997a). This has had significant implications for fostering and has increased the expectations of carers and their families. Not only are foster children likely to present a wider range of needs in terms of their day-to-day care, but carers are now also expected to complete a number of other tasks, including enabling contact with birth parents, attending court and meetings, and completing paperwork. Poor levels of recruitment and retention of carers has meant that appropriate placements, or indeed any foster placements for children, have in many cases been difficult to find (as discussed in the previous chapter). The placements which are hardest to find are typically those for children over the age of ten, sibling groups, minority ethnic groups and children with special needs (ADSS 1997; Waterhouse 1997). There are also often difficulties finding suitable foster homes for children which are near to their own homes and friends (Waterhouse 1997). There is considerable official and professional concern about the implications of this for the quality of children's placements (ADSS 1997; Utting 1997) and the subsequent number of placement breakdowns and multiple placements that children experience (Baldry and Kemmis 1998; Kendrick 1995).

The extent of the work which foster carers undertake and the centrality of the fostering service to local authority care of children and young people is now more widely recognised than in previous years. This recognition has been illustrated by the publication of several major reviews of the foster care service in recent years. These reviews acknowledge past failings and problems (ADSS 1997; DoH/SSI 1995b, 1996; Utting 1997; Warren 1997a, 1997b; Waterhouse 1997). The failings of the fostering service are particularly centred around organisational and management issues (ADSS 1997; DoH/SSI 1995b, 1996). The reports show that the service is not currently meeting acceptable standards in many areas which have a direct impact on the experience of being looked after. There are a number of particularly worrying findings: a lack of strategic planning of foster care; children not having separate care plans (a legal requirement of local authorities); unsatisfactory reviews of children; and a lack of choice in placements (DoH/SSI 1996). The Utting review (1997) also raised considerable concerns about the safety of children in foster care and the lack of regulation and inspection in this area. At the time of writing, many new and positive initiatives are taking place in this field. A UK Joint Working Party on Foster Care was set up in 1997, which has worked on the production of National Standards for foster care and a new code of practice for the recruitment and selection of foster carers. The Department of Health Quality Protects Initiative in 1998 demonstrates present government commitment to try to improve services provided for children by social service departments. The White Paper *Modernising Social Services* (DoH 1998d) also refers to the introduction of an independent regulatory system for fostering services, both independent and local authority, and sets out proposals for new inspection systems (see also Chapters 8 and 10).

Professionalising foster care

One possible answer to some of the difficulties already outlined is the 'professionalisation' of the fostering service. This has seemed, to some, to be the logical direction of future services, if the recruitment, retention and training problems in foster care are to be properly addressed. The contribution of the British Association of Social Workers (BASW) to the House of Commons Health Select Committee on this point was endorsed by a number of other witnesses:

> It is important that fostering schemes in which carers receive fees or a salary are further developed. The task is increasingly a professional one; foster carers are or should be treated as colleagues by social workers ... The number of carers able and willing to provide such a service on an 'expenses only' basis (i.e. a fostering allowance) is likely to continue to decline. (House of Commons 1998b, p.xxxii)

Bebbington and Miles (1990) also suggested that there are few people willing to take on the task of fostering and economic and demographic factors and pressure on women to go out to work mean that this is unlikely to change. Other social policies, such as community care and schemes to get single parents back to work, are also likely to have the effect of further decreasing the number of those willing and able to foster. As noted earlier, foster care is also more expensive to local authorities than first appearances suggest. As Triseliotis *et al.* point out:

> ... the payment of expenses and allowances to foster carers make up only a small proportion of their overall costs though even these are increasing. The recruitment, training and assessment developments of the foster care service contain hidden costs associated with social work and administrative staff time. Additionally, services which foster children receive such as psychological counselling and speech therapy add considerably to the costs involved. To put it simply, fostering is no longer a cheap option. (Triseliotis, Sellick and Short 1995, p.99)

In spite of the financial implications of moving toward a wider use of foster care, many professionals continue to invest their faith in fostering because they believe it to be the better alternative form of care for most children who cannot remain with their families (ADSS 1997). As in other areas of social policy in previous years (such as community care), there is a fundamental belief in the family and in the ability of the family to care and nurture which underpins this faith. The real debate begins when such faith is subjected to studies of the outcomes of this preference in practice.

Some outcome studies of foster care are very positive about the level of care provided by foster carers and the child's experience of it. However, we have already noted Berridge's (1997) conclusion that outcome differences between foster and residential are not, when properly analysed, very significant. On the other hand, with regard to more specific issues there are a number of researchers who do note significant differences. The difficulties of caring for troubled young people in group settings are well known and several research studies have suggested that certain types of anti-social behaviour may be more likely in a group environment (Sinclair and Gibbs 1998). Evidence about issues of control in foster and residential care suggest that aggressive and threatening situations are less frequent within the family environment (Hayden and Gorin 1998). However, foster care is not immune to these problems. Also, it can be argued that abuse of young people in foster homes may be easier to disguise (Utting 1997, pp.35–36). Regardless of differences, most commentators agree that there is a need for a broad range of services to meet the diverse needs of children and that foster care, despite being more widely used, is not best suited to meet the needs of every child.

The National Foster Care Association's (NFCA) Foster Care Charter envisages the recognition of foster carers as full partners working in a skilled profession. More specifically, this implies clear terms, conditions and tasks and the payment of a fee which is worthy of the tasks they undertake, in addition to the payment of the usual (though highly variable) maintenance allowance for the child (House of Commons 1998b, pp.xxxii–xxxiii; Lowe 1989). This would also include the provision of good quality support for foster families and training which could be made compulsory. The NFCA has developed a blueprint for the development of a three-tier career structure and a draft contract for foster carers. Some local authorities, such as Norfolk, already use career scales in order to encourage the improvement of skills and to cater for those who wish to care for children with more diverse needs (Warren 1997a). The development of National Vocational Qualifications and their Scottish equivalent (NVQ and (S)NVQ), which may be undertaken by residential workers or foster carers, will provide a framework for career development if they are made use of by local authorities and foster carers.

Life inside foster families

In considering the potential professionalisation of fostering, it is important that the dynamics of foster families and the impact of caring on them is given full consideration. Research shows that the motivation behind fostering for most carers and their families remains altruism (Rowe *et al.* 1984; Triseliotis, Borland and Hill 1998). Carers enjoy looking after children and find rewards in nurturing them and helping them through what is often a difficult time in their lives. Payment for providing care for these children is rarely a motivating factor, but economic necessity may mean that payment allows them to foster rather than having to go out to work (Rhodes 1993). A research study carried out in Canada found that foster mothers were often reluctant to view their role as a professional one because they considered the care which they offered to be that of 'mother care' (Miedema and Nason-Clark 1997). Anecdotal evidence suggests that many foster families stay in touch with the children they care for, although this is less apparent in one of our studies referred to in Chapter 7. The after-care impact of foster carers is, however, discretionary and cannot in any sense be relied upon by policy-makers. It is often there, but as a valued extra rather than an expectation (McMillen 1997, pp.475–476; SSI 1997, pp.21–23). Fostering often does not stop at the age of eighteen and some children continue to visit their foster carers during their adult lives.

There is a dearth of research evidence about the impact of fostering on the lives of the families of those who foster. The most detailed consideration of the impact of caring on foster families focuses on the effects of caring for foster children with learning difficulties (Ames Reed 1993; 1994; 1997). One survey found that eighty per cent of the sons and daughters of foster carers said that they enjoyed fostering (Part 1993). Having children already in the family may also help foster children to adjust and feel happy in their new surroundings. However, the long-term effects of having foster children living in the household, who may be demanding on their parents' attention, may at times cause frustration and distress for the children of those who foster. Studies which have considered this latter issue illustrate the wide-ranging effects that caring can have on the children of foster carers and how children's reactions are not always positive (Ames Reed 1997; Doorbar 1995; Gorin 1997). One study found that parents reported that they felt their own children lost their innocence quickly because of the exposure to the life experiences of the foster children. This meant that many of them developed an emotional maturity beyond their years and they experienced feelings of sadness, confusion and guilt (Pugh 1996).

The physical safety of the children of foster carers can also be a concern, in light of cases where foster carers have not been informed of the full abusive background of their foster child's behaviour (Clark 1997; Thompson 1996; Utting 1997, pp.37–38). Research and practice highlights the frequent occurrence of foster carers not receiving the appropriate information about children before they arrive (see Chapter 3). This may be detrimental not only to the foster family but also to the foster child; for example, in cases where vital health information is not passed on.

Research findings

The research findings we present in this chapter are drawn mainly from the work of Gorin (1997) and partly from that of Lynes and Goddard (1995). Both projects investigated a wide range of issues which have a bearing upon the debates that we have discussed so far (see Appendix, sections 3 and 2 respectively). We will focus here upon three key themes:

- the motivation of carers and the growth of professionalisation
- the impact of caring on the foster family
- the impact of foster care on young people looked after.

The motivation of foster carers

Trying to find out how to attract new foster carers is one of the main preoccupations of most local authority fostering teams. Clearly, the motivation of foster carers is closely linked to the reasons for starting to foster as well as those for giving up fostering. Our research found very similar results to previous studies on the issue of motivation to foster (Collins and Grant 1994; Dando and Minty 1987). Foster carers had clearly chosen to foster for altruistic purposes and because they felt that they had something to offer a child, as a family. The opportunity for carers to nurture a child and to help support a family provides, for many carers, a great deal of personal satisfaction. A typical comment from a carer in this study about why they continue fostering was: 'Because the rewards of seeing a child smile far outweigh the problems. Because I can help them experience another way of life that may sow the seed of a better future being possible.' For those carers providing respite care for children with disabilities (family link carers), a common motivating factor was an empathy with families because they themselves had a child with a severe illness or disability. Long-term, family link and respite carers in particular said that they felt they had a commitment to a particular child or their family and this meant that they would continue to foster. Some of the male carers said that their partners were keen to foster and that they supported them. Others reported that caring enabled their partners to do an additional worthwhile activity whilst at home caring for other children. As other studies illustrate, very few carers felt motivated by the financial incentive.

Closely linked to motivation to care and to the question of profession-alisation is the way in which carers view their role. The research asked carers whether they perceived their role as that of being a parent, a professional, both a parent and a professional, or in some other way. As Figure 4.1 illustrates, the majority of carers said that they perceived their role to be both that of a parent and a professional. Almost a quarter said they felt that their role to be one of a parent and under a tenth of respondents viewed their role

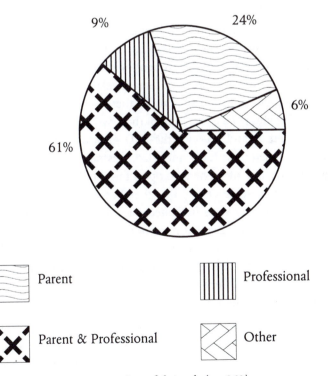

Figure 4.1 Foster carers perceptions of their role (n= 360)

as predominantly that of a professional. Those whose answers fell into the 'other' category said, for example, that they felt they acted as a friend, or 'an auntie' to children they look after.

Despite the strong motivation that carers clearly feel towards helping children, a worryingly high number of carers (46%) in the study said that they had thought about giving up fostering. Those carers who provide emergency care, short-term care and project care were the most likely to say that they had thought about giving up fostering. Respite carers were slightly less likely to have thought about giving up (41% had thought about it), but family link, in contrast, had very few carers who had thought about giving up (only 9%). Evidence from the rest of the study suggested that family link and respite carers may have a very different experience of fostering because of the different nature of the caring task and the often close relationship which develops with birth families. Unsurprisingly, sharing the care of a child and caring for them in short bursts allows families more breathing space and means that the time spent with children is often seen more positively.

The reasons that foster carers gave for thinking about giving up fostering fell into three broad categories. The first and the most common of these were factors related to the social service department or individual social workers (52%). The second set of factors were placement-related and this included the behaviour of the foster child (21%). Thirdly, there were factors relating to foster carers' own families (27%). Over half of those who responded said that their frustrations were bound up with the SSD or with individual social workers. These comments typically included frustration at bureaucracy, decision-making and a lack of adequate support for both foster children and carers. Of these, over one-quarter said that they had experienced a lack of support and another quarter were frustrated with decisions that had been made or with organisational issues. The remainder said they were fed up with the demands of the work, were angry about poor handling of allegations from children or young people, or felt that fostering was costing them financially. For example, one carer's response encompassed a number of these concerns, with regard to feeling like giving up:

> Many, many, many times due to sheer frustration of the system – lack of finance/support – having to be in crisis before getting attention for [a] child. Hard work going to waste when a placement ends unnecessarily. Hurt and pain we have felt but always overcome for sake of [the] children,

but after 10 years we will now do it our way to ensure demands are met or not do it at all any more.

Just over a fifth of carers cited a placement related factor being the reason which caused them to think about giving up. Respondents discussed finding some children's behaviour very difficult to cope with and others reported a sense of failure if the placement had not worked out and this had made them feel disheartened and unsure of whether to continue. This finding is supported by several research projects which have linked placement breakdown to ceasing to foster in many cases (Baxter 1989; Berridge and Cleaver 1987). One carer who felt this way said:

> After having a particularly difficult little girl who did not fit in with the family very well, we had to ask for her to be placed somewhere else. This left us feeling inadequate and that we had failed, both her and us as foster carers.

Other reasons that were expressed by over a quarter of respondents included factors to do with their own family. Most of these mentioned the emotional strain that fostering can place not only on the carer but also on the rest of the family. Some people referred to the negative effect that placements could have on their own children. A carer described how one placement affected her daughter: 'My daughter was so upset that she had nightmares for approximately a fortnight after our foster daughter left.' The remainder of responses were related to personal difficulties which may make continuing caring difficult and some individuals said that they were just getting too old to continue much longer.

MONEY AND MOTIVATION: PAYMENT FOR CARING

Full professionalisation of the foster care service has significant implications. For local authorities, the most important are the significant financial implications. If a full skills-based service were to be introduced in all local authorities, it would involve both direct and indirect costs. The main direct cost would be payment of a fee to carers, in addition to the maintenance allowance. Indirect costs would include, for example, more training and support schemes which would be expected to be more widely attended and assistance with, or provision of, child care facilities whilst carers attended.

At present the payment system across England is very variable. Most foster carers, however, remain 'volunteers' who receive a maintenance allowance to care for children. This allowance varies in different areas and a recent survey found that the majority (64%) of county councils, metropolitan boroughs and London boroughs in England are still paying allowances below the NFCA recommended amounts (Waterhouse 1997). The recommended allowances in 1997 varied from £55.79 (or £65.45 in London) for a child aged 0–4, increasing to £111.58 (or £130.90 in London) for a young person aged sixteen or over (NFCA 1997). Some authorities provide enhanced maintenance allowances for some carers because the child they are looking after is considered to have special needs. However, these enhanced allowance schemes are often problematic because the carer can have the extra money taken away if the child's behaviour improves. In different parts of the country, schemes already exist which provide carers with a fee to care in addition to the maintenance allowance. These schemes are usually used for children who are considered a challenge to look after or those who are particularly difficult to place. Fees vary across the country. However, this fee is then taxable. The fee is intended to cover some of the indirect costs that carers experience, such as lack of income from employment and loss of leisure time. Some local authorities have even moved towards paying fees to all of their carers (ADSS 1997).

Our research sought to find out how satisfied carers were with their current maintenance allowance and what their feelings were about the payment of a fee. In the authorities in which the research was carried out, the majority of carers received only maintenance, although a small number of carers were paid a fee as part of the project care scheme. Nearly two-thirds of carers who responded said that they were very satisfied or satisfied with the maintenance allowance, leaving just over a third who said they were not very satisfied or very dissatisfied. The level of satisfaction with the maintenance allowance did not vary significantly according to type of care provided, though it was interesting to note that carers whose households were earning a combined income of over £25,000 (the highest category of household income in our survey) were the most likely to say that they were 'not very satisfied' with the level of the allowance.

Carers were asked whether, in their opinion, there should be a fee paid to care for a foster child on top of the maintenance allowance. Just under two-thirds thought that there should be a fee to care. There was little variation in attitudes towards whether a fee should be paid across the different income levels. Foster carers were asked what they considered would be an acceptable fee. The amount of money that carers were asking for was relatively small. Almost three out of four respondents said that under one hundred pounds would be acceptable as a weekly fee and of those almost three-quarters said that under fifty pounds would be acceptable (see Figure 4.2). The remainder of respondents suggested either over one hundred pounds or that carers should be paid along similar lines to other child care professionals such as residential care workers.

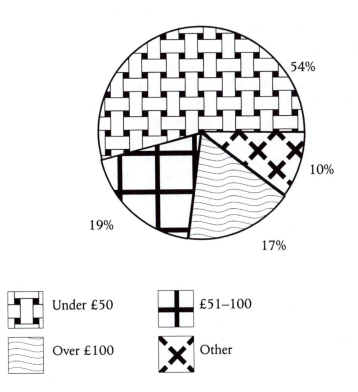

Figure 4.2 Level of fee carers thought would be acceptable per week (n=96)

The majority of carers were not asking for a great deal of money a week as a fee but did overwhelmingly feel that more people would be willing to care if a fee was paid.

The research demonstrated that administration of payments caused most frustration in one way or another. Three-fifths of respondents said that payments were sometimes late. This seemed to vary considerably according to the type of care provided. Respite carers most often reported that they experienced difficulties. There were a large number of responses that expressed a view that claiming for reimbursement of damages or losses could be problematic. Carers felt guilty about asking for money to replace items and said that they sometimes felt that they were not believed that items had been damaged or broken. As one carer said: 'Payment is usually made, but often [be]grudgingly and carers are made to feel guilty for asking.' When carers did make a claim for reimbursement, the money could take a long time to come through. This point was also made by carers many times about claiming for extra expenses for outings or for things the children needed. In some families, waiting for these payments caused added financial difficulty. For example: 'As a single mother I have difficulty supporting three small children with no clothes for three weeks until the cheque clears.'

There were various other comments about frustrations with payment, such as the itemising of pay slips, requests for payment directly into bank accounts, difficulties with getting insurance cover and making claims, as well as levels of pay. A widespread view from the research was that foster carers felt that they often lost out financially through fostering and this angered them as they were told initially that they would never be 'out of pocket'.

The impact of caring on the foster family

Fostering is a very different experience for all families but this research illustrated the significant impact that it had on the lives of all family members. For many children of carers, it was largely a positive experience. Half of the children who responded to the questionnaire said that they were happy about fostering, a third said that they felt 'OK' about it and a small minority said that they felt angry or sad about it.

Most of the children who responded found something that they liked about fostering. Children said that they liked having someone to play with, someone to talk to and share things with. They described certain activities they liked doing with foster children, such as watching television together, playing football or on the computer, listening to music, dancing or reading to younger children. Many of the children and young people felt that it was rewarding to feel that they were helping the foster child and they liked having a bigger family. One child said:

> I like to play games if my brother/sister [foster] are quite young ... I like to read bed-time stories to them before they go to bed, because it helps them sleep and not [be] frightened of being in a strange house.

However there were many aspects of fostering that could clearly be very disruptive at times to the lives of foster carers' families. Some families of foster carers live with very damaged and disruptive children, with behaviour that could have a big impact on the lives of foster carers' children. Children listed the things that they disliked about fostering. Among these were many comments about the behaviour of foster children, particularly aggression, shouting, swearing and situations when foster children were 'horrible' to their parents. Many of the children found it particularly difficult sharing a bedroom. For some young people this was seen as an invasion of privacy, especially if foster children went through their things or disturbed them whilst they were doing their homework or had friends round. Fostering often raised a range of ambivalent and strong feelings for children. One young person wrote that they disliked 'sharing a room, people touching my stuff, people shouting and hitting my parents, reviews at my house, seeing a baby leave.' Children also frequently mentioned that they felt they missed out on their parents' attention because of the immediacy of a foster child's needs. This could cause children to feel jealous of a foster child: 'Mum and Dad sometimes spend more time with them and makes me a bit jealous. They spend more time like when they eat and go to bed.'

Some foster carers felt that at times they were placing their own family at risk through fostering. This was not only through the foster child's immediate behaviour whilst in the household but also after the child had left the family. Foster carers frequently mentioned feeling concerned that foster children who had left may come back to steal property themselves or inform friends who might do so. Those families with older children were also concerned about allegations of abuse made against them and the worry of how these allegations could potentially affect their family. For those families who had experienced allegations of abuse, the effect on their lives and the bitterness that they still felt about the perceived poor handling of allegations was very evident.

The impact of foster care on young people looked after

Having looked at the experiences and views of both foster carers and their own children, it is worth considering the perspective of children in foster care about their situation. Lynes and Goddard's study of young people in care approached this subject through a variety of questions. The responses received on the subject of care experience were overwhelmingly (81%) from children in foster care rather than residential establishments. It is these responses that are examined here. Two questions asked what children liked and what they disliked about their carers. When asked what they liked about their carers, the responses suggested that the 'parenting' role dominated all else in their perceptions. The most common answer in this area was some variation on the theme that their carers were loving, caring or kind:

> They're loving, caring, kind. They're always there if you need a shoulder to cry on or get a problem. (girl, 14)

> They're loving, thoughtful, cuddleable. (girl, 13)

> They are nice and kind and play with us. (girl, 12)

> She's caring, understanding and has an open mind. (girl, 15)

> Kind, they listen, help with homework, cook good food. (boy, 16)

In the same vein were those who found their carers to be good at listening and being helpful:

> They listen and they love me. (boy, 11)

> Listen to problems and help and don't turn me against my family. (girl, 14)

> They help me with my homework, they teach me new and different things and above all they really do care about what I do. (girl, 13)

More directly related to the parenting role were those comments from (seven) young people who were explicit on this point:

> They treat me like their own son. (boy, 15)

> My carer has been with me ever since I was a baby.
> I am one of the family. (girl, 14)

Where one got a useful sense of the general level of satisfaction in these foster homes was, paradoxically, with regard to the question about things that these young people did not like about their carers. Over six in ten of those who answered this question put 'nothing' or some variation on it. One in ten children complained about their carers being strict or bossy and two individuals about them living in a rural area. Amongst the remaining responses (28%) not all of which were negative in tone, there were a few that were, nevertheless, indicators of unsatisfactory placements:

> They make fun of me. (boy, 14)

> Their son, he beats me up. (boy, 13)

That said, the results of this study were more positive than the nationwide study carried out earlier by the Who Cares? Trust (Fletcher 1993). The latter study found higher degrees of dissatisfaction amongst young people in both foster and residential care. While neither study can claim to be representative, for various reasons, the higher numbers in the Who Cares? Study (600 questionnaires returned), together with its national coverage, suggest that its indications of dissatisfaction in many cases (Fletcher 1993) may be a better reflection of the wider picture in foster care.

Given that the questionnaires in this study were sent to the foster (and residential) homes and, presumably, filled in there, we have no way of knowing to what extent there was any 'vetting' of responses. This point also applies to Fletcher's study (1993). Very few replies were so blandly positive and uncritical as to suggest this. Only one reply, from a young man with severe educational difficulties, was explicitly assisted by a foster carer (who explained the reasons for this in a detailed letter to us). There were certainly many replies whose detailed comments and criticism of aspects of the care experience gave the impression of unrestricted response rather than the opposite. There was also explicit departmental instruction to both foster and residential carers to facilitate and ensure confidential replies (see Lynes and Goddard 1995). In the end, however, as with all studies of this kind, we cannot be sure of how far this was the case.

Discussion

Our own research illustrates what others have also found: that foster carers are still motivated by altruism and many make significant sacrifices in order to care for children. Few carers discussed their motivation solely in terms of having a desire to help families to reunite. The messages from carers are contradictory with regard to professionalisation and it is clear that many still view their role, at least in part, as an extension of parenting. Research shows that carers' attitudes to birth parents are often ambivalent (Waterhouse 1992) and anecdotal evidence suggests that they do not always find working with them an easy task, despite knowing that it is encouraged by SSDs and the Children Act 1989. It is difficult to know whether carers are likely to persevere more with a child if they view them as a member of the family or if the child's success (in terms of either their return to birth parents, educational attainment, or improvements in health or emotional and behavioural difficulties) is seen as a reflection of their professional skills.

Several arguments are frequently used by those in favour of maintaining the spirit of voluntarism in foster care. The first of these is that children should know that they are not being looked after for money but because a family cares about them and wants to help them. Little is known about the likely effect of professionalisation on carers' relationships with children. However, some argue that even if payment of a fee is introduced, it is unlikely that it would be enough to convince a child that it is an easy way to make a living (Berridge 1996). Triseliotis *et al.* (1995, p.40), citing their own research, suggest that young people in foster care would not be antagonistic to payment. On the contrary, the young people in their inquiry felt that existing payments were inadequate and were critical of social services in this regard for exploiting the perceived good will of their foster carers. That said, foster carers in our research, as others have previously, did voice concerns about payment attracting the wrong type of carers.

Payment of foster carers is not just about financial support but is also an issue of status. Many carers feel frustrated about the connection which is often made between voluntarism and amateurism. The roots of foster care lie in substitute parenting, yet the task has become much more than this. The lack of status that foster carers are generally awarded, and the subsequent treatment of foster carers by some professionals, causes much anger and frustration. This contributes more frequently to carers giving up than does the lack of a fee to care. Research by Triseliotis *et al.* (1998) also found that dissatisfaction with the social service department represented the largest single reason that carers gave for giving up fostering. Many foster carers feel that they are not listened to by social workers when it comes to the foster children in their care and that information is not shared openly (ADSS 1997; Gorin 1997). Social workers are currently provided with very little training on family placement in the Diploma in Social Work (DipSW) and the result of this can be a lack of knowledge and empathy with foster carers (Warren 1997a). Previous research has shown that foster carers feel that they are rarely included in decision-making, planning, reviews and case conferences and do not always have regular reviews (DoH/SSI 1996; Waterhouse 1992).

Despite the potential for professionalisation of fostering to overcome many of the problems that foster carers face, there are still problems endemic to fostering which will not be altered with professionalisation. These problems focus around a family being used as the placement for a child who may be presenting extremely challenging, and in some cases even dangerous, behaviour. Many families who foster are very resilient and continue to do so despite negative experiences with foster children. In one of our case studies a foster carer told of how their house had been set on fire by a foster child causing thousands of pounds worth of damage, yet they offered to have the child back in their home. In the same family the husband and wife were currently having to sleep separately to allow their foster daughter to sleep in the same room as the wife because of concerns that another foster child may try to sneak into her room at night. Caring for some children may put families under too much pressure, particularly if family routines have to be totally rearranged around the child. This can mean that placements break down or are unsatisfactory either for the rest of the foster family and/or other foster children.

The impact that fostering may have on foster carers' children remains under-researched. It is clear that many children enjoy fostering for the most part, but there are aspects of it which can cause disruption to their lives and bring them undue distress. Aggressive incidents in foster homes, although less frequent than in residential homes, do occur and foster carers and their families are vulnerable to attacks from foster children. Unlike residential staff, they are not generally advised to try to restrain children because of the lack of adults usually available when such situations occur and their lack of training (see Chapter 5).

The difficulties surrounding concerns of abuse in foster families and the handling of allegations is another area which will not be resolved by professionalising the service. Families, by their nature, are not easily monitored. This means that there must be close checks made of families before they foster and whilst they are fostering. This, however, may be seen as overly intrusive by the foster families and many potential carers can be put off fostering by the length and detail of the approval process. Foster carers and their families also face the worry of an abuse allegation being made by a child. In the case of an allegation being made, carers can feel extremely isolated and humiliated. The priority for the local authority must clearly be to protect the child involved, but many carers feel that they are not treated in the appropriate manner by social services departments and are not given adequate support in the event of an allegation (Nixon 1997). The ambivalent nature of some allegations may make them very difficult to prove or disprove. Once made, these may cause not only extreme distress at the time, but can also have long-lasting implications for the whole family (Nixon 1997).

Conclusions and implications

The spirit of voluntarism and the desire to help children who have often had a difficult start in life remains strong. There appears to be a 'hard core' of carers who would continue fostering regardless of a fee. However, it is becoming clear with the crisis in recruitment and retention experienced by most authorities that there are not enough of this 'hard core' to provide a high quality service. A measure of professionalisation may target those people who cannot currently afford to be foster carers but would enjoy doing so. Many carers report becoming worn down by the frustrations of tasks which go beyond parenting and the lack of recognition they receive for their efforts. The demands of fostering seem, to many, to be too great an undertaking without adequate recognition of both the skills and the time invested in providing care. Professionalisation of foster care is also about the status of carers within the service as well as payment to care. However, not all foster carers would welcome the introduction of a more professionalised approach. Not every existing carer may want to become more professional, particularly if it involves undertaking more training or qualifications. This suggests the need for flexibility in incorporating those carers who do not want to stray too far from their existing role as well as those who want to build careers in fostering.

Pressure for changes to fostering have become particularly apparent with the production of the National Standards for Foster Care and the launch of the Quality Protects initiative. However, whether full professionalisation takes place more widely than at present is largely dependent on the financial implications for local authorities. Whilst professionalisation is espoused by some policy-makers and researchers as an ideal, there is often a mismatch between this and what is possible for local authorities working within tight budgetary constraints. It may also be hidden fears about cost that underlie national government resistance to the concept of professionalisation (House of Commons 1998b, p.xxxiv).

CHAPTER 5

Managing the Behaviour of Looked After Children

We have already seen in Chapter 3 that children who come into care are likely to have suffered a range of difficulties and that the experience of coming into care may be viewed as stressful (Kahan 1989). In combination, these circumstances can mean that children in care may present behaviour which adults find difficult to manage. Children enter care for a variety of reasons. Some of these are connected to their own behaviour; others are connected to the behaviour of the adults in their lives. Although many young people in care do not conform to the unfortunate stereotype of being 'difficult' or 'disruptive', there is growing research evidence that difficult to manage behaviour has posed increasing problems for staff and carers, as well as for the young people themselves, in recent years (Berridge and Brodie 1998; Packman and Hall 1996; Sinclair and Gibbs 1998). It is generally acknowledged that many children who enter the care system are more damaged and have more complex difficulties than in the past, partly due to the reduction in admission numbers to the most urgent or necessary cases (DoH/SSI 1997). Alongside these behavioural concerns, there is increasing interest in the health of looked after children, both emotional and physical, as well as their educational status. These concerns often interrelate with, and are pertinent to, the ability of staff and carers to exercise appropriate care and control with the children that they look after.

However, managing the behaviour of children and young people as a whole, regardless of whether they are in or outside the care system, is a concern which has long preoccupied society at large. This concern is bound up with parenting issues, the development of anti-social and delinquent behaviour, congenital and developmental disorders, mental health issues and special educational needs. In other words, we must not lose sight of the fact that a substantial proportion of all children and young people are likely at some time to present behaviour which is difficult to manage for adults, and for a variety of reasons. Furthermore, behaviour viewed as 'problematic' is to some extent in the eye of the beholder and is certainly influenced by a range of environmental factors. It is also true that children's behaviour may be both a form of communication and a symptom of their experiences and unmet needs. Chronic family illness, difficulties in family relationships, neglect and abuse, unpredictability and disruption are among the factors that are known to increase the risk of severe emotional and behavioural difficulties (Kahan 1989). Some looked after children and young people will, therefore, be particularly vulnerable to emotional and behavioural difficulties because of their life experiences – often the very reasons which led to them entering care in the first place (Cleaver 1997; Kahan 1989).

The behaviour of children in foster placements has frequently been cited as a contributing factor in placement breakdown (see Chapter 3), although studies have differed in their assessment of the significance of this issue (Aldgate and Hawley 1986a; G. Kelly 1995). In Kelly's study of long-term foster care the behaviour of foster children, particularly aggressive behaviour, was found to be an important element in placement disruptions. However, very few studies have looked at the range of behaviour problems experienced by children in foster care whilst they are being looked after. One exception is a study by Keane (1983). Keane's research showed that nine out of ten (92%) foster carers recalled having to face one or more of a wide range of behavioural problems at some stage during a placement. Nearly one in three children showed a degree of disturbance, as measured by the Rutter (A) behaviour rating scale. Despite this, a low level of support was found to be available for carers in Keane's study, whether from social workers or psychological and psychiatric staff. Published research has not provided evidence of which behaviours carers find most difficult to deal with and how the carers manage this alongside provision of care for the rest of the family. Some of the research about behaviour, mental health and looked after children has tended to be retrospective studies of adults, and often women, who have been looked after. Studies by Rutter, Quinton and Liddle (1983) and Wolkind (1977) present a similar picture of high rates of psychiatric disorder, poor relationships, difficulties in parenting and economic disadvantage (although, of course, there were women in both studies who were doing well). Studies of men have more frequently described the criminal histories of some individuals subsequent to leaving care, which has been found to involve both more serious crime and recidivism in comparison with control groups (Bamford and Wolkind 1992). Stein (1998), on the other hand, points to the fact that although estimates suggest that some 23 per cent of adult prisoners and 38 per cent of young prisoners have spent some time in care, these estimates include individuals who have spent only short periods of time in care.

Emotional and behavioural difficulties

'Emotional and behavioural difficulties' is a term used to describe a wide range of behaviours which are often divided into two main types: disruptive or externalising behaviours and non-disruptive or internalising behaviours. Disruptive or externalising behaviours include aggressive behaviour such as fighting, disobedience, tantrums, destruction of property, bullying and attention-seeking. More covert types of externalising behaviour include theft, school truancy, running away and lying. Non-disruptive or internalising behaviours include depressive and anxious behaviour. Symptoms of this encompass tension, feelings of inferiority and unhappiness, a sense of worthlessness, timidity, social isolation and hypersensitivity (Goldstein 1994). By their very nature, many of these internalising behaviours are less likely to be recognised publicly as problematic, though they may be far more significant for the young person concerned.

Explaining precisely why individuals behave in the ways that they do has led to the development of numerous theories and models of intervention, behaviour modification and behavioural management programmes. The published literature in this field is vast and particular professionals (and branches of professions) can have strong allegiances to particular theories. Blau and Gullotta (1996) have identified four broad categories for theories which inform different ways of working with behaviour: psychological, social-psychological, socio-cultural and biological. Psychological theories tend to focus upon individual factors and view behaviour as emerging from within a person. Social-psychological theories focus on the interaction between the individual and his or her environment (which would include home, school and neighbourhood). Socio-cultural theories examine the influence of social structure on society and behaviour. Finally there are biological theories which focus upon genetics and congenital conditions. These four types of theory inform different models of intervention and practice and, as we have already noted, not only do they differ between professionals but they also do so within professions. Therapeutic residential communities have typically had a clearly defined model of working, even if it does not align completely with a single theory. Such models of working can serve a dual purpose: not only can they provide carers with a consistent framework for how they work with individuals, but they can also act as an explanation when things go wrong. Berridge and Brodie (1998) found in their investigation into residential care that the quality of care offered to children was best when the head of home could articulate a clear theoretical/therapeutic orientation or specific method of working with children. This allows for a clear and consistent approach when dealing with educational and behavioural difficulties.

The understanding and management of emotional and behavioural difficulties of children and young people who are looked after is clearly central to a consideration of the ability of carers to exercise appropriate care and control. This is an especially complex task for care staff, who often do not have appropriate social work or recognised counselling and therapeutic qualifications and who operate in a context of enquiries into abuse and evidence of inappropriate coercive regimes in residential care. Some staff in residential care can feel vulnerable and that children have been empowered at their expense, in a way that makes it difficult to exercise appropriate care and control. Also, particular staff report that they do not feel that they will be supported in their decisions by their Department (Berridge and Brodie 1998).

Gorin (1997) has shown that this latter situation also occurs in foster care. Whilst these concerns of carers are likely to be influenced by a relatively small number of experiences in both environments, they can nevertheless be perceived as very influential to the task of caring. Given the overwhelming evidence of adult abuse of looked after children in recent decades (see Chapter 2), one can argue that it is quite right that carers should be particularly vigilant about the balance of care and control that they provide. However, some observers suggest that this concern may lead carers to 'back off' rather than address certain behaviours which may in fact leave young people at risk and staff in an untenable position (Berridge and Brodie 1998; Wilson 1993). For example, Berridge and Brodie (1998) write of young people being allowed out late at night from children's homes in areas in which they, as adults, felt unsafe.

As we have already noted, levels of emotional and behavioural difficulties among the population of looked after children and young people have, some claim, grown. However, this is unsurprising given the evidence which exists that 'psycho-social disorders' amongst children and young people in the general population have increased Europe-wide during the last fifty years (Rutter and Smith 1995). The prevalence of emotional and behavioural difficulties (EBD) and mental health problems in children varies according to definition and assessments about the severity of the problem. The overall prevalence of diagnosable mental disorder in the child population is estimated at up to 25 per cent, with 7–10 per cent having moderate to severe problems (Graham 1986, quoted in NHS/HAS 1995). Mental health problems severe enough to be described as 'disabling' are estimated to be found in 2.1 per cent of all children under sixteen years old (NHS/HAS 1995). This latter percentage approximates to the proportion of children who have a statement of special educational need (that is, the more severe forms of educational need). However, only a small fraction of these statements are expected to be for 'emotional and behavioural difficulties' (Warnock 1978). A recent medical study has claimed that some level of psychiatric disorder is significantly more prevalent in both residential care and foster care (McCann *et al.* 1996). This study claimed that looked after children were four times more likely to develop psychiatric disorders and five times more likely to have a major depressive illness than those not looked after. Whether or not this is the case, it is clear that better acknowledgement of and support for the emotional and behavioural difficulties of looked after young people, particularly those in residential care, merits serious consideration. For example, Sinclair and Gibbs (1996) found that nearly four out of ten young people in residential care in their study across five local authorities had thought of killing themselves in the last month and the majority said that they easily became upset and angry. Packman and Hall (1996) add to the growing evidence that significant numbers of looked after children now manifest difficult to manage and distressed behaviour.

The extent to which the different 'looked after' environments may add to existing emotional and behavioural difficulties must also be considered. Morris *et al.* (1994), reporting on calls to Childline, found that reported problems differed between residential and foster care environments. Children in residential care were more likely to ring about bullying (10% of residential callers) within the residential environment and current sexual abuse (9% of residential callers). Sinclair and Gibbs (1996) found a higher proportion of young people reporting that they had been bullied in residential care (40%) and a quarter (25%) of girls reported that they had been taken advantage of sexually. Added to these latter issues, Sinclair and Gibbs note exposure to illegal drugs and criminal behaviour.

Morris *et al.* (1994) found that children in foster care reported different problems in relation to their placement, relating to their ability to make their own decisions (especially boys) and general living conditions. Children in foster care have been found, perhaps unsurprisingly, to present more problematic behaviours the more placement moves that they have experienced (NFCA no date). Foster placements have been shown to be variable in their capacity to hold on to children and help make a difference with their behaviour. In particular, young people who do not form an emotional bond with their foster carer have been found to experience their carer as unhelpful and restrictive, whereas young people who form an emotional bond with a carer report that they have been helped to mature, control their more violent outbursts and keep out of trouble (Cleaver 1997).

Research findings

In this section of the chapter we will use our own research in order to explore further some of the issues already outlined. We explore two main areas in the research conducted by Gorin (1997) into foster care (see Appendix, section 3) and Hayden (1997a) into residential care (see Appendix, section 1), relating to carers' perceptions of looked after children's behaviour:

- carers' experience of aggressive and threatening behaviour from looked after children
- the range of problem behaviours that looked after children might present.

Carers' experience of aggressive and threatening behaviour from looked after children

Both research projects asked carers about the extent to which they had experienced physical and other types of threatening behaviour when looking after children. There is a dedicated recording system for monitoring violent incidents towards staff in the authorities in our research and there was concern about the large proportion (44%) of these reports coming from children's residential care staff. There was also concern about the experiences of foster carers in this respect, but a lack of systematic recorded evidence. It has long been recognised that social work more generally is an occupation in which violence from clients towards staff is likely to occur (Hester 1994; Prins 1975) and that both staff and different social services departments vary in their response to it (see also other relevant literature, for example Lupton and Gillespie 1994). Staff in children's residential care have been claimed to be in the most violence-prone settings (Leadbetter 1993). However, this claim must be considered in the context of the violence which we know that many children have suffered from abusive staff (see Chapter 2). Likewise, aggression and violence against foster carers does occur and foster carers may also be abusive. Whilst acknowledging the significance of the abuses that some children have suffered at the hands of their carers, our research task was to focus on the extent to which carers felt that they were on the receiving end of violent and aggressive behaviour.

There are, of course, problems in assessing the extent to which violent and aggressive behaviour is endemic in particular environments, not least because individuals have different tolerance levels and different perceptions of risk. In addition, in the residential setting in particular, children's homes not only have different 'cultures' or ways of working, but also particular attitudes towards recording and reporting incidents. So, with these cautionary points in mind, we will now explore the extent to which residential staff, foster carers and children who foster report that they *feel* threatened by some of the children that they look after.

RESIDENTIAL STAFF – EXPERIENCE OF THREATENING BEHAVIOUR

Most residential staff (85%) in our study reported feeling physically threatened at some point in their career from particular individuals or a particular mix of residents. Nearly nine hundred records of violent incidents were received by the authorities over a one year period of monitoring from the thirty-one residential units. Disturbances in some units were such that one unit was closed during the period of our research because of the damage done to the fabric of the building by residents. Closer analysis of violent incidents revealed that a disproportionate amount were clustered around a small number of individual residents (eight across the three authorities) who had been involved in violent incidents with over fifty different members of staff, or about one-sixth of the residential workforce, in a three-month period of monitoring. The majority of these individuals had been the subject of unplanned and emergency placements in the units where the violent incidents occurred. As most residential staff had already reported that they had experienced violence in the course of their work, we were interested in *how often* they felt threatened physically or otherwise. Staff responses to this question are shown in Figures 5.1 and 5.2.

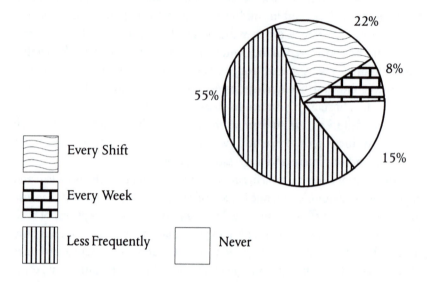

Figure 5.1 Frequency with which residential staff feel physically threatened at work (n=113)

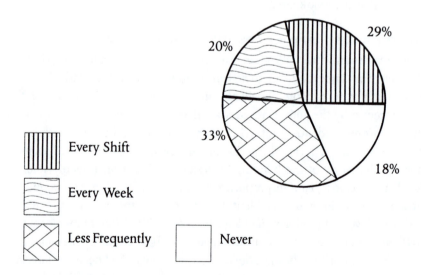

Figure 5.2 Frequency with which residential staff feel threatened in other ways (n=112)

Responses in Figures 5.1 and 5.2 reveal that only a minority of staff feel physically threatened every shift, but that nearly a third of staff feel threatened in other ways every time they go to work. Unit managers were less likely to feel physically threatened, or threatened in other ways, in comparison with care staff. Only a small minority of staff report that they 'never' feel threatened in any way during their work in residential care. The picture of the emotional and behavioural climate in children's residential care given by these responses suggests that staff are having great difficulty in managing (and sometimes understanding) some of the behaviour with which they are presented. About nine in ten care staff reported that they have used physical restraint during the course of their work, despite the fact that four in ten staff have had no formal training in the use of such restraint. More than six in ten staff had actually been involved in the use of physical restraint in a six month period of monitoring. While this latter point shows that physical restraint is not used regularly or routinely by all staff, the great majority of staff claimed that they could not have avoided the use of physical restraint the last time that they used it.

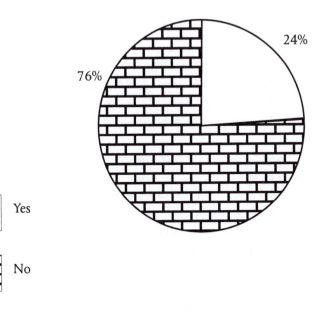

Figure 5.3 Whether foster carers have felt physically threatened (n=362)

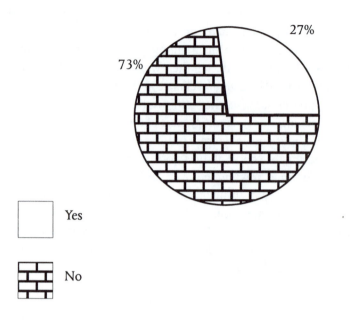

Figure 5.4 Whether foster carers' own children have felt physically threatened (n=328)

FOSTER CARERS AND CHILDREN WHO FOSTER

Foster carers and their children (children who foster) were asked whether they had ever felt threatened, physically or otherwise, by a child that they were caring for. The results of these questions are shown in Figures 5.3 and 5.4.

Foster carers were much less likely than residential workers to report that they or their children felt physically threatened by a foster child, although about a quarter did report that this had happened. However, project carers, providing a more specialised form of care for hard to place children, had felt physically threatened more frequently than mainstream foster carers (50% of project carers). Carers were much less likely to report feeling physically threatened if they were family link carers (6% of family link carers). Other types of perceived threats to children who foster, that is non-physical, were less frequent but were still reported by almost one in five of the carers' children. Foster carers may also come into contact with birth parents of the children that they look after and one in five said they had been threatened by a birth parent. A minority reported that they had been assaulted (1%) and a similarly small proportion (4%) said that they had had their property damaged by a birth parent.

When the research findings are compared from the two settings it seems clear that children present less extreme behaviour in foster care, as is suggested by the work of McCann *et al.* (1996). While it may also be the case that full-time carers are better at managing children's behaviour, it must be remembered that foster carers usually care for between one and three children at a time, whereas the children's homes in our research care for about eight individuals at any one time. There are, thus, a greater number of children in residential placements who may present these challenges. Also, we have noted elsewhere that young people in the two environments are likely to have different characteristics – particularly age. One must also acknowledge the possibly multifarious, though difficult to quantify, effect of group living on children's behaviour (which, however, can be positive as well as negative; see Frost *et al.* 1999). Furthermore, children in residential care have to cope with a team of staff on a shift system and the inconsistencies and frustrations which can arise from this. Finally, different residential staff groups will have particular cultures which may be skilled (or not) at dealing with difficult and sometimes extreme behaviour.

The range of problem behaviours that looked after children may present

In residential care, the best documented evidence about children's behaviour related to violent and aggressive incidents as well as absconding. Self-harming was not uncommon, as well as attention seeking and inappropriate sexualised behaviours. There was also evidence of the bullying of children by other children within the residential setting. Nearly a quarter of all staff made a comment which connected feeling threatened in their workplace to the placement of specific individuals, for example:

> Until recently it [i.e. feeling physically threatened] was an everyday occurrence from one particular resident. He left the unit … and the unit is much calmer as a result.

Whilst some staff rarely felt physically threatened, verbal abuse was reported to be frequent. For example one member of care staff emphasised that whilst he never felt physically threatened, verbal abuse was a feature of every shift. Some staff held the view that the behaviour of young people in residential care had become more difficult to manage. For example, a unit manager with over ten years' experience in residential care said:

> I have witnessed a change in the last three years in young people. There is much more anger and aggression towards staff and systems ... The young people are very verbal. They have damaged several staff cars, made complaints which are threatening and damaged the house where they live.

Staff made references to the use of alcohol and illegal drugs by young people, which could compound their difficulties in managing young people's behaviour:

> Use of alcohol, drugs and substances leads to physical threats and blocks the use of relationships to diffuse situations, as at this time young people are unable to relate ... Verbal abuse and intimidation [are] now a predominant feature of residential work [when young people pursue] rights without responsibilities.

Staff working with younger children did not feel so physically threatened but also reported 'verbal aggression' and threats of allegations against staff. Staff working in respite care with children and young people with severe learning difficulties (SLD) reported regularly being scratched, pinched, kicked, having their hair pulled or being spat at, but were less likely to feel threatened by this than staff in 'mainstream' children's homes.

In many ways, the data presented above replicates what is already well known in relation to residential care. However, there is a relative lack of research evidence about the range of problem behaviours and conditions that foster carers are asked to cater for, although there is much anecdotal evidence and discussion about this issue. We found in our survey of carers that nine out of ten had at some time cared for children who had presented very problematic behaviour, most often relating to some form of abuse. This could sometimes be associated with a learning disability. More than four in ten carers had looked after a child whose behaviour had resulted in an exclusion from school. Eating disorders, self-harming, running away, stealing and vandalising were all behaviours which between a third and half of all carers (depending on the behaviour) had coped with during their time as foster carers. Less frequent behaviours and activities, experienced by fewer than one in five carers in their caring role, were drug and alcohol misuse, depression, animal cruelty, joyriding and arson. Although these proportions relate to experiences by foster carers in providing a placement, rather than individual children, the evidence does illustrate the demanding role undertaken by foster carers, many of whom are facing a wide range of emotional and behavioural difficulties with some of the children that they foster.

The most common problem behaviours from foster children, according to foster carers and their families, were lying, aggression, attention-seeking and stealing. Independently, carers' own children reported the same types of behaviour, with periods of bad temper in addition to the other behaviours already mentioned. Of course, large numbers of children, whatever their background, may exhibit such behaviour at various points in their childhood. The implication from the reports of these foster carers was that these behaviours were exhibited in a more extreme form by some of the children they fostered. The everyday reality of some of these behaviours is well illustrated by the following quotes:

> [It is] difficult to detect truth/lies and trust severely suffers. Problems build up and threaten to disrupt [the] placement.

> It is hard not to be able to leave things around the house without thinking that they will be stolen. The biggest problem is having to hide money away from temptation.

A particular problem with attention-seeking behaviour seemed to be the difficulty that this caused for carers in dividing their time equally between foster children and their own children and the jealousy that this could cause: 'Attention seeking [is the most difficult to deal with behaviour] because there often seems to be a constant battle between my child and the foster child to gain my attention.' Jealousy between foster children and carers' own children was only one of the issues for carers and their own children. Carers' own children often had a number of other behaviours to contend with: 'Theft and destruction of my daughter's property. She could not understand her "friends" treating her property in that way.' Some of the experiences of carers were quite extreme; for example, one carer reported: 'I was kicked and threatened with a knife.' Only a minority of carers (9%) reported no difficulties with the behaviour of children placed with them.

Discussion

Whilst much of the behaviour of foster children is fairly commonplace, other behaviour from some children is clearly more problematic and involves actions which could place the foster children, their foster family, or others in serious danger. This has significant implications regarding the status of foster carers, the training that carers receive and the potentially vulnerable position in which some carers' families are placed. One of the needs of children often identified by social workers is 'consistent boundaries', the provision of which relates to issues of managing behaviour. Understanding and managing children's behaviour, particularly when this behaviour may be an expression of traumatic experiences and complex needs, is a skilled task. If this task is done well it can make a tremendous difference to individual lives. There is a danger when this understanding and skill is not there that carers may use inappropriate, even abusive, forms of control. Behaviour management is fast becoming an issue of concern for a range of professionals and other adults in contact with children, both inside and outside the care system. However, it is an especially pressing issue for substitute carers who have extended or full-time contact with children who present difficult and/or distressed behaviour.

Residential care

Evidence supplied by residential care staff in our authorities confirm many of the familiar concerns about residential care, in relation to staffing, which Utting (1997) describes as 'a chronic problem', and the number of placements that some young people have, which he has described as 'extremely damaging' (p.21). Utting also raises the issue of 'inappropriate placements', which are acknowledged to make the situation in some homes 'impossible' (p.21). Although unit managers in our research were all qualified social workers, most of the care staff did not have social work qualifications and staffing arrangements in many units were characterised by staff absence and the use of casual staff. Staff were very conscious of the relatively low status of their work. Although some homes were more successful than others in providing a calm and purposeful atmosphere, this situation could be dramatically altered by certain emergency placements. The evidence collected in a range of ways in this research supports the view held by many front line staff that violent and aggressive incidents relate to particular placements, rather than to the nature of residential care in general.

The current situation with respect to advice, training and recording of violent incidents leaves staff, and indeed social services departments, in a vulnerable position in relation to allegations that inappropriate methods of control (in particular the inappropriate use of physical restraint) are being used. It is clear that the great majority of staff feel that they need the option of using physical restraint on occasion. It is also clear that a range of untutored methods of restraint and 'holding' are used by staff. Clearer advice from social services departments about safe methods of restraint or 'holding', appropriate to the age, size and disability of children and young people, is needed.

A starting point for improving the experience of children and those looking after them is better assessments and more detailed and realistic care plans. These should incorporate an analysis of pertinent stress factors in children's lives and, in relation to the central concerns of this chapter, a thorough examination of what behaviours are presented in which context, time of day and with what consequence, with a view to beginning to work constructively with individuals in this respect. Relevant outside professional help, such as from psychiatrists, would be useful in this context. Residential staff also reported that they needed immediate and practical support but were also insistent that even some recognition from their own departments of the difficult job they do would help. For example, some staff appreciated getting a letter from a service manager offering sympathy and understanding if they had been involved in a violent incident. Managers of homes wanted to be properly consulted about placements and clearly resented it when their decisions were overridden by service managers desperate to place a child.

Staff from different units held distinct views about whether residential care *could* provide a positive experience for children but tended to be most positive about it when they felt that they had a degree of autonomy in their work. In particular, staff held strong views about the placement of individuals that they felt unable to 'make a difference with'; such placements could have a very negative effect on whole staff groups as well as other children resident in a home. In sum, although the behaviour of children in residential care can be difficult to manage for staff, it is only in a minority of cases that staff really feel that they should be in a more specialised placement. A 'more specialised placement' is usually taken to mean a therapeutic environment or a secure unit. Emergency placements, as has already been noted, represented the most problematic cases monitored over a short time period. These placements could affect the morale of large sections of the workforce in particular homes. They could also provide very unsettling experiences for other residents. Most staff could understand why these placements happened but often said that, in effect, emergencies must be planned for. That is, many staff believed that there should be a return to a division between short-stay and longer term residential units, rather than the unhappy mixture which could occur in some areas of the authorities studied.

More planned respite care, outreach work and support work with families was also viewed as necessary in order to reduce the number of emergency admissions.

Foster care

Although foster carers do not appear to be as frequently subjected to aggression and violence from foster children as residential staff, there is a serious issue about the ability of foster carers to cope with those very damaged youngsters who may pose a physical threat to themselves and to the families with which they are placed.

The amount of training that foster carers received varied in and across the authorities. Although some had undertaken a large number of courses, others were used for placements by their local authority even before the initial training period had been completed, if social services were desperate to place a child. The research reported upon in this chapter points to a need for initial training to cover in more detail issues such as the nature of some learning difficulties, eating disorders and self-harming behaviour. Foster carers need to be made more aware of the nature of looked after children's likely behaviour, so that they could have the opportunity of devising an agreed strategy for working with the individual positively and purposefully. They also required that social workers were honest with them from the beginning about the child's history, health, and emotional and behavioural difficulties (if any). Evidence from foster carers in our study suggests, as we saw in Chapter 3, that social workers frequently do not provide foster carers with all the information about a child. This is possibly because they are unaware of information themselves, but may also sometimes occur because they are concerned that carers may not take the child.

The research showed that many foster carers worry that they are placing their own children at risk and are concerned about their rights if foster children hurt a member of their family. Several carers reported incidents where they or members of their family had been hurt by foster children and little action was taken on their behalf by the social services department concerned. It is clear that particular caution needs to be exercised when making some placements in homes where foster carers have their own children (especially young children) in order to prevent the development of a new client group of abused children. Carers need to feel they will be appropriately supported by their social services department in the case of allegations being made by either party. The use of physical restraint by foster carers in the home is problematic, but it is clear that training on the handling of aggressive and violent incidents would be beneficial to many foster carers who, as the ADSS (1997) report, often feel 'out on a limb when faced with these situations' (p.8). Foster carers, like residential workers, also need routinely to complete records for violent incidents. This latter strategy could allow carers some protection in the case of any unjustified abuse allegations made against them, as well as provide the opportunity to reflect more systematically about the way that they are interacting with a child.

A wider implication of the reports of aggression against foster carers is the need for local authorities to consider their strategic policies for looked after children. Almost half of the carers in our study had cared outside their approval range, over two-thirds had cared for children for longer than planned and half said that they did not receive enough information on foster children before they arrived. Carers can be faced with a situation in which they are looking after children without adequate information, for an age range/sex/number of children that they are not approved for, without adequate support, training or finance. They may also be looking after children who have complex needs and who may display a range of difficult to manage behaviours, partly as a result of their life experiences. National reports (ADSS 1997; Warren 1997a) have already noted that there is an urgent need for change within local authority fostering services, particularly in a climate where independent agencies are growing and offering carers and foster children the support they need as well as the element of a financial reward.

Conclusions and implications

The two research projects referred to in this chapter provide some illustration of the emotional and behavioural climate in which some carers look after children in England. The values of both residential and foster carers in the research projects were clearly tilted towards care, rather than control. Yet some carers in both settings found themselves in extremely difficult situations in relation to being able to exercise appropriate control. This is confirmed in Berridge and Brodie's (1998) follow-up study on children's residential care. A key issue here is the relationship between adults and looked after children. In the case of residential workers, they are clearly paid professionals. Foster carers, on the other hand, are expected to act as professionals but are not fully trained nor appropriately paid to do so in most local authorities. Professionals (we will include all carers in this category for the purposes of this argument) have a different relationship with children; they are not in a position to act in the way a birth parent might towards their child. This latter point can cause difficulties in setting and enforcing boundaries, especially where children might choose to abscond when carers seek to enforce safe and appropriate behaviour.

There have been a number of key policy shifts since the early 1980s which are impacting upon the ability to cater for looked after children effectively. The move away from specialist provision, both in special schooling as well as in residential therapeutic environments, means that the most distressed children and young people are expected to cope in environments where staff rarely have the appropriate training and a full understanding of how to respond to and manage their behaviour. This is illustrated by the disproportionate over-representation of looked after children amongst those excluded from school (Hayden 1997b). Some of these individuals are also, in effect, excluded from their foster care placements and from particular residential units, or at best may be contained but viewed as an 'inappropriate placement'. In effect, what some staff were saying in these contexts is that the individual is in need of the therapeutic skills of professionals who are trained to understand and respond positively to their needs: skills that these staff did not feel they had.

Occasionally, staff were of the view that a young person should be in a secure facility. Mental health needs were recognised in the majority of cases of challenging behaviour, but both the way in which the service is currently provided and the long wait to see a specialist made mental health intervention seem practically irrelevant to staff and carers coping with the immediacy of a young person's needs.

In sum, the research evidence in this chapter points to the need for a greater recognition of the realities of the behaviour of some looked after children, so that professionals can respond in ways which will not compound their difficulties. Regulations accompanying the Children Act 1989 recommended that there should be a formal system of external consultancy to childrens' home staff, with respect to psychiatric and psychological services. This recommendation had not been put into practice formally and systematically in our authorities eight years later, although some individual managers of children's homes had used personal contacts to set up some level of support for staff and residents. It is also clear that more accessible support from psychiatric and psychological services is needed by foster carers. It is a need which is being recognised by the independent agencies which are providing both mainstream and specialist foster care services.

CHAPTER 6

The Education of Looked After Children

As outlined in Chapter 2, the education of looked after children is of growing interest to both researchers and policy-makers. The responsibilities of social services and education departments, as well as those of other services such as the Careers Service and Training and Enterprise Councils (TECs), in relation to the education of looked after children feature in contemporary debates about corporate parenting and the central place of education in combating social exclusion. As well as being a significant area of research, the poor educational participation and performance of looked after children and young people has now also become a standard item of discussion in official publications in this field (for example, Audit Commission 1994, 1996; House of Commons 1998b, pp.lxi–lxvii; SSI 1998b, p.36). While official interest is still recent enough for the government's Social Exclusion Unit to claim that 'there is a great shortage of data about the educational circumstances and achievements of children in care, and this in itself is a symptom of the low priority often given to their schooling' (Social Exclusion Unit 1998, p.12), it is a claim that is already being superseded by policy developments. We will return to these developments later in the chapter and in the concluding chapter.

Next to time spent in their home environment, time spent in school is the most significant influence upon the development and sense of well-being of children. However, school attendance and educational achievement (and underachievement) have long been known to be related to socio-economic factors and to family-based issues (Davie, Butler and Goldstein 1972; Douglas 1967). We also know from school improvement and effectiveness research that 'schools make a difference' (Rutter *et al.* 1979; Sammons, Hillman and Mortimore 1995). On the other hand, they do not always make as much difference as current political interpretations of school improvement and effectiveness research would tend to assume (Gibson and Asthana 1998). Rutter and colleagues emphasised, in *Fifteen Thousand Hours* (1979), the quantity of time that most children spend in secondary school. Since then, there have been numerous studies and special projects in the education field to tackle underachievement. More recently, we have seen the development of specialist support services (or special projects) in some local authorities, with a remit to support the education of looked after children (Fletcher-Campbell 1997).

Looked after children are a tiny minority of those in the education system (estimated at 0.4% of the school population in 1996, in DoH figures quoted in Fletcher-Campbell 1997). Indeed, they are a tiny minority of all children who either do not achieve their potential (underachieve) or have limited capabilities in terms of gaining academic qualifications. Just over half (53.9%)of all children leaving school at sixteen achieve fewer than the five-plus GCSEs (General Certificate of Secondary Education) grade A* to C considered to be the benchmark in compiling league tables in school achievement. It is within this broader knowledge and context of the potential of schools to compound or act positively to combat social disadvantage, underachievement and disaffection from school that we should consider the issue of the education of looked after children.

However, we must also remember what is different about looked after children: it is likely that they will come from particularly vulnerable circumstances and the state has either sole or shared responsibility for their welfare. In this latter sense, we may judge the educational experience and outcomes of looked after children in the context of the quality of corporate parenting. However, the bald figures are not suggestive of good parenting. While the vast majority of children (93.4%) achieve at least one GCSE grade A* to G (DfEE 1998a), '75% of those looked after leave school with no qualifications whatsoever' (DfEE, in House of Commons 1998a, p.xxvii n.156). One must, though, balance this sense of the role of corporate parent with an acknowledgement that the looked after population is a dynamic group and many young people will spend only short periods of time in care. For this and for a variety of other reasons (the most important of which is, of course, experience prior to being looked after), the looked after experience itself cannot always be blamed for poor outcomes.

Jackson (1987) undertook one of the first serious attempts to document the level of knowledge and understanding about education within the care system. She found very little written specifically about the education of children in care, reflecting the low priority given to this issue at that time by policy-makers, practitioners, carers and researchers. This low priority for education has long historical roots. In the field of the education of children in care, Jackson (1989) noted elsewhere a gradual shift away from a focus on the saving properties of vocational education for such children (typical of nineteenth-century reform movements) and onto an attempt, influenced by the twentieth-century growth in psychoanalytic thinking, to deal with their deeper emotional problems. This shift is one that Jackson views as not always a positive development, since as a result of focusing on the emotional needs of looked after children, social services as well as other professionals may undervalue or fail to exploit the therapeutic potential of education itself. The obvious connections between educational achievement and self-esteem may be missed, as well as the practical benefits of enhanced employability in the future. Jackson notes in particular, and strongly disagrees with, the view that children with severe emotional difficulties cannot be expected to give their attention to academic learning:

> I would also take a pessimistic view of social workers' ability to compensate children in care for the terrible emotional handicap of knowing that no one in their families cared enough about them to provide them with a home. Perhaps we should concentrate on things we can do something about. (Jackson 1987, p.38)

However, as we have seen, during the 1990s there has been a growth in research and government interest in the education of looked after children. Guidance to the Children Act 1989 stated that local authorities have a responsibility to provide opportunity and support for educational achievement and to take the long-term view of a child's education (DoH 1991a, Vol. 4, para. 2.33). The Act requires that every child looked after should have a written care plan and that this should set out the child's educational needs and how they are to be met. Both the Utting (1991) and Wagner (1988) reports had raised the issue of the importance of educational achievement for looked after children. This issue also featured as one of six circulars unfortunately entitled *Pupils with Problems* (DfE 1994). This circular emphasised the significance of schooling for looked after children, the need wherever possible for continuity of school placement, the roles of teachers and care providers and the need for service planning and collaboration. An SSI/OFSTED (1995) report published in the following year was a damning critique of the failure to provide even *adequate* education for looked after children. During the same period, researchers were advocating the need for 'exceptional' inputs to overcome the earlier adverse life experiences of many looked after children (Heath *et al.* 1994). Reducing exclusion from school and improving the attainments of looked after children has since featured in the recommendations of the first report from the Social Exclusion Unit (1998). This recommended that effective education should be considered a key outcome of relevant social services intervention involving school age children and that targets should be set for the educational achievement of looked after children. These recommendations have been taken up by the Quality Protects initiative, referred to elsewhere in this volume and discussed in detail in the concluding chapter. By the time that Jackson had completed her investigations into the factors that encourage educational success for looked after children (Jackson 1998b), there was greater hope that its lessons, and those of others, might lead to the promotion of greater educational achievements for this group of young people.

There are a number of particularly relevant themes which run through the research on this subject. Before examining what our own research says about the education of looked after children, it is worth considering these themes further.

Attendance and exclusion

School attendance and exclusion have received a high public profile during the 1990s. This is not least because of a general acceptance that the numbers of exclusions have been increasing in recent years and that this is somehow related to educational league tables and the consequent competitive pressures between schools (Hill and Tisdall 1997, pp.126–127; Social Exclusion Unit 1998, pp.8–11). Even before the recent level of interest, an SSI/OFSTED (1995) report on this subject revealed non-attendance and exclusion to be significant features of the educational experience of many looked after children. In the census of educational placement in this latter study, 12 per cent of all looked after children of statutory school age did not attend school regularly or were excluded from school. The proportion of non-attendance and exclusion was higher (25.6%) for children in the last two years of schooling (Key Stage Four), which is likely, clearly, to have adverse implications for both gaining qualifications and obtaining access to post-sixteen education. In addition to children not attending school, a further 7.6 per cent of children were educated otherwise than at school: at Community Homes with Education (CHEs), Pupil Referral Units (PRUs) or by home tuition. The Audit Commission (1994) provided a higher estimate of non-attendance from residential units at about 40 per cent and Scottish research has estimated that a child in a Lothian residential unit is eighty times more likely to be excluded from school than one living at home (Maginnis 1993). More generally, official publications have continued to point out the high level of school exclusions among looked after young people (House of Commons 1998a, pp.lxi–lxii; SSI 1998b, p.36). Comparison with the general school population shows that only a tiny proportion of this latter group (0.17%) are likely to experience a permanent exclusion from school in any particular year (DfEE 1998b) and similarly only a very small proportion (0.5%, measured as a proportion of possible half-days of attendance) are absent without authorisation. The Social Exclusion Unit quoted a National Foster Care Association estimate that children in care are ten times more likely to be excluded than those outside the care system (Social Exclusion Unit 1998, p.9, ref. 28). However, fixed term exclusion (for a matter of days) and authorised absence affect much bigger proportions of the school population. While reliable national figures for fixed-term exclusion do not exist at the time of writing, we know that authorised absence amounts to 5.7 per cent of possible attendances. Some of this absence will include parentally condoned absence, for example for family holidays during term-time (DfEE 1998c).

Research in the field of school exclusion reveals that children excluded from school often have had or have social work involvement with the family. Indeed, it has been argued that children excluded from school are usually 'children in need' or 'children with special educational need' (Hayden 1997c). A high proportion (45%) of primary aged children were found in one national study (Hayden 1997b) to be looked after during the year in which they were excluded from school. However, the association between these two issues may be reciprocal rather than causal. That is, some children appear to stop attending or get excluded from school before they are taken into care (the exclusion may be part of the overall situation which precipitates reception into care) and for some children educational breakdown happens after they are taken into care. The latter may occur through poor planning of placements, the low priority accorded to education in the new placement and/or poor management and understanding of the child's behaviour during this period of disruption (Hayden and Martin 1999).

Expectations and achievement

It has frequently been noted in accounts from young people who have spent time in care that teachers have low expectations of them (Sinclair 1997). In these accounts, it is often assumed that there is an association between being looked after and these expectations. However, some studies do not support this picture of low expectations (Heath *et al.* 1994). It also appears that social workers may have limited expectations for young people in their care. Residential staff in particular are generally unlikely to have professional and higher educational qualifications and may lack confidence in dealing with the education system and senior school staff (Berridge and Brodie 1998). Firth and Horrocks (1996) contrast the expectations of parents and of people working in the care system with respect to young people: 'Natural parents talk about further, higher education and career development and the family support necessary for this while care system professionals talk about jobs, claiming benefit and independent living' (pp.87–88). Looked after young people often lack a significant adult with enough knowledge, interest and responsibility to provide support in this part of their lives in the way that a concerned parent might (SSI/OFSTED 1995). Jackson (1998b) has found that many previously looked after young people who have achieved educational success (defined as those who have achieved five or more GCSEs at grade C or above) had a role model or mentor to support them and to advocate on their behalf. As well as this, a high proportion of these young people were enthusiastic and early readers. In general, however, many of these young people took the view that in light of the difficulties in their way, their success had been achieved *in spite of* the care system rather than because of it.

There is no national monitoring system on the educational achievement of looked after children at the time of writing. However, systems are being developed through two routes sponsored by the government. The first of these is the piloting of new data collection systems in ten local authorities in 1998/99. The second is the use of Educational Development Plans to improve monitoring of local performance (DoH 1998g, p.33). Up until the present, evidence cited has frequently been known to suffer from gaps in information as well as poor results and comes from a wide variety of sources (for example, using data from the National Child Development Study –

Essen, Lambert and Head 1976; Jackson 1987, 1998b; Osborn and Sinclair 1987; Stein 1994). According to evidence provided by the National Children's Bureau and the Who Cares? Trust to Parliament, between 50 per cent and 75 per cent of looked after children leave school with no qualifications (as opposed to 6% in the general population). Likewise, between 12 per cent and 19 per cent go on to further education, compared with 68 per cent in the general population (House of Commons 1998a, p.lxi). The consequences of this are unsurprising, with between 50 per cent and 80 per cent of 16–24-year-old care leavers thought to be unemployed (Biehal *et al.* 1994). The incomplete nature of the records that some of these figures are based upon is significant in itself: Stein (1994) found that nearly one in five social workers did not know whether individual young people on their case loads had any qualifications. He also noted that there is some evidence that children in foster care are more likely than those in residential care to achieve some academic qualifications.

As discussed in more depth in Chapter 3, children who come into care tend to come from more disadvantaged homes than the average. This disadvantage is associated with reduced social and cognitive development. In addition, many children will also have suffered trauma and neglect, which is likely to be associated with difficulties at school. Self-esteem, which is known to be crucial if children are to be enabled to develop into self-reliant and responsible adults (Sinclair 1997), is improved by educational achievement. However, children with low self-esteem are likely to underestimate their own potential. This may lead to a lack of effort, or to seeking attention by disruptive behaviour, possibly resulting in exclusion from school (Jackson 1987). Thus, a vicious circle of low achievement, low motivation and disruptive behaviour can become established. Such a pattern may also be an indicator of special educational need. Disproportionate numbers of looked after children have an identified high level of special educational need in the form of a statement, frequently for emotional and behavioural difficulties (EBD). However, it must be emphasised that although EBD can affect a child's capacity to achieve or may relate in part to intellectual ability, it is not in itself an indication of low intelligence. Special education needs are, though, a significant feature in the looked after population. One in five (20%) of children had a statement of special educational needs (across a range of identified needs) in the SSI/OFSTED (1995) report, in comparison with about 2.9 per cent of children in the general population (DfEE 1998a). About a quarter of the children in the

SSI/OFSTED study were educated outside mainstream school provision, compared with only a fraction of a per cent of the general population.

Education and the looked after experience

Fletcher-Campbell and Hall (1990) found that becoming looked after carried with it a high risk of educational failure. Research has repeatedly shown that an overriding theme for children and young people looked after is the lack of stability in child care placements (Biehal *et al.* 1992). Changes of placement can often also mean changes of school (Fletcher-Campbell and Hall 1990; Kendrick 1995). Stein (1994) has written of the 'assault on personal identity' (p.353) occasioned by the multiple placements and disruptions which can characterise the care experience and notes an association between movement in care and poor attainment: three-quarters of those who had four or more moves in comparison with half of those who had experienced no moves whilst looked after. Improved educational attainment has been found to be linked with planned long-term placements in foster care (Aldgate *et al.* 1992) and for care leavers who had stable care careers (Garnett 1992; Jackson 1998b). To add to this, residential children's homes have tended not to be educationally enriching environments; there are often few books, learning resources and quiet places for study (Berridge *et al.* 1997).

The SSI/OFSTED report (1995) pointed, like the NFER study (Fletcher-Campbell and Hall 1990), to a past absence of policy for the education of looked after children. Firth (1995) has identified education as the second largest problem facing social workers after child protection, yet he notes that most social work departments maintain an ambivalence and lack of real understanding of the issues involved. A range of issues to do with interdepartmental working and understanding have been identified, such as the lack of mutual understanding and communication between residential social workers and teachers and practical difficulties relating to how, when and why meetings are held about individuals. There is sometimes a failure to understand that meetings during the school day are usually difficult (sometimes impossible) for teachers to attend. Changes in the balance of responsibilities between local LEAs and individual schools are not always well understood by social services departments, who can expect LEA officials to have more power over schools than they in fact have. In reality, local management of schools has diminished the power of LEAs and means that real negotiations often have to be undertaken at the individual school level.

More recent research by Fletcher-Campbell (1997) found some progress, with a higher profile for the education of looked after children in many local authorities: half of the local authorities responding to her survey had a focused initiative for this group. On the other hand, no common patterns were found in the types of services and initiatives which were supporting the education of looked after children.

Post-sixteen education

While post-compulsory education for looked after children and care leavers appears, now, to be a significant item of official concern (DoH 1998g, p.26), there has been very little research published to date investigating access to post-sixteen education for this group. Neither the DfE circular (1994), nor the SSI/OFSTED (1995) report pays much attention to this issue. Perhaps the explanation for this is, in part, the traditionally low numbers of looked after children taking up this option. Broad (1997) has raised the key issue of financial support for looked after young people wanting to continue in education beyond the age of sixteen and/or go on to some form of training and notes that financial support for care leavers has actually reduced since the Children Act 1989. The background to this reduction in support can be located in both wider social policy developments (reduction in income support access for young people) and resources available to local authorities for particular client groups or issues, but also in the priorities then decided upon within local authorities.

Research findings

In what follows, we explore some of these themes in a number of ways. First, by considering Lynes and Goddard's (1995) research into the views of young people in care and care leavers (see Appendix, section 2) and second through Van Der Spek's (1998) focus on the transition period for those in care and care leavers from school into post-compulsory education, training or employment (see Appendix, section 4). We will focus upon research evidence from these studies in the following two areas:

- experiencing school whilst being looked after
- academic achievement and post-sixteen education.

Experiencing school whilst being looked after

As Blyth and Milner note, 'relatively few studies have sought to ask directly care recipients about their educational experiences' (Blyth and Milner 1997, p.48). The data reported on here falls within that small group. The questionnaire sent by Lynes and Goddard to young people in care asked a range of questions about their educational experiences. We concentrate here upon the responses to the question of whether young people thought that their education had got better or worse since entering care. Of the 118 responses, there were a significantly higher number who felt that things had improved (44%) than who thought it had got worse (12%). On the other hand, a very large percentage (43%) felt that it had stayed the same. These figures are better than the earlier national survey by the Who Cares? Trust, in which respondents were more evenly divided between those who stated that things had got better (36%), those who indicated that they had got worse (30%) and those who said that their education had stayed the same (34%) (Fletcher 1993, p.26). Respondents in our study who thought that their education had improved wrote about feeling settled or safe, getting encouragement from carers and of being cared for better by teachers. They expressed this view in various ways:

> Because I am more settled and safe. (girl, 14)

> My carers give me lots of encouragement. (girl, 16)

> If there are no problems at home then there are no distractions. (boy, 14)

> Better because I have to work hard at school to go home. (girl, 13)

Those who had more negative experiences tended to be more precise in their identification of the factors involved. Those who thought that their education had got worse wrote about being unsettled and having extra worries:

> I don't live at home and so sometimes I don't care if I get into trouble and so I mess about. (girl, 14)

> Worse as I cannot get to school and not having a home makes it hard. (girl, 14)

> Because when you're in care you have to concentrate on improving your family life more than school. (boy, 14)

> Because I've been moved about a bit. (boy, 17)

It's worse because being in care produces worries – moving homes, change of carers, meeting parents. (boy, 15)

We also wanted to know whether these children thought they were treated differently by fellow pupils and by teachers as a result of being in care. In relation to pupils, the majority (79%, or 90 children) reported not being treated differently. However, from those who said that they were treated differently, it was clear that this could often take acutely painful forms. In focusing upon this subject, and in asking the young people involved to expand upon their experiences of being treated 'differently', we went beyond Fletcher (1993) and into territory that has not, as far as we are aware, been similarly explored elsewhere in published research. While negative experiences of school are hardly unique to those in care, some of the comments were related to particular aspects of the care experience. For example, one boy of thirteen in residential care said that he was treated as though he was a troublemaker. An eleven-year-old boy in foster care said that he was bullied. A further six children said they were teased or 'picked on' as a result of being in care. This included 'name calling' (boy, 16) and, from one girl of fourteen, 'being called horrible things about being in care.' One girl of ten wrote, enigmatically, of 'comments from children', a girl of fourteen in foster care wrote that 'they whisper about you and leave you out so you feel lonely' and a girl of fifteen in foster care identified her educational experiences as worse because 'some people think that if you are in care there is something wrong with you.'

On the other hand, being treated differently sometimes had positive implications:

People tend to think that I've had a hard life and be more friendly. (boy, 17)

They think that you have a need for attention and they try being a lot nicer, to find out things. (girl, 13)

My friends have supported me when my mum didn't like me. (girl, 12)

Being treated differently by teachers had other implications. On the one hand, Jackson notes that 'small kindnesses and sympathetic responses from teachers are remembered with gratitude' and on the other that 'they [looked after children] didn't want to be treated differently from other children' (Jackson 1987, p.14). With our sample, however, the percentage (19%) who reported being treated differently mostly saw it in a positive light:

Because they're supporting me until I'm back with my mum. (girl, 14)

> They are more understanding and kind because they think you have problems. (girl, 15)

> They treat me more delicately and always have excuses for me. (girl, 15)

> They always ask me how my placement is going and how I am. (girl, 15)

Occasionally, though, this extra interest could be experienced as 'patronising' or 'over-caring', with some teachers seen as inclined to 'worry too easily'.

Interestingly, however, a more open-ended question asking about how being treated differently made these children feel produced responses even from other children who had not indicated earlier that they were treated differently. About a quarter of respondents (26%, 32 children) answered this question. These were among the most sharply personal responses that we received. Most were negative, though not all. The negative comments about how being treated differently made looked after children feel included the following:

> Puts you down because it makes you feel as though you've got a sign on your back saying don't talk to me. (girl, 14)

> Angry, upset and very sad. (girl, 14)

> It makes me the odd one out and I don't want to keep being reminded that I am in care 24 hours a day. (girl, 13)

There were several brief answers, where the children simply said that such treatment made them feel 'sad', 'upset', 'terrible', 'pretty bad' or 'angry'. More positive were those, fewer in number, who indicated feeling more 'wanted' or 'cared about'.

Academic achievement and post-sixteen education

Overall, the group of 143 young people in Van Der Spek's (1998) study exhibited many of the characteristics that are familiar from the studies of the care experience cited earlier. Implicit within many of these characteristics are explanations for why social services departments and other agencies either failed or were unable to improve the educational performance of these young people. Of particular note in this study is the fact that about one in five children had experienced between five and ten placement changes since the age of five. Further, over a quarter (28.5%) had either a learning difficulty or physical disability.

The precise nature of the relationship between this sort of background data and subsequent educational performance is a matter for some dispute, as has been already noted. Nonetheless, some of the links will be fairly obvious. Analysis of the school history of these young people showed a number of features, some of which echo similar or related research (for example, Jackson 1989). Although over half (56.8%) of these young people were recorded as being in mainstream day school and a similar proportion (58%) were seen as regular attenders of whichever school they were registered for, almost four in ten (38.4%) had experienced some form of exclusion (see Table 6.1). Almost half (44.5%) of these young people had had three or more school changes since the age of five and a minority (7.4%) were known to have changed school since starting exam courses. Finally, in relation to social work input, about a quarter (26%) of care managers did not know who, if anyone, provided support with homework, though the majority (79%) of them did know who went to school to discuss academic progress.

With regard to the looked after experience of these young people, we have already noted that changes in placement can have significant knock-on effects in relation to educational outcomes – an extreme example of just how serious these can be can be found in Jackson's (1989) account of the experience of Mike Lindsay, former Children's Rights Officer for Leicestershire County Council, whose bright start in education was almost thrown into reverse by a placement change at a crucial time. In the case of these young people, reviewing the reasons for changes in placement is useful in indicating to what extent moves were planned. Whilst over half of the placement changes were planned (57.3%), of those young people where information is known (a total of 117) approximately 10 per cent of moves were related to a foster carer or residential unit being unable to continue care. Also, in excess of 17 per cent of placements broke down because (in part) of conflict between the child and the placement, or due to challenging behaviour.

EXCLUSION AND OUT OF SCHOOL PROVISION

Table 6.1 clearly indicates that more than four in ten (43.4%) of these young people had recorded periods of time outside full-time school provision. In most of these cases time out of school was recorded as exclusion, with only a minority (4.9%) officially known to the out of school service, referred to as the Home and Hospital Teaching Service (HHTS) in this local authority. The HHTS does not only deal with excluded children, but also provides for other groups such as school phobics and children who are hospitalised or otherwise unwell. On the other hand, not all looked after children who are excluded would be entitled to HHTS intervention (for example, fixed-term excludees). These services are generally referred to as part of 'Education Other Than At School' (EOTAS) in most local education authorities and are a statutory obligation for LEAs. In over one in five cases in our study (21.7%) more serious exclusions of individuals were involved (indefinite – now no longer used – or permanent exclusions); in these cases children could be out of school for months and longer with minimal or no educational provision.

Table 6.1 Education other than at school, and exclusion status		
Exclusion status	Number	%
Has not come to the attention of the HHTS service	81	56.6
Officially known to the HHTS service	7	4.9
One fixed period of exclusion	14	9.8
Two or more fixed periods of exclusion	10	7.0
One or more permanent/indefinite periods of exclusion	16	11.2
Combination of fixed period and indefinite/permanent exclusions	15	10.5
Total	143	100

(Snapshot of status from data supplied by Home and Hospital Teaching Service, April 1996)

GCSE RESULTS

While careers data was available for the period up to June 1997, GCSE exam results are not released until August and were therefore not available by the time that this particular piece of research had been finished. For this reason, only the GCSE results of those young people leaving in 1996 have been included and percentages have been calculated on this basis (eighty-one young people in all). These results are presented in Table 6.2. There are also problems with obtaining GCSE results: they are not always recorded by careers services, particularly where they are so low as to be discounted when devising future plans. However, if results are good it is reasonable to surmise that they are more likely to be recorded or known about within a social services department. We found no records of any GCSEs passed or nothing known about this in nearly seven in ten (69.1%) cases.

Table 6.2 GCSE results for young people leaving school in 1996		
Grade	Number	%
Mainly E, F, G	1	1.2
Mainly C, D	10	12.3
Including 3 at A, B, C	9	11.1
Minimum of 4 at A, B, C	5	6.2
Total with known GCSEs	25	30.1
Missing/no GCSEs recorded	56	69.1

However, three in ten young people *did* obtain GCSE passes and a significant group (17.2%, 14 young people) obtained several high grade GCSE passes. Five (6.2%) young people are recorded as achieving four or more passes at grade C or above. One of these latter individuals is very able by any measure, achieving ten GCSE passes at Grade C or above. For those who had done relatively well, careers service support seemed to be easily available. All five young people with four or more passes had at least one careers interview. Also, of those nine achieving a minimum of three passes at A, B or C, seven had been interviewed by the careers service. Two had not (destinations for these two individuals were not available either).

Overall, about eight in ten looked after young people (79.7%) were known to the careers service that served the area and a little over half (56%) of the entire target cohort were known to have received careers interviews. Further to this, about three-quarters (73.8%) of those looked after young people known to the careers service, and who were of school leaving age in summer 1996, had received at least one careers interview by June 1997. About two-thirds (67.3%) of those looked after young people known to the careers service, and who were of school leaving age in summer 1997, had received at least one careers interview by the end of June 1997. There was, as in the non-care population, a small group of young people who required and received extra help. In this case, it was a small group (14% of the total) of young men known to the careers service who had between eight and twenty interviews.

POST-SIXTEEN EDUCATION AND DESTINATIONS

However, post-sixteen destinations for the whole cohort – or, rather, careers service and social services knowledge of these destinations – presents a

bleaker picture, but one which is again incomplete because of gaps in records
in nearly half (48.3%) the cases investigated.

Table 6.3 Post-sixteen destinations			
Destination	Number	%	Valid %
FE vocational course	11	7.7	27.5
FE A-levels	2	1.4	5.0
FE GCSE resits	3	2.1	7.5
FE basic skills/entry level	3	2.1	7.3
FE NVQ2	1	0.7	2.5
School (Vocational)	3	2.1	7.5
School (A-levels)	2	1.4	5.0
School (Resits)	2	1.4	5.0
School (NVQ2)	1	0.7	2.5
School (NVQ3)	1	0.7	2.5
Special School	9	6.3	22.5
College of Agriculture	2	1.4	5.0
Sub-total	40	28.0	99.8
Other (training or employment)	34	23.8	–
On records but destination not known	20	14.0	–
Missing/no records	49	34.3	–
Total	143	100	

These post-sixteen destinations were investigated using a snapshot of last
known or intended destinations in June 1997. They included actual
destinations of young people who left in 1996 and intended destinations of
young people leaving school in 1997. Taking into account the limitations of
the data, only 22 per cent of young people who are looked after are known to
be continuing in full-time education. This compares with a county-wide
combined average for full-time college and school participation of 73 per
cent and a similar rate nationally at the time. Eleven young people planned to
follow a vocational route via further education (FE), making this the largest
category. Some perspective is given to these figures by the realisation that the
next largest category would be that of 'special schooling', with nine young
people (6.3%).

Table 6.3 also shows that four young people (3.3%) of those completing
statutory schooling in 1996 planned to continue study to A-levels. Of these,
two achieved a 'minimum of four' A, B or C grade GCSEs and had plans to

study at FE, one other achieved 'at least three' at A, B or C and had plans to study at school. The young person with ten GCSE passes planned to stay on at school to take A-levels. Of the other nine with a minimum of three A, B or C GCSE passes, seven chose to pursue vocational courses at FE. The remaining young person with a minimum of four passes chose to undertake a vocational course at school. It would appear, therefore, highly unlikely, though not impossible, that more than three or four young people would have higher education as their next destination.

About a quarter of the young people (24.3% or 30 individuals) who left school in 1996 were on some form of training provision in June 1997. This included some young people who had experienced multiple placement. Of these, sixteen were female and fourteen were male. This proportion of looked after young people going on to training rather than further education at age sixteen compares with a county-wide average of 6 per cent. Eight young people in our group (6.5% of those who left in 1996) had experience of employment. Fourteen young people (11.4% of those who left in 1996) had either experienced unemployment or were unemployed at the time of the research. In comparison, unemployment for school leavers county-wide in 1996 was 3 per cent. What is evident again in this part of the study is the fact that there was no data available for just over a third (34.3%) of the young people.

CARE MANAGERS' PERSPECTIVES

The 83 care managers who provided responses to open-ended questions about this subject held some views in common and diverged on others. In many instances the existence of negative influences, or experiences, in the educational background of young people who are looked after was taken almost as a constant by care managers. Discussion about how barriers to the problems involved in post-sixteen educational participation might be overcome were encouraged from the starting point of 'where the young person is' rather than 'what should have been done' in the past, as this was seen to be the most constructive approach.

Three main barriers were seen as directly contributing to poorer post-sixteen education participation levels amongst looked after children, in comparison with the general population. These barriers were: first, under-achievement in mainstream school; second, lack of entrance qualifications; third, young people's lack of awareness of opportunities available to them. These three barriers were intrinsically seen as outcomes linked to other specific primary factors in three areas. The first of these areas concerned the individual characteristics that affect the young person's capacity and ability to access or use existing resources. Usually this was related to prior experience before being looked after. The second area concerned existing or associated stress factors that would be experienced around the transition from statutory schooling. These concerns related to lack of consistent long-term support, and uncertainty. Third, and finally, care managers were concerned with agency considerations including funding issues and the practical constraints involved in collaborative working. Comments in these areas were particularly centred around two concerns.

The first concern related to the lack of information and uncertainty about the roles and responsibility of different agencies. The sharing of information between agencies was further characterised by, it was claimed, a lack of understanding about the statutory roles and responsibilities of agencies outside social services, as well as a lack of confidence and appreciation of different agency cultures. These concerns were also reflected in the comments from other professionals in education psychology, the careers service, education welfare, teaching and those in the voluntary sector. Young people themselves were very often aware of these difficulties. The second concern related to funding problems. More specifically, the competitive nature of departmental resource allocation. Problems were encountered in agreeing funding with the education department over therapeutic inter-ventions and the financial limitations of statutory responsibility. One care manager voiced particular disquiet at the number and nature of accomm-odation changes; changes that were felt to be resource-related rather than needs-led. Training and financial recompense for foster carers was also identified as an issue.

Care managers recommended various ways in which support could be improved; in particular, improvements in the sharing and communication of information between different agencies. Some felt that access to and information about non-statutory funding opportunities should be examined, and the exploration of the role of 'sponsorship' for individuals who wished to undertake higher education courses was also suggested. (A ring-fenced budget of £90,000 for care leavers going on to further/higher education was later established in this authority.) Other suggestions included the allocation of funding to provide extra (non-school) tuition for young people and training for care workers, this latter to enhance the educational environment and support available in residential homes. Training for foster carers to help them, also, to cope with educational and general issues particularly related to adolescence was also suggested, along with the need for longer term strategies to help address uncertainty over accommodation. Inevitably, despite initiatives within this area, it was still felt that there was a need for increased cooperation and communication with schools through, for example, liaison with named individuals about specific school exclusions.

Discussion

Our research adds to the growing evidence about the educational experience of looked after children and the debate about corporate responsibility for this issue. Although some of the findings about the experience of education whilst they are looked after may be seen as encouraging, in that for the majority in Lynes and Goddard's (1995) study their situation either improved or stayed the same, rather than got worse, we may want to consider these findings further. Whether or not children perceive the situation as better, worse or the same begs the question (first raised in the discussion in Chapter 1 of the 1834 Poor Law Amendment Act) of the starting point for this assessment and whether or not being looked after is expected to improve an individual's life chances. Of course, some children may not need improvements in their education, but as Van Der Spek's study shows, in academic terms at least there is usually a clear need for more support for looked after children.

Van Der Spek's (1998) study illustrates too that there are still too many gaps in the basic record-keeping about looked after children – such as whether or not they achieved any examination passes or their destinations after compulsory schooling. Judged by the standards of the interested and well-meaning parent, it is hard to explain why local authorities as 'corporate parents' do not have adequate recorded evidence about whether or not children have achieved any GCSE passes. It is also hard to imagine the interested parent simply not knowing what their children were doing or planned to do beyond the age of sixteen.

Time spent out of school, whether through exclusion or non-attendance, can be part of the system abuse (discussed in Chapter 2) which looked after children suffer and is related to their looked after status in a number of ways. Disruption in and of itself is disadvantageous and when disruption sometimes involves both a change of home, carers, school and friends it is hardly surprising that some children do not settle easily. On the other hand, schools have to enforce acceptable standards of behaviour. While schools may make exceptions and be flexible in certain cases, they also need to be kept informed about children's home circumstances. However, in order to be flexible and make any special provision schools usually expect the support of parents, which in the case of looked after children will mean, in practice, foster carers or social work staff.

Young people's comments about the experience of being in care while also in school remind us of the need to be sensitive to children's individual needs, though not singling them out and thus enhancing feelings of difference. Although, on balance, individuals report not being treated differently by other pupils, we need to consider this in the context of wider issues of bullying and discriminatory behaviour amongst school children when interpreting the negative experiences of school for some looked after children.

The connections between school achievement and possibilities beyond school leaving age and leaving care are obvious. Some of the confusions and lack of understanding within social services departments about post-sixteen options are hard to justify. Returning again to our 'interested parent': when this time arrives, they will generally acquaint themselves with the necessary information to support their child, if they have not done so earlier. The reported lack of understanding about the roles and responsibilities of different agencies has long been talked about, but little progress has been made despite most organisations having clearly published information about the nature of their services. On top of this, the funding problems come about largely because of the permissive nature of the legislation in relation to supporting looked after children beyond the age of sixteen.

Poor experiences and outcomes from the education system are both symptoms and causes of social exclusion. Attending school for the majority of children is about some opportunity for achievement, as well as spending time with friends. The majority of children now stay on in education beyond the age of sixteen and nearly a third of young people can now expect to go on to higher education. Any existing difficulties that a child has when they enter the care system can be compounded by the disruption of placement changes, the lack of priority accorded to education in comparison with welfare issues and disproportionate patterns of poor attendance and exclusion from school amongst the looked after population. In these ways, many looked after children are also excluded from more positive and varied social networks and experiences, as well as the possibility of academic achievement. The limited possibilities and horizons which characterise social exclusion are the landscape for which many children leave the care system, as we shall see in the next chapter.

Conclusions and implications

The case for the effect of early experience affecting educational performance is well established by a number of studies, as we have already noted. However, the National Federation for Educational Research (NFER) study (Fletcher-Campbell 1997) and the Oxford-based study both point out that this need not be accepted as a deterministic feature of looked after children's histories, but rather, as the Oxford study (Aldgate *et al.* 1992) suggests, as an indication of the need for 'exceptional inputs' to ameliorate factors which could be controlled. The recognition of the institutional barriers to the educational attainment of looked after children of statutory school age that has arisen out of the research in the area has been the basis for many recommendations concerned with best practice. In particular, the attention the above research has brought to the way looked after children have 'fallen through the net' of education departments and social service policy has done much to highlight the need for practical guidance in the liaison between the two services, a need which the DfE circular 1994 attempted to address.

However, guidance contained within such publications as the DfE circular is just that, and the way that such guidance is implemented and its resource implications are dependent on the interpretation and priorities of individual local authorities. For post-sixteen education, policy with regard to looked after young people is fragmented. Neither the SSI/OFSTED (1995) report nor the DfE circular explore the ways in which 'exceptional inputs' could be used to directly further post-sixteen participation. With regard to post-sixteen education and training, recent reports indicate that care leavers are unlikely to be well placed either to make, or to implement, an informed post-sixteen career choice directly on the completion of their compulsory education and that their living circumstances are likely to reduce their motivation to place post-sixteen education or training high on their agenda of priorities whilst in their teens (Action on Aftercare Consortium 1996). Once again, the development of supportive systems and resources is identified as a prerequisite for ensuring that SSDs, careers services, TECs, local training providers and other agencies work together to plan and deliver services which are more likely to ensure that care leavers receive equality of opportunity in accessing quality training and education. It must be stressed that these young people would not be positively discriminated towards by the targeting of resources in this manner. It is, rather, a matter of restoring and safeguarding an entitlement.

To summarise, all available literature suggests that looked after young people suffer additional disadvantages in the education field; disadvantages which relate to the looked after experience. Both our studies support this, though the first study suggests that the everyday experience of school for looked after young people is more mixed and not without its compensations. From the point of view of some of the young people concerned, going into care can often have very positive educational impacts. The need for a more realistic policy of practical and constructive support for the education of looked after children is illustrated in a range of ways from our research and that of others. High levels of special educational need, very high levels of exclusion and time outside mainstream schooling, as well as the general disruption associated with being looked after, point to the obvious need for policies and funding arrangements which reflect this situation. For many looked after children there is a need for additional time and resources to support any 'catching up' necessitated by the upset, time out of school and other disruptions experienced. The state must be financially responsible for the education of looked after children beyond the period of compulsory education and provide the necessary support to young people leaving care so that they are able to benefit from the opportunities on offer. The extent to which policy proposals on education under the Quality Protects initiative measure up to these requirements is discussed in the final chapter.

CHAPTER 7

Leaving Care

This chapter examines leaving care preparation, support and outcomes. We know already from Chapter 2 that when young people leave the care of local authorities, whether foster or residential, they experience disproportionate problems in adjusting to independence and adult life. These problems are compounded by poor educational attainment and include vulnerability to unemployment, homelessness and young parenthood (Action on Aftercare Consortium 1996; Biehal *et al.* 1994; Garnett 1992; Hazelhurst and Tijani 1998; SSI 1997; Stein 1998; Stein and Carey 1986; Utting 1997; West 1995). Young people often carry with them many disadvantages as a result of being in care: the disruption associated with placement changes and break-downs, added to the dislocation of coming into care in the first place. However, it is worth considering what we mean by 'leaving care' in this con-text. Over fifty thousand young people spend time in care during a one year period, of whom about six in ten start to be looked after during this same time period. More than half (59%) of children are looked after for less than six months, and many of these for less than eight weeks. During 1997–1998, 7900 young people left care aged sixteen years or older (less than 1% of their age group); 2900 were aged eighteen years or older, thus the majority (63%) of these care leavers were aged sixteen or seventeen years (DoH 1998c). It is this group of post-sixteen care leavers, particularly those that were looked after for long periods, that we are concerned with here.

This relatively small and identifiable number (7900) of young people is known to be amongst the most vulnerable in its age group. Part of this vulnerability is related to the age of leaving care. In the 1990s, the proportion of young people leaving care at the age of sixteen has increased: from 33 per cent in 1993 to 40 per cent in 1997 (Stein 1998). It is particularly those individuals who are leaving care in the sense that they are also leaving their home who are the focus of most leaving care studies. However, certain high-profile outcome measures (for example inmates in prisons, homeless young people and claimants for DSS severe hardship payments) are somewhat misleading in that they can include individuals who have spent 'some time in care', however brief (SSI 1997). Baldwin, Coles and Mitchell (1997) also caution us to remember the complex biographies which lie behind the statistics about outcomes from care. Alongside differences of gender and race, reasons for original admission to care, age of admission, number of episodes of care, and number and type of placements there is, of course, the overall length of time spent in care in comparison with the rest of an individual's childhood and young adulthood.

The policy response to the well-known problems of care leavers is laid out reasonably clearly in the 1989 Children Act and in post-Act regulations. Two difficulties arise, however. The first of these concerns the level of discretion given to local authorities in determining the help that they give. The second difficulty is the general political and social climate, which often works in a negative direction when it comes to the welfare of young people. Important elements of the policy response, under the 1989 Act, are as follows: section 27 of the Act states that Housing Authorities should comply with requests for help from social services departments (SSDs); under Section 24, local authorities are given the power to 'advise, assist and befriend' up to the age of 21 (however, young people must be 'in need' and some of the powers are discretionary); local authorities must provide a leaving care policy document. Two ways in which the wider political and social climate cuts across these objectives are that, first, the 1996 Housing Act removed the capacity of local authorities to give priority status to care leavers (and also single parents, in relation to which the Act received most publicity at the time). Second, lower benefit levels for the under-25s had already been introduced by the Social Security Act 1986. Measures in this Act assumed parental support and made life inevitably more difficult for those young people without such support. There are two further problems, relating to the Act itself. The first of these is that Section 24 assistance applies only to those in care after their sixteenth birthday, and thus unwittingly encourages local authorities to shift young people out of the care system prior to their sixteenth birthday in order to avoid the consequent responsibilities. Second, the Section 24 power to 'assist' – in cash or kind – is discretionary. Utting (1997) has since recommended that assistance be made a duty, in light of SSDs' frequent tendency to wash their hands of young people once they cease being 'looked after' by them. The current government plans to replace the discretionary power with a 'duty to assess and meet needs' (DoH 1998g, p.27).

Inter-agency cooperation and coordination

Inter-agency cooperation has been a long-standing problem in the field of state child care, especially in child protection (Hallett 1995). The requirement for inter-agency working under the lead of social services departments is made clear under the Children Act 1989. Health, education and housing authorities are particularly highlighted as having an obligation to assist social services where reasonable and practicable (Children Act 1989, s.27, (3)). The permissive nature of the legislation means that there is no requirement from agencies outside social services to assist with the needs of looked after children, or indeed children in need more generally. This lack of statutory requirement on top of the differing priorities of agencies outside social services can result in care leavers being in a vulnerable position and case holders being frustrated in their attempts to do their best for young people. These issues are well recognised at an official level (Audit Commission 1994, 1996; House of Commons 1998b; SSI 1998b; Utting 1997). It is a particularly relevant concern, of course, at the key points of transition faced by young care leavers. Without adequate cooperation between the relevant agencies in the fields of education, housing, employment and social services, many young people can fall into the worlds of homelessness, joblessness and crime. Even after these outcomes have occurred, there is often failure to integrate service responses. As the Audit Commission noted:

> In most areas there is a duplication of service; different teams of social workers are looking after care leavers and young offenders separately, although they are providing equivalent services to these different groups of young people at risk, often with little idea of the cost. (Audit Commission 1996, p.81)

As well as a failure to work adequately or in a coordinated manner between state agencies, there are also problems of coordination between state and private sectors. Recent research into existing levels of involvement between social services and the business community in supporting leaving care schemes (Meegan 1997) found that fewer than one in twenty SSDs worked with employers on a regular basis and that only one in eight SSDs worked with Training and Enterprise Councils (TECs) or Local Enterprise Companies (LECs) on a regular basis. It was also found that nearly half (45%) of SSDs did not work with careers' services to support leaving care schemes. This is clearly likely to limit the access which care leavers have, not only to employers and the types of network which can facilitate this, but also to impartial and informed advice on education, training and employment opportunities.

Youth transitions

Coles (1995) has characterised youth as a series of interrelated transitions: education, training and labour market entry (the school-to-work transition); domestic careers (from families of origin to families of destination); and housing careers (from living with families or surrogate families to living independently of them). The interplay between these interrelated transitions, young people's own choices and perceived options and their carers' understanding of and commitment towards supporting these transitions is the context in which we should consider the particular situation of care leavers, in comparison with their counterparts in the rest of the population.

In 1988, the UK government introduced a Youth Training Guarantee scheme which stated that no young person would be without education, employment or training. The intention was to tackle the then growing problem of long-term youth unemployment. During the 1980s patterns of school leavers' participation in education and employment changed dramatically. It became increasingly the norm for young people to stay on in education beyond the age of compulsory schooling and increasingly unlikely that young people would go into paid employment at the age of sixteen. The proportion of all young people staying on in full-time education rose from under five in ten in 1986 to about seven in ten in 1996. Conversely the proportion of young people leaving school and going into paid work has declined from about five in ten young people in 1979 to one in ten young people in 1996. Government-supported training has generally failed to date in its aim to equip this latter group of young people with qualifications. Whilst the introduction of Modern Apprenticeships is said to have helped to raise standards for those in work-based learning, the track record of government schemes has not been good (Pearce and Hillman 1998). Furthermore, there is plenty of evidence that thousands of young people still 'vote with their feet' in relation to options which are not valued (Williamson 1997).

Although the vast majority of 16–18-year-olds are in some form of education and training, there is a proportion of young people which is neither employed nor undertaking any learning. Those young people not participating in education or training have been termed 'Status ZerO' by some policy analysts, a term which is viewed as contentious (Williamson 1997). The exact number of young people not in education, training or employment is a matter of debate; one estimate suggests 7 per cent of sixteen-year-olds and 8–9 per cent of seventeen-year-olds (Robinson 1998). Local analyses tend to show much larger figures for non-participating young people, far in excess of either official local figures or estimates from national data sets. This is partly due to the fact that there is no longer a claimant count of sixteen- and seventeen-year-olds (Pearce and Hillman 1998).

Since the election of a Labour government in May 1997 there has been a great deal of interest in these issues as they relate to other concerns, such as disaffection from school, truancy, exclusion from school, delinquent and anti-social behaviour in particular neighbourhoods and the relationship of all of these issues to social exclusion. Initiatives such as New Start for disaffected young people in the 14–19-year-old age group and the New Deal for people aged between 18 and 24 are targeting efforts on young people at risk of entering 'Status ZerO' and those already there. Whilst these initiatives are not particularly targeted at looked after young people, their obvious relevance to this group will soon become apparent as we explore our research findings in this chapter.

Research findings

In order to illustrate and illuminate some of the issues for young people leaving care we again report upon aspects of our own research in this field. First, we consider the views of care leavers themselves about many aspects of their experience from Lynes and Goddard's (1995) survey (see Appendix, section 2) of care leavers. Second, we continue tracking the careers advice input and subsequent employment details (as far as these can be established) of the care leaving sample in Van Der Spek's (1998) study (see Appendix, section 4). The themes we explore are as follows:

- the experience of leaving care
- inter-agency cooperation: careers and leaving care.

The experience of leaving care

'DON'T LEAVE CARE': YOUNG PEOPLE'S VIEWS OF THE LEAVING CARE EXPERIENCE

In this study, we were interested in the general experience of leaving care for young people and how that experience varied. It is worth noting at this point the views about care-leaving of the 121 young people who responded to the in-care questionnaire in the same county as we conducted our research (Lynes and Goddard 1995). They are a useful point of contrast with the views of the 65 care leavers who responded to our leaving care questionnaire. While the experience of leaving home is usually very different from that of leaving care, looked after young people clearly do not intend it to be so and their hopes for the future are the ordinary hopes of most teenagers as they look forward to independence.

ASPIRATIONS WHILST BEING LOOKED AFTER

There were a wide range of responses to our question: 'What do you want to do when you leave care?' and many of these young people gave more than one response, making them difficult to categorise. However, there are several general points worth making. First, there was a small proportion of children (6%) who focused primarily on their desire to go home after leaving care or to renew contact with their family. Leaving care was seen by these young people as a chance to heal family wounds and repair damage. Equally, there was a small proportion (5%) who wished to stay in care. Some individuals focused simply on having their own home and others on further or higher education. However, a much larger proportion (notwithstanding that some of the choices implied further or higher education) focused on career or work ambitions. The range here was wide: graphic designer or illustrator, fireman, doctor, accountant, footballer, police officer. In other words, the same sorts of careers that children outside of the care system may aspire to. There were a number who wanted caring careers with children or elderly people, but no more than those who were interested in the police or armed forces. Only two individuals wanted to be social workers. Many of these children, despite their ages, were quite specific about what they wanted to do, such as one girl of fourteen who wanted to 'get into the police force, that's all I ever wanted to do when I was a little girl.'

In general, what was most obvious about the responses (apart from the occasional exception, such as an ambition to 'live on the streets' from a boy of fourteen and those few who wanted to stay in care) was the normality of the ambitions, the extent to which these children came across as diverse and yet as alike as the non-care population. A few of their comments serve to illustrate this:

> Go to university and get a degree in physics. Then find a nice place to settle down and have a family. (boy, 17)

> Be an artist, travel all over the world and look after children. (girl, 16)

> Just continue to be happy. Get my GCSEs, go to [local technical college], go to [local university] and get a nice job and a nice future. (girl, 15)

'ALL ON YOUR OWN': THE EXPERIENCE OF LEAVING CARE

The contrast between the above ambitions and the realities of the post-care experience of young people in the county in our study was a striking one. There are, of course, a wide number of explanations for the wide gulf between the apparently positive experience of most young people in care in the county and the generally negative experience of care leavers. One of its implications, however, was that the quality of care had less relevance to explaining post-care outcomes than did the abruptness of exit from care and the level of support between the ages of sixteen and eighteen and the generally poor planning and preparation for leaving care (in line with the criticisms levelled by a wide range of other leaving care studies).

The number of placements that young people had experienced varied considerably. However, although over three-quarters of the young people had experienced five placements or fewer, there were eight young people (11% of the total) who had experienced eight placements or more. The long-term effects of frequent moves are difficult to isolate from other factors which may have influenced young people whilst they were living in care or, indeed, before they had entered care. However, it is worth noting that of these eight individuals, six claimed to have received very little training in independence skills prior to leaving care, six could not get help from their last carer after leaving, six stated that social services could have kept in touch better and six had been involved in criminal activity. Of these latter six, five had been (or still were) in prison. Lastly, seven of them reported difficulties with money. It is such extreme dislocation, and its consequences, that is the focus of current government targets to reduce the number of moves whilst young people are looked after (see Chapter 10).

This particular group of young people were, in fact, very quick to draw inferences concerning the relationship between their in-care and their post-care experiences. With specific regard to the effect of frequent moves, one young woman of sixteen echoed Sonia Jackson's (1989) point that in moving young people while they are being 'looked after' too little notice is often taken of potential educational impact:

> When I was in care I was moved from place to place all the time and that really pissed me off because all I have done is move from school to school to school and now my education is fucked up because of Social Services pissing me around and I would like to say tell Social Services when someone is in care leave them where they are or move them so they can go to the same school so they do their GCSEs and get an education.

Another young woman, of eighteen, noted the effect that being moved had had on her ability to form trusting relationships of the kind that are often vital in overcoming the hurdles of moving to independence: 'because I don't trust anyone – being pushed from foster home to foster home – it feels as no one wants you so you don't trust or get close to anyone.'

We asked questions about the length of the last care episode and the final placement type. The former question was particularly important as it indicates what sort of opportunity was available for social services to engage in training these young people in independence skills. Of those who responded, the great majority indicated that their last care episode had lasted for more than six months; time for at least some leaving care preparation. In relation to final placement type, fewer than half (46%) were in supportive lodgings or rented accommodation. Nearly half (49%) were either in residential or foster care prior to leaving care. Both the length and type of the last care episode indicate, therefore, that there was a reasonably large group of young people who could have derived substantial benefit from local authority based leaving care preparation.

PREPARATION FOR LEAVING CARE

One of the crucial features of the leaving care experience about which we sought feedback was the preparation that young people had received. We sought this information in forms that we could quantify but we also sought qualitative feedback. On the former, we asked about the extent to which young people had been taught a range of basic skills. Only about six in ten care leavers (62%) in our survey claimed to have been taught basic cooking skills. The proportion drops to about a half for the other basic competencies, such as washing and ironing, budgeting, where to go for help, job hunting and claiming benefits. Just over a third (37%) of the group claimed to have been taught how to both budget and cook before leaving care. Fewer than one in five (17%) said that they had received help with all six activities. As well as this, some difference emerged between residential and foster care: the former gave noticeably more help with budgeting and cooking skills and the latter was more useful in teaching young people where to go for help and about seeking employment. Although, given the above, much of the inadequacy of preparation can be linked to insufficient time in care during the last care episode, this clearly cannot explain away all of the problems.

Given these findings, it is not surprising that asking these young people's views of the preparation that they received for leaving care elicited more negative comments than positive. Indeed, the question about what was 'good or useful' in relation to this preparation produced negative responses from twenty-one young people (32% of the total), as against twenty-seven (42% of the total) positive responses (the rest gave no answer). These 'negative' responses to what was a 'positive' question were often couched in emphatic terms:

> Nothing, because I didn't get any preparation until I had been living by myself for three months. Social Services left it too late. (young man, 18)

> The people were useless they didn't help me at all. (young man, 18)

> I was taught nothing, everything I have learnt was down to watching others. (young woman, 19)

Of the positive responses, many identified the teaching of a specific skill, such as cooking, washing or ironing. The sense that there was somewhere to turn to if necessary after leaving care was also identified as important by a few young people. In the words of one young woman of 17: 'there was always someone there to care for me. I knew I was loved and welcome there.' This sense of a place to retreat for support, of something or someone in the background, turned out – as we shall see later – to be more important than leaving care preparation. Finally, the manner in which skills were taught could also be important: 'Going through it with me first, then getting me to do it, but with someone with me and the support' (young woman, 18), or 'Being in a flat on my own in the grounds of a children's home' (young man, 17).

When we asked what had been 'bad or not useful' about leaving care preparation a small minority responded 'positively' by stating 'nothing'. Overall there was a higher proportion of dissatisfied young people from residential care than from foster care. Some young people denied receiving any leaving care preparation at all, while some said that social services had 'left it too late'. Several others complained of a general lack of follow-up support, or of a rather shallow approach to teaching such skills, such as:

> Bad. I think when I was in care they did not teach me about life on my own and what it was going to be like for me. (young man, 19)

> They taught you how to do these things in groups and not as an individual. (young woman, 21)

> Not being told enough or the right things I really needed, they expected you, once you know how to do it, to do it all on your own, 'you've been told once, now that's it' attitude. (young woman, 18)

LEAVING CARE GRANTS

Approximately two-thirds (65%) of the young people reported receiving a grant (for such things as bedding, furniture and rent deposit) on leaving care. Nearly a third, 32 per cent, did not receive a grant and 8 per cent didn't answer the question. Of the ones who were given financial help, three-quarters received £300 or less. One young person recorded having received £2000, but this had come from a voluntary body in another county and not from the local social services department. The average grant across the group was £286. This compared very poorly with the average local authority leaving care grant of £731 in 1992, as calculated by First Key, the leaving care advisory service, from information provided by eighty-eight social services departments (Roberts and Morey 1992, p.21). However, the provision of this information by the local authorities rather than by young people themselves should encourage us to treat this latter figure with caution. In any case, both figures are well below the figures, of £2000 and similar, recommended by most leaving care studies (for example West 1995, p.38). Finally, our local authority could provide no clear information on how the amount of leaving care grant was calculated and what criteria were used – a situation common to many other local authorities (Roberts and Morey 1992).

AFTER LEAVING: THE FIRST SIX MONTHS

We wanted, here, to get some account of the feelings and thoughts of these young people during this initial period after leaving care. We also wanted to know about the extent to which they felt that they could get help from their last carers and also who had helped them the most since leaving care. In response to the first question, about how they coped during this time, more than half responded positively, a fifth negatively and a few gave an ambiguous answer. Among the positive responses there was considerable variation. One young man of nineteen stated that 'I was still in supportive lodgings but when I left care the supportiveness was dropped and I thoroughly enjoyed it.' A young man of eighteen, similarly positive, noted that 'after the first six months everybody who I knew said that I had grown up a lot.' However, among these positive responses were a number who qualified their view about how they fared on leaving care: 'Not too badly as I had money but it was very hard' (young woman, 19); 'I seemed to cope very well, but did not receive a lot of help from Social Services, especially when I needed it, when I had to find somewhere to live' (young woman, 18).

Of those who answered negatively, two-thirds indicated that life had been very difficult. Again, the intensity of the responses varied:

Not very well. Very confused and unsure why it was worth living. (young man, 20)

I wasn't able to cope very well due to being alone and no life skills. (young woman, 19)

I did not cope very well as I soon became homeless and was living on the streets and around friends. (young man, 17)

When these young people went on to describe how they felt during this time, rather than how they coped, the balance shifted and there were more negative responses than positive. Of those who described their feelings during the first six months, six in ten had felt either unhappy, frightened, insecure, isolated or lonely. Their fuller comments about how they felt in the months after leaving care are illustrated by the following:

On my own, frightened, worried, isolated and nowhere to turn for help. (young woman, 20)

Lost and alone – trying to hang on to anyone that was left. (young woman, 18)

One young woman of 20 reported feeling: 'very depressed, suicidal. I still feel depressed now [four years later] because I can't seem to live in the community without taking drugs and now I am in prison for it.' On the other hand, a third of these young people did record more positive feelings, even though this varied through various shades of 'OK', 'fine' and 'great'. Some, who had earlier reported coping, nevertheless admitted to feeling unhappy during the process.

When it came to getting help from their last carers, nearly six in ten (59%) said that they could and four in ten (41%) that this had not been possible. The latter group were then asked why they could not get help. Responses varied, but included a few where the young person had fallen out with their foster carer, some where they had simply felt unable to ask for help and a few who claimed implicit or explicit messages from carers that no more help would be forthcoming, such as one young woman of seventeen who noted that: 'My foster parents who looked after me were pleased to get rid of me (but I say no more).'

There are a couple of major issues worth noting from all of this. The first of these is that the proportion of those able to get help from their last carer varied between last placement type. This ranged through 70 per cent for supportive lodgings, 60 per cent for rented accommodation, 58 per cent for residential care and 50 per cent for foster care. These proportions are based on small numbers so caution must be exercised in making any general-isations, but the figure for foster care is interesting because it suggests an important limitation on the extent to which foster care can be simply assumed to replicate the traditional family model. The comments of many of the young people, together with our own experiences when telephoning round many of these foster parents and seeking to trace former foster children, confirm that such an image would be a false one. Although many foster carers clearly did make enormous efforts to keep in touch beyond the period of formal care, many others did not. The increasing shift towards foster care may not, therefore, be helping to improve leaving care preparation and assistance. A further point is that of those who felt unhappy, frightened, insecure or isolated, only four in ten (41%) had been able to get help from their last carers, whereas nearly eight in ten (78%) of those who felt they had coped pretty well, well or fine were able to access such help. After-care support appeared, from our study, to be more significant than independence training for ensuring that young people successfully dealt with leaving care transitions.

The impression that foster carers do not give as much help after care as might be supposed is confirmed when young people are asked who gave them the most such help. Although 'foster carer' was not included as a separate category in our question, making it conceivable that more young people would have picked it if it had been, the level of stated support still appears remarkably low when compared with that provided by social services or by friends and family, with only 8 per cent of young people naming foster carers as their source of significant help, as against 50 per cent naming social services and 43 per cent citing their friends.

Finally, in this section, we also asked what more could have been done to help in the first six months after leaving care. Of those who responded (46), just over a quarter identified more help from social services. To be more precise, they were concerned that contact should not be cut off so abruptly once care had ended. In the words of one young woman of 18: 'Not trying to get me to switch off from them so quickly, telling me I didn't really need them anymore, when I knew damn well I did, I mean they can't tell me whether I feel I do or don't.' A further quarter returned to their preparation for leaving care and identified this as an area that should have been better. One young man of 17 echoed what some of the leaving care literature also says: 'I should have left care two years after I did realistically.'

LIFE AFTER LEAVING CARE

Either during or after the first six months of leaving care, about a quarter of the young people reported approaching social services. All but one of these young people were under twenty-one years of age when they did so. They needed help with money, housing, past or current abusive relationships or to find their birth relatives. As to whether social services should have kept in touch with them better after they left care, two-thirds of the replies on this issue said that they thought that social services could have done better. Many of them identified with the *in loco parentis* role of local authorities and considered it a dereliction of parental duties to cut ties so swiftly. It is not surprising, in light of this view, that over three-quarters preferred after-care support to be provided by social services departments rather than by some other agency.

More general questions provided a wider picture of what life had been like for these young people since leaving care. About a quarter of our respondents reported that they had experienced periods of unemployment and only one in eight had significant experience of full-time employment since leaving care. With regard to experiencing difficulties with major areas of life, the exception was the young person who did not experience such difficulties. For our group, difficulties were experienced with respect to money (81%), relationships (68%), work (67%) and housing (61%). Many of these young people were experiencing multiple difficulties after leaving care – a depressing if not uncommon finding. More detailed responses on these topics highlighted loneliness, practical hardship and stigma as being problematic. The first two of these we have come across before. The stigmatising effect of a care background was seen by some as an additional burden:

> People's attitudes towards children who are in care or have been in care. (young woman, 18)

> There is a 'stigma' attached to people who have been in care as being troublesome, at job interviews explaining why I didn't live at home was difficult. (young woman, 19)

More positively, the majority (83%) also indicated that they had what they considered to be successes and achievements. Most young people cited achieving or surviving independence as their main success. Educational qualifications, finding a job, maintaining a steady relationship or having a child also featured. Not surprisingly, given the above, these young people were more likely to ascribe these successes to themselves than to anyone else, although a few individuals credited social services or voluntary agencies. Six individuals identified their partners ('my husband has shown me I am important and am loved') and only one identified former foster parents.

Table 7.1 'Please indicate if you have had experience of any of the following since leaving care' (n=59)		
Description	Frequency	%
Unemployment	38	61
College	22	36
Drug abuse	21	34
Criminal activity	21	34
Parenthood	21	34
Renewed contact with family	18	29
Lost contact with family	18	29
Alcohol abuse	16	26
Attempted suicide	16	26
Counselling/therapy for childhood abuse	14	23
Medication for depression or anxiety	14	23
Severe financial debt	12	19
Homelessness	11	18

We also asked about personal issues, in an explicitly optional section that asked about sometimes very specific experiences. The responses of the fifty-nine young people who replied to this part are given in Table 7.1. This table encapsulates much of what this chapter has been about. Young people leaving care are often dealing with multiple problems, usually at too early an age. They are usually doing this with some 'baggage' either from their care experience or from the experiences that led them into the care system in the first place, often both. That so many of them therefore experience major problems in adjusting to adult life is not surprising.

Finally, we offered the young people who responded to our questionnaire the opportunity to offer advice to both the Director of Social Services (who received a collection of the full responses in due course) and to other young people leaving care in the future. Fifty-two individuals took the opportunity to proffer advice to the Director. The comments were understandably diverse, but common themes included the provision of more information (on services available, for example), greater after-care support, more financial support and better initial preparation for leaving care. To other young people such as themselves, fifty-eight of our sample offered advice. It was often, naturally, more personal than that offered to the Director of Social Services. It included comments such as the following:

> I would say to them are you sure that you want to leave if you were to ask me I would say stay in care because you are better off and you will find it hard to cope with everyday problems, so make sure that you are making the right choice. (young woman, 17)

> Don't be big and say I don't need you anymore, I've got rid of you all, at least I'm on my own. Swallow your pride and hang on to every last person you can hang on to. Don't let go until you know that everything is going smoothly and you have got yourself sorted out in your new place and have been going for at least a few months. (young woman, 18)

> Don't get in with the wrong people who are into crime. Don't take drugs – it's the worst thing that can happen to you. I found out the hard way. (young man, 21)

The tendency for local authorities to fail to deal adequately with the problems of young people before passing them on to other agencies is very apparent from both our research and that of others. It was less evident in Van Der Spek's research, in which agency coordination (or, rather, the lack of it) was a more significant issue. Nonetheless, the problems are much wider than this. They are, for example, partly political and a response to political agendas, whether they be those concerning the threats of juvenile ill-discipline or a concern with social exclusion. We deal with a subset of those problems but, more importantly, with issues that are given too little attention (careers service links) or that are insufficiently informed by the complexity of the experience of individual care leavers. We consider Van Der Spek's (1998) study next in so far as it focused on careers service involvement with care leavers.

Inter-agency cooperation: careers and leaving care

Since 1993, the social services department studied in Van Der Spek's (1998) research had been highly proactive in the development of its after-care provision for looked after young people, with the development of several major policy initiatives. In particular, two After-Care Coordinator posts were created to develop services for care leavers aided by a dedicated budget, and with a brief to raise awareness within social services about the particular needs of this group. The importance of a senior officer with responsibility for the development of leaving care services has been identified as highly necessary to the success of such services (Biehal *et al.* 1995); thus the creation of these posts has been crucial to the acquisition of specialist knowledge and dissemination of advice to both young people, carers and care managers and to raising the profile of this group and liaising with other agencies. In October 1995 a new After-Care Policy was developed which set out the local authorities' obligations and provided guidance about how they should be met. The responsibility for planning for independence and the financial and practical support for young people leaving care was delineated. It is worth noting that around the time of these developments the Audit Commission (1994) had found that two-thirds of the local authorities they studied still had no procedures to ensure that leaving care plans were prepared. A dedicated ring-fenced budget of £90,000 to financially support care leavers in Further or Higher Education was also established. The budget was to meet assessed need in both term-time and holiday periods, with planning to be undertaken prior to the start of the course to identify resources and support to be given throughout the duration of the course. It was anticipated that this would be formalised in an agreement with the young person and the department which would be subject to annual review but with the understanding that top-up funding would not be withdrawn unless other sources of income increased or the young person withdrew from the course.

CAREERS ADVICE

The careers service, a national network of individual organisations, works to a clearly specified contract on behalf of the Secretary of State for Education and Employment to provide careers information and guidance to young people. Formerly run by local education authorities, these services are now contracted out to a range of organisations. In this particular context, the careers service had been contracted out to an organisation that also operates in another county and which operated from several centres of population. This organisation employed over two hundred staff across both counties. These staff conducted over 70,000 interviews with young people in the school year 1996/97. New initiatives in 1996/97 included the creation of a database providing access to information on all local, full-time, vocational and A/As level courses as well as youth training and modern apprenticeship schemes and new approaches to young-person-led Action Planning.

The 1997 Education Act (section 43) provides that all publicly funded schools shall be required to provide a programme of careers education to all pupils in Years 9–11. From September 1997, this included the provision of access to careers services to enable them to fulfil their contracted duties on behalf of the Secretary of State (section 44), and working with careers services to ensure that pupils have access to materials providing careers guidance (section 45). The Act effectively provides that all young people have a statutory entitlement to impartial information and guidance provided by the careers service. However, no previous research has addressed the way in which looked after young people have accessed the careers service and whether, given the other problems experienced by these young people, there is a need to further ensure this entitlement.

Given the fluctuating and seasonal nature of careers service contacts, records were updated as late as possible in June 1997. They provide data from computer records that are kept about the incidence of contact between looked after children in the cohort in the county and the careers service over the period. Of the subsection of the cohort who were of school leaving age in 1996, the data provides details of verifiable careers contacts to one academic year later. Of those in the cohort who were of school leaving age in 1997, the data covers the time period up to the point of leaving.

Of the 143 young people described as 'looked after', the names of 114 (80%) of them were found on careers service roll records in our authority. It was not possible to ascertain verifiable careers information about the remaining 29 (20.3%). By cross-checking with questionnaires and social service records it was found that of the unaccounted-for twenty-nine, thirteen were placed in some form of 'out of county' placement. For the remaining sixteen 'in county', it was much less easy to find specific reasons why they might not be known to the careers service. Three care managers had failed to return questionnaires, and information on the remaining thirteen showed a variety of problems. Whilst not originally listed as 'out of county', two had 'moved on' or were living elsewhere, one young person was described as having 'no fixed abode' and a further four were found to be living out of county. One young person had since been adopted. Of those five remaining, no immediately obvious cause for their apparent 'disappearance' could be found.

Further investigations revealed that nine of the unaccounted-for young people had used one or more different aliases, often relating to their complex family and personal circumstances. This again complicated the search for careers data. Generally, tracking the post-sixteen destinations of individuals not 'known' to the careers service proved very difficult. At least five of the missing twenty-nine are believed to have some form of contact with the careers service in other areas. Social services records indicated that at least three young people were undertaking some form of course at college. One young person was said to be undertaking A-levels with the intention of participating in Higher Education.

Table 7.2 illustrates the proportions of looked after children who were known or not to the careers service and, if known, whether or not they were interviewed. Over half (56.6%) of the entire target cohort were known to have received interviews, with some individuals having a very high number of interviews: five individuals between them received over eighty-four interviews. The mean number of interviews (for those interviewed) at 2.7 is partly a reflection of this. However, nearly three in ten (28.9%) of looked after children known to the careers service had not received interviews, in addition to those we have already identified as not known to the careers service in our study.

On the other hand, the figure is slightly distorted by the fact that the second group in the cohort had not received their grades by the end of the study and might, therefore, have been delaying their careers interviews. This hypothesis, with its implication that young people who have left school over a year ago might be more likely to have made contact with careers, is supported by the smaller percentage of young people in the 1996 cohort who had had no careers interviews (26.2% of the 1996 group as opposed to 32.7% of the 1997 group). Where reliable data is known, a total of 73.8 per cent of the 1996 cohort had received careers interviews one year after leaving school, and 67.3 per cent of those who had just left in 1997 had received careers interviews by the time of leaving.

Table 7.2 Careers interviews and looked after young people in one local authority			
Interviews	Number	%	Valid %
0	33	23.1	28.9
1	27	18.9	23.7
2	19	13.3	16.7
3	10	7.0	8.8
4	4	2.8	3.5
5	6	4.2	5.3
6–10	10	7.0	8.8
11–20	5	3.5	4.5
Missing	29	20.3	–
Total	143	100	100

However, this represents a difference of just 6.5 per cent between the two groups. In short, the likelihood of attending a first careers interview is not substantially increased by the lapse of time after leaving school. The 1996 cohort is more fully represented in the higher numbers of young people receiving multiple interviews. (12.3% of this cohort had ten or more interviews compared with 2% of the 1997 cohort.) This appears consistent with the original hypothesis that the difference in time since leaving school is likely to be influential in the number of interviews attended. Unfortunately, data on the interview rates for the rest of the population in this county was not made available and it is therefore difficult to set these results in context and thus to make comparisons with the non-looked-after population in this area. One can only guess at the reasons why this information was never forthcoming. However, as the interview rate is intrinsically related to the penetration rate used as a performance indicator by the organisation who are contracted to supply the careers service in the area, it seems not unlikely that this was a factor. Penetration rates (i.e. number of action plans delivered to Year 11 pupils) are also used by the DfEE as a comparative measure of performance. It therefore seems reasonable to speculate that research data that deviated significantly from careers service targets, such as those for looked after young people, is unlikely to be welcomed.

In relation to the interviews, there was an interesting gender divide. Nearly two-thirds (64%) of females had between one and three interviews, whereas the corresponding percentage for males was just over one-third (36%). On the other hand, the majority of those with instances of high multiple interviews were male. Overall, it thus appears that males are less likely to be interviewed, for whatever reason, but are more likely to figure amongst the complex cases requiring continued help.

Generally, there was a lack of sufficient information on careers input and destinations. Tracking down the 'unaccounted-for individuals' proved to be very difficult. Although guidelines for reciprocal working arrangements for those young people living out of county do exist, the lack of readily available information on some of these young people indicated some problems with their implementation. Careers input with the young people was sometimes good but often patchy. The length and detail of case note comments was indicative, in some cases, of considerable perseverance and willingness to help preserve benefit entitlement and assist in similar ways. Nonetheless, combining those 'missing' with those known but not interviewed, 62 young people (43% or the entire cohort) were not recorded as having received careers interviews.

Discussion

As mentioned at the start of this chapter, one of the most revealing features of the Lynes and Goddard study was the examination of in-care and after-care experiences in the same county. The contrast between an apparently relatively happy and contented group of young people in care and a group of care leavers with, in most cases, significant problems, suggests the importance of the structural factors (both in wider society and within the care system) identified by the other leaving care studies referred to earlier. In other words, it is what is left out of the care experience that matters, rather than what is included. It is not enough to provide well-run, caring homes (in residential or foster care) if the peculiar circumstances likely to face most care leavers are not addressed.

The post-care ambitions of those who filled in the questionnaire on living in care show that young people in care may have a very wide range of goals in life. The reality of the after-care experience is, for many, very different. This contrast is a depressing one. There are a number of positive stories to be told that reflected well on individual carers and social workers, but also many negative stories reflecting well on no-one. However, this is not something new. As we noted at the start of this chapter and in Chapter 2, leaving care studies have been saying much the same thing for many years. Our findings confirm the universality of these findings and some complexity and richness through these young people's comments about their particular experiences. Van Der Spek's study once again illustrates that major gaps in information exist about looked after young people, so that it is difficult to establish just what is happening to them overall as a group. Clearly, given the evidence in Chapter 6 about the multiple issues which affect the pre-sixteen educational experience of looked after young people, it is perhaps unsurprising that careers advice is minimal or non-existent for a significant proportion. That the scale of non-attendance at school, disaffection and exclusion are known to increase in the final years of school (and particularly for looked after children) will mean that some looked after young people are simply not present to take up offers of careers interviews. As with other issues to do with services for the general population, such as the education, careers and health services, there are clearly special issues with regard to the looked after population. Whilst some of these issues might be concerned with agency coordination and cooperation, there is a clear issue about what case holders and key workers within social services consider a priority, record on case files and follow up. Looked after young people are a small proportion of all those likely to use the careers service in a given year. This means that it should be possible to set up targeted arrangements with clear lines of responsibility and accountability within and between agencies. With such targeting, backed by the appropriate resources, careers services could act as gateways to looked after young people seeking access to post-care development resources.

Conclusions and implications

There are many specific problems that have been picked up by this chapter. However, the more central problem is structural and cannot be stressed enough: young people leaving care are moving on into independence far in advance of their non-care peers (where the average age of leaving care remains the early twenties). Leaving care preparation cannot hope to deal with the major problems that stem from this. A balance needs to be struck. There is an obvious need to prepare as well as possible for leaving care at eighteen or before, but also a need to accept that the tacit assumption of leaving care preparation being completed by the time that young people actually leave care is thoroughly unrealistic for the majority of young people in this situation. The commitment of a Labour government to legislate to improve support up to eighteen and discourage care-leaving prior to that age where it is 'premature' is a step in the right direction (DoH 1998b, p.60), though in the light of the evidence presented in this chapter it is by no means certain to make a major impact on the wider problem. Section 24 of the 1989 Act is the key avenue for progress here, in its recognition of the need to provide help (in the form of 'advice' and 'befriending') for young people between the ages of eighteen and twenty-one, should the relevant social services department decide that they need it (subsection 5a). Many of the young people in the Lynes and Goddard survey could clearly have benefited from section 24 help, including the 'assistance' (financial or otherwise) this makes available by discretion (subsections 6 and 7). It did appear that although some young people were receiving such after-care help from their social workers others were not. A central issue is the provision of the kind of advice, befriending, but also practical support which will make possible the complex and interrelated youth transitions we outlined earlier. As we have seen, these transitions are often more acutely difficult for looked after young people. Current central government proposals to provide greater assistance in this transitional period are reviewed in Chapter 10.

Acknowledgement

This chapter was written jointly with Dee Lynes.

Dee Lynes is Policy Assistant to the Director of Community Services, York City Council. She also has experience of campaigning for children's rights.

CHAPTER 8

Training, Support and Service Quality

Training, support and service quality are clearly linked. It is often assumed, for example, that more training and support for carers might produce a better quality service for looked after children. However, the evidence about the impact of training is less clear than that about support for carers. With regard to training for those working in residential care, the Department of Health's review of the most recent research on this topic, a study of 48 children's homes by Sinclair and Gibbs, found that 'high staffing ratios and high proportions of qualified staff were not shown to affect performance' (DoH 1998c, p.80). Similarly, a study of Diploma in Social Work (DipSW) training for managers found only tentative and anecdotal evidence of an impact on service quality (DoH 1998c, pp.36, 82–85). That said, these findings raise more questions about the adequacy and relevance of contemporary social work training for residential workers than they do about the usefulness of training *per se*.

While there are a large number of discussions of training issues for residential workers and some with regard to foster carers, less is written about what is really meant by 'support' for carers and any link between support and service quality. Also, training for foster carers in particular is known to be patchy and little research has evaluated the kinds of training that foster carers find useful or indeed want. As most looked after children are now in foster care, much of this debate also relates to the growth in the professionalisation of fostering (see Chapter 4). The quality of the fostering service has come under scrutiny in recent years and reports have repeatedly stressed the inconsistent nature of foster care provision across the country and some poor levels of standards, organisation and planning (Warren 1997a). Authorities have been accused of failing to meet children's needs in a number of respects. These include strategic planning for foster care, the use of quality control systems, care planning and assessments, case recording and in relation to choice of placements (DoH/SSI 1995b, 1996).

As we have seen earlier, residential care in particular has laboured under the negative effects of being a reducing service and one in which a number of major scandals of abuse of children has occurred. These factors, coupled with a more challenging resident group and insecurities and misinformation about children's rights since the Children Act 1989, have affected the morale of staff in residential care, something which is likely to have an impact on the quality of the care that they provide (Berridge and Brodie 1998; Chaplain and Freeman 1994). Whilst once again acknowledging that residential care is an essential part of the range of provision for looked after children, Utting (1997) concludes that 'urgent action is needed to raise standards, but the sector now lacks enough providers of sufficient size to organise this from within' (p.2). Less criticism is levelled at foster care, although it is acknowledged that there is evidence of abuse of children in foster care, as in other settings where children are looked after, and that foster care is not always a positive (or even preferred) experience for children (Kahan 1995; Utting 1997). Indeed it would be fair to say that much of the emphasis in discussions about training, support and service quality for looked after children still focuses on the minority of children who are in residential care (for example, DoH 1998c). Many of the major reports and reviews which have followed scandals in child care services in recent decades have pointed to a lack of suitably trained and supported personnel, a degree of isolation from the rest of social services and inadequate regulation (Berridge and Brodie 1998; Chaplain and Freeman 1994). In general, the systems and checks and the ethos of care for looked after children have improved in recent years, due in part to the findings from inquiries and the implementation of the Children Act. However, Utting (1997) warns that even in the best environments in which children are looked after, people who wish to exploit children will seek occupations which will give them access and that institutions can be corrupted by particular individuals or 'decay internally through neglecting their primary purpose of serving the interests of children' (p.1).

Training

Despite the concerns about the efficacy of training that we have already noted, training continues to be perceived as important for both residential staff and foster carers while tending to be focused on residential staff. The 1990s has seen attempts to improve the level of training and qualifications in residential care. In particular, effort has been expended upon ensuring that unit managers of homes have a DipSW, as managers are known to be the biggest single influence on the quality of care provided in the residential setting. Utting (1991) found that eighty per cent of managers of homes were social work qualified at the start of the 1990s. Towards the end of the decade, this figure is thought to be near to one hundred per cent, partly as a result of the Residential Child Care Initiative (RCCI). However, there is still a large gulf between the level of qualifications of unit managers and that of care staff, the majority of whom remain unlikely to have a social work qualification (Berridge and Brodie 1998). More recently, Utting (1997) recommended that CCETSW should go even further in specifying the content of child care training on DipSW courses and CCETSW, shortly to be replaced by a General Social Care Council (DoH 1998b), is working on developing standards for a post-qualifying award in residential child care. This may meet some of the earlier concerns of the Warner Report regarding the need for specific qualifications in residential child care (DoH 1992, pp.116–129).

Training of foster carers was only introduced in the 1970s following the introduction of specialist carers. The most popular training packs include the NFCA's *The Challenge of Foster Care* and the Open University course *Caring for Children and Young People*. However, there are sometimes particular difficulties in offering training to foster carers, such as ongoing training once they are in service, because of the demands of their caring responsibilities (Gorin 1997). While very little is known about the level of training that foster carers have received, more is known about the backgrounds and previous qualifications of foster carers. Bebbington and Miles (1989) found that almost a quarter (23%) of foster carers' present or most recent jobs were child-related; for example nursing, social work or teaching. In Scotland the number of foster carers connected to a social care related job was higher, rising to approximately two-fifths (Triseliotis *et al.* 1998). On the other hand, Triseliotis *et al.* also found that the majority of foster carers had left school at sixteen and that 70 per cent had no qualifications.

Utting (1997) notes that there has been an increase in the training available for foster carers since the early 1980s, but does not provide evidence about the extent to which this training has been taken up. The NFCA recommend that training for foster carers should be a requirement and some local authorities now link level of training to approval and payment. Triseliotis *et al.* (1995) suggests that training opportunities for foster carers are still uneven, with half the carers in one sample reporting that they had no training at all. SVQs and NVQs have been developed for foster carers and additional funds from the DoH are to be made available specifically for such training. The NFCA are keen for S/NVQs to be obtained by foster carers as a means of promoting the status of carers, raising the quality of care for children and meeting required standards. The potential importance of initial training is underlined by evidence from Berridge and Cleaver (1987) that foster care placement breakdowns are fewer when carers have had even rudimentary induction training.

The assumption that more trained carers should lead to better care for children may need further consideration. Ward (1998), making explicit criticism of the DipSW, notes that residential staff see the DipSW either as irrelevant or inadequate to their needs, or as insulting to their professional integrity by virtue of a continual denigration of residential services. Hudson (1998) writes of what he views as the 'structural ignorance' about residential care amongst social work academics and field social workers, and the negative messages dominant about work in this setting. In other words, the nature of the training available to staff in the Sinclair and Gibbs study may, at best, be not particularly relevant, and at worst positively unhelpful. Ward (1998) suggests with respect to managers of residential homes that they undertake training comparable to the Headteacher qualification.

Support

Staff turnover and sickness in residential care, loss of foster carers and placement breakdown in foster care are some of the indications that demands often exceed the ability of carers to meet children's needs. For children, the result of placements which cannot or do not 'hold them' is more disruption to their lives, often with an accompanying sense of loss and rejection. Nixon (1997) has identified a range of possible sources of support to foster carers, most of which are equally relevant to the residential task. These might include practical support from social workers, emotional and psychological support, professional development including training, task-focused problem solving, respite care and community support. Sellick (1996) adds realistic and reliable financial support for foster carers to this list. For residential workers, supervision and staff meetings should be routine; for foster carers 'staff meetings' are likely to be seen as an alien concept and visits from social workers may or may not be experienced as 'supervision'. Provision of support requires assessment and planning to ensure the elements are present in an appropriate combination for particular circumstances. Yet in reality residential staff and foster carers are physically isolated from the support of social services departments on an everyday basis.

It is now common in both mainstream and specialist fostering schemes to provide carers with access to social work support in their own right, separate from the child's social worker. These social workers might be located within the same social work team as those for children and families, or might form a different team. In different parts of the country these social workers go by different names. For example, they may be called family placement social workers, link workers or fostering officers. The system of having 'link workers' was introduced following the use of such social workers on specialist schemes. The capacity of link workers really to be available to families when needed is, however, variable. Despite this, research has shown that link workers are valued by foster carers. They believe them to provide an invaluable form of support. The extensive research by Triseliotis *et al.* (1998) in Scotland found that 90 per cent of foster carers rated their relationship with their link worker as very good (68%) or good (22%) and nine out of ten carers also said that the frequency of visits was good or very good. However, foster carers were not so happy about the support received from the children's social workers and here ratings for general relations, frequency of visits, interest, availability and appreciation were all lower.

Group support as a supplement to individual support is encouraged by most authorities. However, many support groups have attendance problems. Lowe (1990), in a study of local authorities in England and Wales, found that the majority provide for teenage fostering schemes and monthly support groups, usually led by link workers. Support groups have two main components, that of training and that of providing carers with an opportunity to share their experiences. The way in which support groups are managed and run can be an issue and support groups can be more successful if led by foster carers. Many of the NFCA local branches organise a mixture of social events and training, but such events are often not attended by all foster carers (Cliffe with Berridge 1991). Shaw and Hipgrave (1989) have noted that some support groups have struggled with the notion of voluntary or compulsory attendance. If attendance at support groups were to become compulsory for some carers (such as specialist carers), these support groups may more aptly be renamed 'supervision'. Support groups and training sessions run by independent fostering agencies often require compulsory attendance, but also offer reimbursement of expenses and alternative child care provision. Some authorities have made use of mentoring schemes, where new foster carers are introduced to a more experienced carer. These more experienced foster carers can be more accessible to new foster carers, both in terms of feeling able to talk openly with them and being able to reach them easily by telephone, in comparison with social services staff (Cambridgeshire County Council 1990).

Service quality

Service quality is both a nebulous concept and an obvious issue in child care. Social services, like other public sector services, monitor their own services through 'arms length' service quality units as well as being monitored from a national level by the Social Services Inspectorate (SSI). Of particular importance to children's services in this context is the Quality Protects initiative, launched in September 1998. This has been referred to in earlier chapters and is discussed in depth in Chapter 10. Here, however, we focus on developments prior to this initiative.

When researchers have sought to investigate service quality for looked after children, they have varied in their approach. Much of this work does not focus upon quality explicitly. On the other hand it is known both anecdotally, as well as through inspection evidence, that particular residential homes and placements can clearly make a difference to individual lives. It has long been known that apparently similar establishments can vary greatly in their regimes and in the behaviour and morale of those in them. Berridge and Brodie's (1998) up-date on children's residential care is useful in this area, both because it explicitly looks at quality which is clearly operationalised as a concept and also because the study makes comparison with the situation in the same authorities a decade earlier. Overall, an unevenness in quality of care across the homes in the Berridge and Brodie study was noted. In comparing this study with Berridge's earlier work (1985), they conclude that there has been a reduction in both good and poor quality care and a clustering around the 'average'. A thirteen-point list of variables is used to assess quality, including such issues as relationships between staff and young people, whether the institution was judged to be child-centred, the adequacy of the educational environment, staff morale, family contact and community links. They found that homes showed quite a high degree of consistency across variables, homes with high scores in one area having high scores in another. In a similar vein, Sinclair and Gibbs' (1996) investigation into the quality of residential care found that troubles did not come singly. Homes which had individuals with a higher than expected level of criminal convictions and running away also tended to have young people who experienced the resident group as less friendly and more delinquent, felt that they had less of a say in how the home was run and felt that there was little value in being resident there. Manageable homes in the Sinclair and Gibbs study were found to be relatively small; their role and purpose was clear and stable; staff agreed with the home's philosophy and worked together well. Staff in successful homes tend to have adequate autonomy to do their work, consistency in their approach and a clear theoretical or therapeutic orientation in their work. These latter findings are very much in keeping with the Berridge and Brodie study and also that of Chaplain and Freeman (1994).

Child-centredness is often seen as an important dimension of quality provision for looked after children. Colton (1992) has made a useful comparison of the context of caring in residential and foster care environments. Care practice in the foster homes studied was generally found to be significantly more child-orientated than that in children's residential homes. Explanation of these findings includes consideration of such issues as the number of children cared for in each setting and the bureaucratisation of children's homes, which inhibits the degree to which residents are able to lead the sort of life experienced by the majority of children. As we have seen elsewhere, however, opinions on the relative merits of foster and residential care do vary. Although measuring quality in foster care is not an easy task, because of its inevitably private nature, the importance of ensuring that there is a quality framework for foster care, as in residential care, is increasingly being recognised. The introduction of the DoH Looked After Children materials, DoH/SSI Inspections (1995b; 1996) and the SSI/OFSTED (1995) report on the education of looked after children have all raised considerable concerns about aspects of the fostering service (ADSS 1997). Although few research studies have focused solely on measuring the quality of provision in foster care, many findings of studies have implications for improving this aspect of the service. Outcomes from the care experience are one way of judging the quality of certain aspects of that experience.

Research findings

The research findings in this chapter elaborate on some of the themes that we have just outlined and draw upon the work of Gorin (1997) on family placement and Hayden (1997a) on residential care, as well as that of Lynes and Goddard (1995) on user views (see Appendix, sections 3, 1 and 2 respectively). The work of Gorin and Hayden provides evidence largely on training and support issues, while that of Lynes and Goddard gives a user perspective on service quality. Accordingly, our analysis concentrates upon the following three issues:

- training, staffing and caring
- support: staff and carers' needs
- user views of social workers and the care experience.

Training, staffing and caring

RESIDENTIAL CARE

All unit managers in the 31 units in our study (see Hayden 1997a), and one in six care staff, were social work trained (either CSS, CQSW or DipSW). Other care staff had a range of qualifications, of marginal relevance to the residential task, and about a third reported that they had 'no relevant qualifications'. Although this profile of residential care staff is better than in some studies, it again provides evidence of the least qualified staff at the sharp end in the most demanding situations. However, the focus upon the training of staff employed on a contract in residential care masks the impact of the use of agency and casual staff, for which no such qualification or training profile was readily available. Staff availability for work was a key issue for the majority of children's units in our study: two-thirds of units did not have the full complement of staff needed to run the unit and more than eight in ten units had staffing issues which had implications for the efficient running of the unit. These problems meant that casual staff were a strong feature of the staffing in most units.

Residential staff were generally confident in their approach to the care and control of young people and most staff reported that their unit was consistent in their approach. This was not always borne out in the case studies of individuals in our research. Staff were more divided about whether young people's awareness of their rights within the care setting was a positive development, with nearly four in ten staff reporting that they felt that young people in residential care had more rights than staff. However, the most significant issues for staff groups were whether they felt that young people were appropriately placed in their unit and whether they had the right amount of autonomy to do their work (see Chapter 5). Whilst the majority of staff believed that residential care could provide a positive experience for young people who need a period of time outside the family home, this view was most positively correlated with staff groups who felt that young people were appropriately placed in their unit and who also reported that they had the right amount of autonomy to do their work.

FOSTER CARE

Most of the 376 foster carers (85%) who responded to the survey in our authorities (see Gorin 1997), had been on the initial training course and the great majority found this training at least useful. Those carers who had not even had initial training (50 carers, 15%) tended to be those who had been caring for a long time and who had started before training was introduced or were family link carers (those looking after children with special needs). Over six in ten carers (62%) had more than the initial training. The great majority (85%) of carers wanted more training, some of the areas identified (in order of priority) being: behaviour management; caring for an abused child; caring for a child with disabilities. Carers were also asked to say how they thought training could be improved. A quarter of the carers responding suggested the use of existing foster carers in training sessions; others mentioned wanting to meet children in care as part of their programme of training. Some carers suggested the potential involvement of their own children in the training programme. Carers clearly wanted to be given a realistic picture of what they could expect of the children they were likely to care for and how best to understand and cope with behaviour difficulties and children who had been abused. Although the majority of carers felt that they were adequately prepared before they cared for a child (many individuals making comments to the effect that they had worked with children and/or brought up their own children), three in ten carers did not feel adequately prepared. Some of this latter group reported that it was not a case of a lack of training but rather that there are some things that training, however good, cannot teach you and that it was a case of learning from experience: 'There is no adequate preparation! Every child/family is different and experience is the best preparation.' Respite and family link carers were more likely to report that they had been adequately prepared to care for their first foster child.

Foster carers were generally positive about the experience of caring for a child and their ability to make a difference: 85 per cent of carers reported positive changes in children that they had looked after. The kinds of positive changes reported included an increase in positive behaviour and self-esteem, improved social skills, improvements in attendance and behaviour at school, and improvements in school work. Nearly three-quarters of foster carers had generally positive experiences of working with birth parents, with many carers describing a friendship relationship and their own satisfaction in encouraging a better relationship between children and their birth parents. However, as we noted in Chapter 5, a quarter of carers had negative experiences with birth parents, such experiences most often involving threats (20% of carers) and, in a minority of cases, property damage (4%) and assault (1% of carers).

Support: staff and carers' needs

RESIDENTIAL CARE

The relative isolation of the 31 residential units in our study from the main body of social services has been noted in other research (Berridge and Brodie 1998). In this context much of the contact with social services for residential staff came via requests for a placement, social workers visiting children, statutory visits and inspections and occasionally via training events. Some of this contact was experienced by staff in our study as supportive, depending upon how the contact was handled. However, there was a strong feeling amongst many residential staff that the rest of social services were happy not to have too much contact with them. The support that residential staff said that they needed related strongly to the immediacy of situations that they could find themselves in. Residential staff often interpreted 'support' as more staff available for particular individuals or situations, as the following quotes illustrate: 'It's not the heavies coming in but when you get a six-foot individual ... coming at you ... you need the staff...', and '[what we need is] sufficient staffing levels to ensure everyone's safety. For recognised needs to be met, that is when one-to-one staffing is identified for the resource to be made available to ensure this can happen.' Some staff wanted more external specialist support or emergency facilities, for example: 'We need to have a group resource where they (the children) are known to the staff there and the young person has fun and play ... and we can use it in an emergency ... They end up going into secure, which is not the answer.'

Whilst some units had built up useful relationships with particular resources or professionals, other units seemed relatively isolated. The local authorities had an education support service staffed by teachers and employed by social services. These individuals were valued, but varied in their ability to get children into school. Relations with the police varied in quality, although in some homes they were the main source of support cited. In terms of support wanted, psychiatric, psychological and similar types of support were mentioned by staff, as illustrated by the following quote:

> [What we need is] more input [from] ... agencies for young people to get help with anger management. All staff within residential care should be automatically offered training in anger management to be able to deal with and support young people during their time in care. Young people displaying continued violent behaviour within residential care should automatically be seen by a psychologist. Staff teams should continue to have contact with a psychologist (perhaps attend one staff meeting monthly) to talk about young people's behaviour and ways of dealing with it or reasons behind it.

Staff also wanted better understanding and recognition of their work from their departments, as well as more response out of hours:

> We need to be listened to when things are getting tough – i.e. physical abuse or sexual relationships between young persons, we don't want to hear 'get on with it'. We need support from the Emergency Duty Team ... I don't feel they are giving us any support at all over the last two years.

FOSTER CARE

Support for foster carers in our authorities was much more clearly identified with social services departments. The departments had specialist social workers responsible for family placement, that is family placement social workers (FPSWs) and family link social workers (FLSWs) for families caring for children with disabilities. As discussed earlier in the chapter, these social workers are responsible for providing support to the foster family. Most foster carers (83%) reported that they were visited enough by their FPSW or FLSW. The frequency of contact between foster carers and social workers was very variable, ranging from weekly (3%) in the minority of cases to over three months between contacts in almost one in five cases (18%). More than four in ten carers reported that they were visited within a three-month period. Carers were also contacted by telephone and they generally reported that they were satisfied with the amount of telephone contact that they had. Two-thirds of carers who made comments about their social worker had positive things to say about the kind of support they provided. Negative comments clustered around three themes: part-time social workers who were difficult to contact when needed; continuity of contact with a social worker; and infrequent visits. Carers were much more positive about family placement social workers than the foster child's social worker and least positive about social services as an organisation. This is also shown in response to a question about how valued by the different parties foster carers feel in relation to the work that they do, as illustrated by Table 8.1.

Table 8.1 How valued foster carers feel

Valued	FPSW/FLSW (%)	Child's social worker (%)	Foster child (%)	SSD (%)
Always	75	46	44	33
Sometimes	22	45	54	51
Never	3	9	2	16
Total responses	358	330	349	331

Three-quarters of our foster carers reported feeling valued 'always' by their FPSW or their FLSW. This proportion dropped to less than half for the child's social worker and the foster child themselves, and to about a third of carers in relation to social services as an organisation. It is also worth noting that carers report that they are often getting the most valuable support from their FPSW or FLSW (60%), rather than from other carers or from family and friends (see Figure 8.1). Indeed, although most carers were aware of support meetings and social events for carers, only about half of the carers in our survey attended these events. Carers' priorities for improving support included: better cover for part-time and absent social workers; more respect from social workers; better organisation and timekeeping from social workers; more contact with the child's social worker; more financial incentive; more support for carers' own children; and more consistency in practice across social services areas.

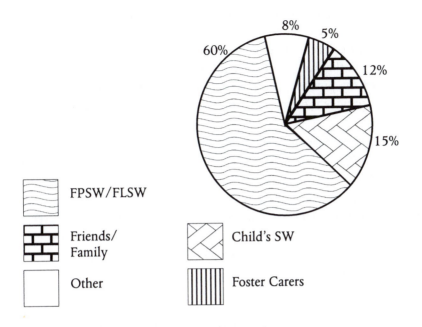

8%

5%

60%

12%

15%

FPSW/FLSW

Friends/
Family

Child's SW

Other

Foster Carers

Figure 8.1 From whom foster carers find support most valuable (n=335)

The subject of the attitudes of some social workers was raised in other parts of the research. Although only one in five carers chose to make additional comments about this particular issue, it is worth further consideration in the context of appropriate support to carers. Comments made by carers included the perceived lack of recognition by some social workers of the commitment made by the foster carers and the importance of the carer's own family life. Some carers felt they had not been listened to despite being the day-to-day carers of the children. This caused a great deal of frustration: '…foster parents should be colleagues. Social workers should take more time to listen to the foster parents who care for children twenty-four hours a day. They are not always right but their views should be discussed not dismissed.' Other comments about social workers included: the damage that could result from tactless remarks; anger over decisions being made without any explanation and children being moved from placements without prior notification to carers; inadequate support during inquiries following allegations; and the negative effects on children from the inconsistencies brought about by a change of social worker. However, it should be noted that many foster carers recognised that the problems they had experienced were not universal. Many social workers were perceived as good at supporting carers and making them feel valued. As one carer remarked: 'The social worker's attitude makes an enormous difference to the placement. We have had more good experiences than bad, but the bad tend to colour the good!'. Furthermore, some carers recognised the pressures on social workers and that sometimes the latter could not provide the support that carers and children might need.

User views of social workers and the care experience

As well as foster carers, looked after children have views of their social workers that are relevant to assessing service quality. As we have seen in other chapters in this volume, there are a range of issues we could raise in this respect. A number of these are covered in the following chapter. However, we concentrate here on two specific areas: the views of looked after children on the performance of their social worker and their views with regard to the care experience as a whole.

SOCIAL WORKERS

In the Lynes and Goddard study, there was a wide range of responses from children and young people about the frequency with which they saw their social worker: from once a week or more (10%) to once a year (1%). However, more than half (54%) the children saw their social worker at least every two months. Children were also asked how often they would like to see their social worker. Responses to this question did not indicate precise frequencies in most cases. The most frequent response was 'about the same' (31%) with only a minority of children explicitly saying they wanted to see their social worker less often and a small number saying they would like to see their social worker more often than they did.

Children were asked to tell us what they liked about their social worker. There were a range of responses here, with the most common response relating to the perceived helpfulness of their social worker (21%), that they were easy to talk to (14%) and that they were kind or nice (14%). Less frequently mentioned positive features related to social workers listening to the young people, being understanding, taking them out and even 'everything'. On the other hand, about one in seven (14%) children responded negatively, stating that there was 'nothing' good about their social worker. The positive responses included the following:

> She is very helpful. She finds out if I can go places and she sorts out any problems if there are any. (girl, 13)

I can tell her things that I would not tell others. (girl, 13)

Supportive, friendly, easy to talk to, always available when I need him. (boy, 17)

He listens and I am friends with him. (boy, 11)

She understands and compromises in difficult situations. (girl, 15)

Children were also asked to tell us what they did not like about their social worker. Of those responding, nearly half (47%) reported that there was 'nothing' bad about their social worker. The children's responses detailing the negative things about their social workers were wide-ranging and seemed to be very specific to both personal relationships as well as perceptions about social workers' abilities to do their job, such as their lack of communication skills:

He gives me the creeps. He always takes ages to get anything done which I need to get done. (girl, 15)

He is a student and he has someone around with him all the time. (boy, 14)

Listens but doesn't act. (girl, 14)

She is always eager to move me on to another foster home. (boy, 14)

He don't listen and jumps to the wrong conclusion. (boy, no age given)

She only listens to what she wants to, she's inexperienced. (girl, 15)

Children were asked whether they could see their social worker on their own. The great majority (97% of those in foster care and 96% of those in residential care) said that they could. Of those who said that they could not see their social worker on their own, one young person qualified their answer by saying that they could see their social worker on their own 'sometimes'. Of the remaining three children, two did not know why they could not see their social worker on their own and one said she preferred not to:

Because he scares me, he gives me the creeps. I have asked for a different social worker. (girl, 15)

As already indicated, there was no significant difference in the ability of children to see their social workers on their own in the two main sectors of residential and foster care and there were no differences in relation to the age of the child.

THE CARE EXPERIENCE

Children were also asked what they felt was good about being looked after in care. One in five children talked about being happy and feeling secure:

> It's better than being treated how I used to be treated at home. People care. (girl in foster care, 15)

> I don't have the stress of looking after mum because they don't drink, also someone is always there. (girl in foster care, 14)

> I am a much better person, have more than have ever had before, am loved and feel secure. (boy in residential care, 17)

A similar proportion said that 'nothing' was good about being in care, although this view was qualified in ways which showed that this response was not necessarily negative:

> There is nothing good about being in care. But it has had to be for me and my sisters and others but for us we found a happy, caring family. (boy in foster care, 11)

> Nothing really, it's just that you don't have to worry about your mum beating you up every time you go near her. (girl in residential care, 14)

Other responses varied, with individuals reporting feeling loved, supported and cared for, having better leisure activities and in a minority of cases getting away from their families.

When asked to tell us of the bad things about being in care, the biggest group said 'nothing' (35%). However, answers to this question were complex and difficult to categorise. Some of the bigger categories such as 'can't see family' and 'can't live with family' (taken together, these constituted 18% of responses) are reminders of the dislocation and loss that children are likely to feel and the difficulties that carers are likely to have in compensating for this. Many of the other responses related to issues to do with feeling different or being treated differently, moving around and a range of issues largely to do with the particular situation of being in care. In short, responses were varied, but there were some patterns. This are illustrated by the following:

> You can't live with your real family. This is found hard with a lot of kids accepting you've got foster parents and can't live with your real ones. (girl in foster care, 14)

> You are not with your proper family and you're not in a family atmosphere. (boy in residential care, 14)

I miss my brothers and sisters. (girl in foster care, 13)

Moving around places and not being happy. I was made to feel different with my old foster carers. (boy in foster care, 10)

You are not allowed to go anywhere without all the information about where you are going, how long you are going for and the people you are going with and that sometimes takes some time. (girl in foster care, 13)

There's always a chance that you can get kicked out of your foster placement. (boy in foster care, 14)

Discussion

The research reported upon in this chapter provides some evidence that the level of training of both residential staff and foster carers is improving, but that there is still some considerable way to go before staff and carers are appropriately trained for the work that they do. Most care staff do not have specialist training. Children are placed in families who have had only a matter of days training and occasionally no training at all. However, looking after children is fundamentally about building relationships, wanting to care for them and make a difference, and the motivations of the majority of care staff and foster carers in our studies had this at their core. Both groups generally wanted the chance to make a difference with children and in many respects foster carers were more able than residential staff to feel that they could so. In particular, foster carers were positive about contact with birth parents and their ability to help improve relationships between birth parents and children.

Most social workers in Lynes and Goddard's study appear to be relatively well liked by looked after children. Children more frequently held positive views about their social workers or found 'nothing' to dislike about them. On the other hand, a substantial minority were critical and could find nothing good to say about their social workers. Furthermore, it is clear that although much of the interpersonal work undertaken is appreciated, children do not always feel at ease with their allocated social worker and criticise what they see as inexperience. It was positive to see that the great majority of children reported being able to see their social worker alone, but nevertheless worrying that even a small minority reported that they could not do so. As we have noted earlier in this chapter, Utting (1997) has warned of the need to be constantly vigilant in effecting safeguards for looked after children. It is perhaps in the infrequency of the contact between looked after children and social workers that one can appreciate their sometimes marginal significance (in the everyday sense) as well as the sense of isolation from support of the main body of social services that is sometimes expressed by both residential and foster carers. One can also appreciate the sense of frustration of carers when decisions are sometimes made by social workers without apparent reference to everyday knowledge about a child.

Many of the difficulties and crises for people directly responsible for looking after children happen out of hours and it is most often residential workers and foster carers who will have to deal with these situations. Some children abscond, misuse drink or illegal drugs, become distressed or aggressive when planned contact with a birth parent goes badly or does not happen. In most of these situations, staff and carers cope but sometimes they may feel they need extra support, or confirmation that they are adopting an appropriate approach. Emergency Duty Teams, by their very nature, were not viewed as useful or appropriate in our research into residential care (see Hayden 1997a), in that they could not guarantee the type of experienced and practical support that residential workers and foster carers were calling for. That is, what was often needed by staff and carers was access to *appropriate* out of hours support. In some cases this included the perceived need for an emergency facility so that children could be quickly taken out of a situation for a period. The kind of staffing wanted was seen as likely to come from particular specialists in other services (such as psychologists and psychiatrists), from experienced residential social workers, or from other support workers. Residential staff were particularly appreciative of outside agencies who did come into the units and spend time getting to know staff and residents. Foster carers were generally appreciative of their family placement social worker and would most often turn to them for support.

Staff and carers were generally keen to have more training, particularly in the context of understanding and managing children's behaviour. Some residential units and carers were more connected to established support structures than others and not all individuals (staff and foster carers) perceived the need for further support. However, there are some similarities in the needs for support across the two sectors which, if taken together, could enhance the morale of staff and carers and their ability to feel positive about their work and which correspond to the findings on better quality care in research about residential care (see for example Berridge and Brodie 1998). The kinds of support needed across the sectors are:

- responsive out of hours specialist advice and practical support services for residential staff and foster carers

- a 'cooling-off' facility or emergency respite placements, where children could be given periods of more intensive help when their situation in a placement had reached a crisis point

- regular access to specialist psychological and psychiatric support services – both for staff, carers and children

- better understanding and recognition of direct work with looked after children from colleagues in field social work and social services management.

Users' views on the care experience remind us that providing a good quality service has a range of dimensions, some of them very personal. Important issues for children are perhaps sometimes obvious but often difficult to address satisfactorily. Some of the children's comments remind us that foster care is not always experienced as 'family' care. At the same time, one is informed by users' views of how hard it is for staff and carers to compensate adequately for a child not being able to live with their birth parents or siblings.

Conclusions and implications

Whilst there is evidence to support some improvements in the quality of care for looked after children, there is also heightened awareness from these studies of those aspects of care in which the state as corporate parent fails children. Kahan (1989), by reflecting upon the trouble that most birth parents take with the health needs of their children, provides us with a common-sense way of reflecting upon what might enhance our ability to provide good quality care for looked after children. Kahan's sentiments are very much endorsed by the DoH stance in the Quality Protects initiative (DoH 1998b). Whilst we have moved away from residential staff and foster carers being viewed as 'parents', they do have (or share) parental responsibility for looked after children. We have noted elsewhere that Action and Assessment Records, as part of the *Looking After Children: Good Parenting and Good Outcomes* (DoH 1995) pack, are not without their problems. Berridge and Brodie's (1998) finding that in practice they were not sufficiently completed to be of use is something which we can confirm from our own research. Whilst there might be valid criticisms of the checklist approach, the cultural assumptions about 'good parenting' (Knight and

Caveney 1998) and their limited utility for children with disabilities (Berridge and Brodie 1998), it is nevertheless clearly necessary to promote methods of monitoring and evaluation as part of the process of improving the quality of care for looked after children. Berridge and Brodie have noted that the most positive model for delivering a quality service in residential care was found in homes for children with disabilities. In this model, there is a strong interprofessional dimension: health, education and social services all play a part in the devising of care plans and care programmes. Relationships with families are largely based on support, rather than child protection. However, there is better public understanding and recognition of work with disabled children and the parents of disabled children utilising residential care come from a wider social grouping. There is also a clearer sense of purpose for staff and institutions in this latter sector. It is worth considering how best we might make these principles more applicable to children in mainstream residential and foster placements.

CHAPTER 9

Involving Young People in Decision-Making

This chapter examines a number of issues regarding the involvement of young people in decisions concerning their care. The focus of the previous chapters – training, professional support and practice monitoring – deals with the subject of improving practice in state child care largely from a professional perspective. However, it has long been recognised in the field of social care more generally that laudable and necessary efforts to improve professional practice need to be balanced, at both a structural and a professional practice level, by a willingness to listen and respond to the views of service users. This recognition has taken place in governmental, academic and professional arenas and has relevance to fields as diverse as child care, disability and care of the elderly (Harrison and Mort 1996; Howe 1992; McCaughan 1992; Wilson 1993). With regard to our more specific focus, the House of Commons Health Select Committee proposals on looked after children (House of Commons 1998b: pp.xlviii–liv) include recommendations for a children's rights commissioner, mentors (or 'adult friends') for young people and the greater use of young people's forums. In a similar spirit, the Utting Report endorses the importance of complaints procedures and telephone help lines (Utting 1997, pp.184–185).

We saw in Chapter 1 that the development of a children's rights approach to state child care policy, which has provided much of the impetus for moves to increase user involvement in this particular field of social care, has taken place over at least the last two decades. As a result of this, a children's rights perspective both preceded and fed into the 1989 Act (Fox Harding 1997, pp.109–156), though some commentators have noted that – in part due to the views of judges – practice has not always lived up to theory in this regard (Lyon and Parton 1995). However, there are wider political and ideological aspects to this development, illustrated most clearly in the drafting of the United Nations declaration of the rights of the child. Numerous and inevitable compromises and different interpretations of the concept of 'rights' (e.g. rights to be cared for as well as rights to be listened to) went into the making of this document (Hodgkin 1994). These differing interpretations involved, for example, a conflict between paternalistic and assertive interpretations of the concept of 'rights'. The positive feature of such a catch-all approach to rights was that it did at least widen out discussion and recognise that rights to social and economic resources need to be considered alongside rights to protection from harm and rights to have a voice or a say in decision-making. Although it can be argued that the commitment of some governments, such as that of the UK, to the Convention is rather ambivalent (Freeman 1996), there is no doubt that the Convention has helped to change the terms of debate on this subject since its adoption in 1989 (Franklin 1995). A further feature of the focus on children's rights in recent years has been the use of such a perspective to support the greater involvement of young people in decision-making about their daily lives while in care. It is at this point that the paternalistic and assertive interpretations of rights can meet. Both are usually found to support the widely held view that it is partly through children exercising their rights to be consulted and to have a say in decision-making that they can adequately protect themselves from various forms of abuse:

> If children in general are a vulnerable group, children looked after by local authorities are acutely vulnerable. It is all the more important that their voice should be heard by people in positions of authority. (House of Commons 1998b, p.xlviii)

However, many see this approach as not solely concerned with child protection issues. It is often associated with empowerment in a more general, everyday sense and tends to reject paternalist approaches to protection (Franklin 1989). It is just such an approach, an assertive view of rights, that is examined in this chapter.

In exploring the practical implications of these arguments in what follows, we focus on Lynes' and Goddard's survey of young people in care, which addressed a number of issues concerned with young people's involvement in decision-making. Young people's views and experience of this in the context of their everyday lives in care is well worth exploring in this context, since their responses provide us with a sense of what involvement, consultation and participation mean for the young people themselves. We also draw on the research of Fletcher (1993) concerning the involvement of young people in decision-making with regard to their own lives. We finish the discussion by assessing the current status of, and future prospects for, the greater involvement of young people as a means of improving state child care decision-making. These issues are also considered in a wider context in the final chapter.

Research findings

Lynes' and Goddard's user-view survey was, in a quite specific sense, itself an extended exercise in user participation in child care services with a view to improving quality (see Appendix, section 2). It shared the philosophy of other studies (such as Fletcher 1993 and West 1995) that have sought to involve service recipients in child care in the development of service improvements. In this particular case, it was conducted with the express objective of influencing policy at local level through making explicit the views of young people about the services that they were receiving. It was also conducted, designed and piloted by members of the local child care and care leavers user group. Included within it were detailed questions regarding young people's own views of the extent to which they were consulted about decisions made concerning them and also questions regarding the extent to which they felt that they ought to be consulted. It is to these findings that we now turn. They concentrate on the following three issues:

- levels of consultation over routine care issues
- the level of involvement of young people in significant child care decisions
- young people's access to resources for promoting and protecting their rights.

Everyday decision-making

Discussion of user views and feedback mechanisms in the child care context is often taken to refer to the development of user-groups, the use of surveys and questionnaires, the co-option of service users onto decision-making committees and other such overt and structured mechanisms for ensuring the influence of young people in care at a policy level. Yet it is at the everyday domestic level – particularly for young people in care, but also for others living in non-home residential environments whilst receiving social care – that decision-making involvement or the lack of it impacts most profoundly on the individuals concerned. In the questionnaire that was sent out to looked after children, they were asked a series of basic questions concerning whether they 'had a say' in the following six areas of everyday life: pocket money, bedtimes, choice of friends, clothes, hobbies and food. The choice of these areas was dictated by the wish to make comparisons with the earlier survey by the Who Cares? Trust (Fletcher 1993), which asked a very similar but less precise question: 'Do you have a say in daily life where you live? (for instance, bed times, food you eat, pocket money, clothes etc.)' (Fletcher 1993, Appendix 1). The overwhelming majority of questionnaire respondents (116, or 96%) answered each part of this question. However, in order to avoid over-complicating the questionnaire, what having a 'say' meant was not specified. This means, of course, that it covers the range from being asked for an opinion occasionally to having sole control over an area of life. Nonetheless, it appeared that consultation and involvement in decision-making at these basic levels was quite high. Over 90 per cent of this group said that they had some influence over their choice of friends, clothes, hobbies and food and at least 60 per cent had some choice over pocket money and bedtimes (both of these latter two will, obviously, also be restricted or controlled by the vast majority of parents). This was similar to the Who Cares? Trust findings which, like ours, found that children in foster care appeared to have more choice than those in residential care (Fletcher 1993, p.11) (though our more detailed question suggested that this was only significant in the area of pocket money).

Other evidence suggesting general (though not universal) contentment in this area came when we asked about those areas of everyday life where young people would like more say. Over half (58%) of the young people gave no answer to this, while one in five (20%) of those who did give an answer specifically stated some variation on 'none', or 'I get enough say already'. Just over one in five (22%) of the total number of questionnaire respondents indicated some area or areas where they would like more say. This finding may have been due in part to young people being able to indicate areas of difficulty in response to the previous question, but it still contrasts markedly with the Who Cares? Trust finding on a similar question. That study claimed that 'virtually all' (Fletcher 1993, p.10) young people indicated areas where they would like more say in their everyday lives.

For our group, out of the twenty-seven children who specified areas where they thought they should have more say, ten identified pocket money, bedtimes or the food that they ate. Five children wanted more influence over what time they had to be in at night or how many nights they were allowed out. The remaining twelve responses covered a wide range of other areas that children were concerned about and included the following:

> Bedtimes, sleeping out more, everything. They treat us like five-year-olds. (girl, 15)

> To know what is going on and what they have decided to do with me. (girl, 14)

> When I should sleep over Mum's and to see her more. (girl, 17)

> Whether I want to be where I am. (boy, 15)

Such comments as the above four remind us that the peculiar situations of many young people in care raise extra issues where decision-making is concerned, issues that go beyond the everyday. It is to these, more care-specific, issues that we turn next. Notwithstanding these, however, for this group of young people at least there appeared to be a generally high level of satisfaction with the level of choice offered to them on an everyday level.

Decision-making at reviews and case conferences

Once again, the overwhelming majority of the group we surveyed expressed contentment with their level of involvement in wider decision-making, at least as far as reviews were concerned. Out of the total number who answered this question (all but two of our questionnaire respondents), 87 per cent thought that people listened to them at reviews and case conferences, with the younger age groups, ten to twelve years, being particularly likely to feel listened to. The Who Cares? Trust survey found lower levels of satisfaction in this respect: a national figure of only 61 per cent who felt listened to in these areas (Fletcher 1993, p.51).

The fifteen children (13%) who said either that they were not listened to at their reviews, or were only sometimes listened to, gave various explanations for this. Two children said that they did not attend their reviews, although they did not say why this was so. There were a further four who thought that they were not taken seriously. These included one girl of fourteen who said that her social worker 'speaks over me' and three other sets of comments in a similar vein:

They don't listen about contact and adoption. (girl, 11)

Yes, but don't take action. When they do it takes a long time. (boy, 10)

They listen but don't do anything, or it seems like that anyway. (boy, 14)

Although the above criticisms came from a relatively small group of children, there was a much larger group of thirty-three children (27%) who felt that reviews could work better for them in some way. Although only part of their views concerned direct involvement in the review discussion process, there were other aspects of 'involvement' where dissatisfaction was experienced. These areas included the provision of information to young people (or, rather, the lack of it) and the failure to implement agreed decisions. There were a number of replies here that suggested that once the surface was probed a little, young people were less happy with the review process than first appeared. More specifically, relating to involvement in decision-making and the provision of information, comments about improvements that could be made covered a diverse range of issues. Some, as indicated, related to general wishes to be taken seriously, listened to or be provided with more information:

If they allowed more time for me to explain what I want and not try to treat me like a baby. (girl, 16)

People listening to my ideas and not trying to put me off the plans which I have made. (girl, 17)

If I had more proof that I am being listened to. I'm fifteen and it's my life not the social worker's. (girl, 15)

Yes, get a chance to say more. (boy, 11)

If they talk to me through the review and not after and when they have decided what is happening they say 'is that alright' but I don't have no choice. (girl, 15)

Some of these young people wanted changes that were less easy to accommodate, such as wanting a family member to attend or not attend a review or case conference. Others made points about the general conduct of some reviews that one suspects some of the adults present on these occasions would endorse:

Not asking pointless questions. (boy, 16)

They could be shorter and less long-winded. (boy, 16)

They could get straight to the point instead of waffling on. (girl, 16)

If people didn't butt in while one person was talking as that happens a lot. (girl, 15)

More serious, however, were various points made which indicated ways in which young people could easily become alienated from the whole review process:

Social workers that actually carried through what we agreed on. (girl, 14)

They are good but I get worried as I have moved so much. (girl, 12)

Discussing more about the future instead of the past. (boy, 15)

Although these are clearly important points (as were those by a couple of young people who saw the main solution lying with themselves having the courage to be more assertive), one should not overstate the levels of dissatisfaction here. Other young people indicated satisfaction with reviews or even a preference to have them less often because of general satisfaction with their care experience and consequent perception of the review as a largely redundant exercise. It is the variety of responses that is most striking, indicating the dangers of making easy generalisations about either young people's satisfaction with the process or their desire for more involvement. The personal, individual nature of their comments on the review process suggests that greater listening and prior consultation with young people would achieve, in most cases, far more to increase their satisfaction with the results than specific structural changes to the process itself.

Consultation and information: files and moving home

As well as the more formal and public methods of involvement in decision-making by looked after children, such as those which take place at reviews and case conferences, there are more subtle and routine forms of involvement. In this survey, these were measured through asking questions about young people's access to their personal files, the extent to which they were consulted prior to moving home and the extent to which their involvement in decision-making could be made easier. By doing this, we were attempting to develop and explore the real meaning of 'involvement' in those areas in ways that cannot be captured through signatures on review forms or social work records.

With regard to the question of whether young people could see their social services files, of the 121 young people only two did not answer this question. The most significant feature of the replies was the level of ignorance on this subject. Just over one in five of looked after children (22%) said that they *could* see their file and 9 per cent said that they could not. This left nearly seven in ten (69%) who 'didn't know' (e.g. 'I've never been told I can, I've never been told I can't. It's a no-win situation', from one girl of fourteen). This compares poorly with the equivalent national survey by the Who Cares? Trust, in which 56 per cent knew that they could see their file and only 29 per cent were unsure (Fletcher 1993, p.51). From those who said they could not see (or were not sure about seeing) their files, thirteen children indicated why this was so. One of these said that they did not want to see their file and two said that they had never asked to do so. Other reasons why children reported not seeing their files included the following:

> Confidential. (boy, 10)

> You have to wait six months. (girl, 15)

> Because I am not 18 which is really silly I think. (girl, 14)

> Been told not old enough. (girl, 15)

> When I ask they are always busy. (boy, 15)

The views of one of the care leavers that we also surveyed is also worth quoting on this point:

> I wish I could see my file but my social worker said 'no', as he said 'no' because of letters about *me* were in there. But the file is about me, so why can't I see them? (young woman, 20)

Despite the relative clarity of the law in this field, it is hard to know whether it is misinformation or misunderstanding that is at work in these cases. Both our own and the Who Cares? Trust survey suggested that young people in residential care are likely to be better off in this respect than those in foster care (Fletcher 1993, p.51). The legal position is fairly unambiguous on this and should be known by most social workers. As in other local authorities, local versions of a child-friendly Department of Health leaflet were available for clarification. This latter leaflet was clear on the relevant points:

> You have had the right to see what is written on your social work file since April 1 1989 if Social Services think that you will understand what is written there when you see it … They will not let you see what is written

about other people, unless these people agree. Social Services will not let you see anything which they think will put you in serious danger. (DoH 1991b, p.10)

While it is almost certainly true that some of the refusals indicated by young people were due to the local authority exercising its permitted discretion with regard to age, understanding and the possible 'harmful' consequences of reading such information, this cannot account for the high level of ignorance. The level of ignorance, even allowing for misunderstanding, confusion and forgetfulness on the part of some young people, suggested a somewhat less than proactive approach on the part of social workers to the task of informing young people about their rights in this respect.

In other fields, the picture with regard to the provision of information was more mixed and somewhat less negative. With respect to being consulted before moving to a different home, just over three in ten (31%) of the young people who answered this question (a total of 106 children did so) said that they were not consulted. This compared with a national figure of 16 per cent who claimed that they had not been consulted in response to a similar question ('Are you asked before plans are made to move you?'; Fletcher 1993, p.51). With regard to looked after young people knowing how to make a complaint, the figures of 82 per cent answering 'yes' and 18 per cent answering 'no' were identical with the Who Cares? Trust figures (Fletcher 1993, p.71). Access to a telephone in private was also similar at national and local level, with 70 per cent at local level indicating that they could use a phone in private if necessary. In all three of these areas, therefore, the overwhelming majority were consulted or informed but a significant minority were either not consulted or not informed.

In sum, the picture suggested was one of properly provided formal feedback mechanisms and structures but less success at providing relevant information. There appeared to be insufficient appreciation of the extent to which knowledge is central to the exercising of rights. What this meant in more concrete terms came across when we asked the young people a further, open-ended question: 'What can be done to make things easier for you to have more say in decisions?'

About half (54) gave no answer at all here and of those remaining a third said that nothing could be done to enable them to have more say. However, it was not always clear from their answers whether this was because they felt that they had enough say already or whether they were pessimistic about the prospects of change. A further 13 (19%) of this group indicated that 'more listening' or 'being asked more' was needed, 13 (19%) said that they did not know and 19 (29%) gave some other reason. In short, as usual, although responses could sometimes be grouped together they tended to exhibit great variety.

Of those who indicated that 'nothing' needed to be done, there were a few who explained that this was a positive response rather than a negative one:

> Nothing. If I want a say or something then I say it or get my social worker on to it. (boy, 14)

> Nothing, I'm quite outspoken and have no trouble in asking things. (girl, 15)

For those who wanted to be listened to more, or wanted greater consultation, the criticism was usually (though not always), directed at social services:

> Take my Mum's voice box out (no). Once in a while for Mum to listen to me instead of demanding which hurts me heaps. (girl, 14)

> They could listen to me more at my planning meeting and reviews. (boy, 14)

> My social worker does what she wants and thinks that by taking me out for 2 hours once a year that makes it all right … they need to listen to me and learn sign language. (see below)

> To be asked what I want to happen. (girl, 14)

(The reference to sign language above was from a young deaf person. Out of the 121 children who returned questionnaires, 7 (6% of the sample) indicated that they had some form of disability. However, on analysis of the questionnaires only one of them raised it as an issue relevant to their care experience. This young person raised their deafness at several points. Whilst happy with their foster carer, who could use sign language, they were clearly very unhappy with their social worker and others who could not use sign language. Gender and age were left out of the original report in order to avoid easy identification of this young person. That practice is therefore followed here.)

Among the less easily categorised responses were those who felt that some form of advocacy would be helpful (a point also raised in responses at other places in the survey), as well as further requests for information and clarification:

I would have liked someone to stand in for me so I'm not on the spot. (boy, 11)

To plan all things well in advance. (boy, 16)

Me sticking up for myself and not let people make me change my mind to what they want me to do. (girl, 17)

To see the person before I move. (girl, 12)

To get someone I can talk to, to speak for me. (boy, 16)

However, it is important to recognise that the provision of individual means of influence and redress, together with relevant and important information, is only part of the picture. Young people in care will always remain in a relatively powerless position within the care system, as individuals facing an apparently well-organised and sometimes daunting social services 'system'. One way of redressing the balance slightly is to allow, facilitate or actively encourage the organisation of young people in care at a group level. This was recognised in the 1980s with state support for the National Association of Young People in Care (NAYPIC) and local support for individual care groups. The frightened silences revealed by the abuse scandals uncovered in the 1990s have led to it again being officially encouraged, with the current government committed both to the involvement of looked after children in decisions on their care at local and national level and also to funding a group to provide a national voice for looked after young people and care leavers (DoH 1998d, p.48). These developments are explored in more depth in the next chapter.

In the county that we surveyed, while over half of the looked after children did not wish to be in touch with others in a similar position (the stigmatising effects of such group identity played a part here, particularly for some children in foster care), nearly half, or 51 children (45%), did wish for this extra contact. The sense of empathy and the desire to help others in a similar position were strong factors in this desire. The reasons given for these responses revealed simple human needs that are sometimes overlooked in the user group or children's rights literature, which tends to focus on the political justifications for user groups and service user contact. The range of responses was wide, but of the 51 children who indicated an interest in further contact with other children in the care system, almost half cited a desire to share experiences, help each other and make friends. This was expressed in the following ways:

To talk to people in similar situations to me or have been in the past when I lived at home and share experiences so may be able to help them. (girl, 15)

Because I would like to find out what it is like for other people in care. (girl, 12)

Because it would help us to know that we aren't alone in the care system. (girl, 14)

As I have been with lots of children in care and lost touch and I miss them, they are my friends. (girl, 14)

Pen pal to tell problems and vice versa. (boy, 16)

Because you can see what different places of care are like and have more friends. (boy, 11)

Although, as noted, some children in foster care were antagonistic toward this sort of contact, on the whole they were slightly more likely than those in residential care to wish for such contact. It is perhaps worth noting that the Who Cares? Trust survey (Fletcher 1993, pp.94–96) found that the desire for meetings with other children in care (even for a 'children's union') was common among the 'wish lists' of their foster care sample.

Discussion

For the majority of the children discussed in this chapter, there were clear indications that influence over their lives was an everyday reality. It is hard to know if this indicates positive change, since we had no previous data to compare our own results with. The results and the comments from both ours and the Who Cares? Trust survey do suggest, however, that the principles of involvement and partnership that were embodied in the 1989 Children Act were being practised with regard to the majority of children. In a sense, this is saying little more than that these children were able to take part in the same sort of bargaining and negotiating processes that are the routine fare of child care in most families outside of the care system (Hill and Tisdall 1997, p.74). Still, that is worth knowing and reassuring in itself. It is in combating ignorance about rights that things appeared to be rather less positive. In those areas of involvement and decision-making that were more peculiar to the looked after experience – reviews, files, moves, complaints – young people were more inconsistently involved or aware.

One might have thought that this 'blind spot' with regard to the importance of information was a teething problem encountered while social services departments came to terms with the importance of information if service user involvement was to be a meaningful concept in practice under the 1989 Children Act. However, this has turned out not to be the case. In one of the key reports to have inspired contemporary reforms by the current Labour government, the Social Services Inspectorate summed up the position in 1998 as being very similar to that which we have already described. Their criticisms (based on a lengthy review of twenty-seven local authorities) were specific:

> **4.27.** All of the SSDs produced some written information for children and their families on services for children looked after. The content and quality was patchy and it was often out-of-date. Few SSDs had systems for regularly reviewing and up-dating such information.

> **4.28.** Children and their families rarely remembered having received written information though many did report receiving some form of verbal briefing. This also applied to complaints where most children indicated they knew how to make complaints but often denied ever having been provided with a copy of the procedure. Children in residential care were usually the best briefed and most confident about how to make a complaint. (SSI 1998b, p.24)

However, just as important as this broad picture was the more narrow focus of individual children in our survey. The individuality of their responses to each of these issues is a useful caution against any blanket assumptions with regard to how children in the care system deal with its various points of impact on their lives and the extent to which they wish to be involved – or not involved – in decision-making.

Conclusions and implications

In a formal, legalistic sense, the provisions and philosophy of the 1989 Children Act were a significant step forward. Complaints procedures and powers to initiate legal proceedings may have seemed daunting to some social workers but have at least provided a framework for redress and influence. However, Lindsay rightly warns us that such 'rights' are of little use without adequate support, information and confidence (Lindsay 1991). It is in these areas of isolation and ignorance that the active exercise of formal rights and opportunities is being held back. The active exercise of rights is also not helped when 'involvement' is either tokenistic or inappropriate. Adult and professional attempts to promote such involvement need to be carefully thought through so that the environment, process and forms of involvement are appropriate to the age, understanding and level of interest of young people. In particular, the rights of young people *not* to be involved, or to choose when they wish to be so, should also be respected if involvement is to be genuine rather than merely a response to adult agendas and needs.

Part of the explanation for the apparent ambivalence about 'rights' in child care appears to lie with the problems that grassroots workers have perceived this concept to present to themselves. Berridge and Brodie (1998) found this ambivalence to be entrenched in the views of many residential workers. While some of these also held more positive views of the 'empowerment' of young people, the problems that this presented were often seen to be more pressing:

> In their attempts to explain serious behavioural problems, staff often referred to the issue of children's rights and children 'knowing too much'. It was felt that children had been empowered at the expense of staff, and that staff were consequently unable to deal effectively with behavioural issues. One member of staff expressed the views of many in saying, 'we're expected to deal with the most difficult young people in society yet we're not given the tools to do it with.' (Berridge and Brodie 1998, p.134)

It is this sort of resistance that lies at the root of the developing consensus that the spirit of the 1989 Children Act in the field of children's rights (and sometimes, also, the letter of the Act) has not taken practice sufficiently far forward. Hence the greater central control and target-setting of current policy approaches, with central government perceiving a need to step in and override the concerns of local authorities and local authority workers with explicit objectives, advising local councillors that they must 'make sure you are consulting children and listening to their views about the services meant for them' (DoH 1998b) and setting a final explicit sub-objective of the Quality Protects programme that local authorities must:

Demonstrate:

(a) that account is taken of the views of children and their families and

(b) satisfaction by users with the services provided. The extent to which these sub-objectives are attained can be measured through consumer surveys. (DoH 1998c)

The will is clearly there at central government level. It remains to be seen how successful the current government can be in removing some of the resistance that remains in the child care field to the practical implementation of measures for the protection of children's rights.

Acknowledgement

This chapter was written jointly with Dee Lynes.

Dee Lynes is Policy Assistant to the Director of Community Services, York City Council. She also has experience of campaigning for children's rights.

CHAPTER 10

Conclusion

This final chapter considers how well we look after children in foster and residential care. It also outlines the ways in which policy and practice are developing and are likely to develop in the near future. Rather than repeating the conclusions and implications of each chapter, we draw upon evidence from across chapters in order to assess those specific features of the state child care system that we have been examining.

At the time of completing this book, there is much to be optimistic about in the clear commitment of the current Labour government to provide a better future for looked after children. This commitment should be seen as part of a wider attempt to address problems of social exclusion. As previous chapters of this book illustrate, there is much room for improvement in the field of state child care. Securing such improvement will not be straightforward, since the problems that need to be addressed are often complex and multi-faceted. For example, shortage of foster placements can lead to ill-matched placements and placement breakdown, thus leading to disruption and further damage to children's self-esteem. This, in turn, is likely to impact upon educational achievement (which should be, ideally, a source of enhanced self-esteem and beneficial peer group relationships) and affect long-term post-care outcomes. With this in mind, the government's particular commitment to actively encourage agencies to cooperate more effectively (DoH 1998h, pp.96–107) – or, in the current jargon, operate a system of 'joined-up government' (Social Exclusion Unit 1998, p.27) – is entirely sensible.

Looking after children?

Chapters 3–9 of this book have demonstrated that the state does not look after children in its care well enough. Using basic measures, such as the ability to match individual needs to placement, the numbers of placements that individuals might experience, the educational achievements of children who have been in care and outcomes for those leaving care, the current system is inadequate. In relation to children leaving care, there is an enormous gap between best practice and what happens in many local authorities. Most difficult to defend is the *increase* in the proportion of young people leaving care at the age of sixteen (DoH 1998j, p.24). At the same time, we need to be clear about the extent to which we ascribe responsibility for all of the poor outcomes for care leavers to the care system. To do this is to neglect the influence of earlier experiences in birth families and the lack of employment and other opportunities for many young people in disadvantaged circumstances, whether looked after or not. In this context, it is worth emphasising that young people themselves are quite capable of recognising when the care system has improved their lives rather than made it worse (see Chapter 9). However, recognising that young people come into care with many problems which it may be difficult or impossible for the state to fully resolve is not a reason for defeatism. Rather, it allows us to debate more realistically the purpose of the child care system. It presents a case for turning the nineteenth-century philosophy of 'less eligibility' on its head and constructing a system which enables young people themselves to rise above or move beyond such problems. Under such a system, it would be the state's role not merely to protect children but also to provide them with the personal resources necessary to compensate for their own past disadvantages.

Residential care

There is an ambivalent attitude on the part of many social work managers, field social workers and some social work academics towards residential care. We know that residential facilities are often viewed as a last resort. This view and its effect on the morale and philosophies of residential workers has consequences for the children and young people who are then sent to units which may not see themselves as able to provide a stable and positive enough environment for them to thrive. However, many social services departments are coming to recognise, as most of the recent enquiries and reviews have done, that a significant residential care sector is needed as part of a range of options to provide for looked after children (Utting 1997). As the recent

DoH review of research on residential care (1998c) concludes: 'Residence has undoubtedly done many children good. It would represent a significant step forward if everyone involved in providing services for children was convinced about the nature of the residential sector's contribution to the overall task' (p.5). At the same time, the review contains a strong message that many residential facilities need to be improved.

Central to the ability to provide appropriately for looked after children is the need to be able to plan across a range of types of placement, whether these placements are in residential or foster care. The Children Act 1989 introduced the concept of a continuum of services. Such a concept encourages local and health authorities to treat services as complementary, rather than compartmentalised or even in opposition. In this context, local authorities have been encouraged to view residential and foster care together (DoH 1998c). However, in reality we have arrived at a situation in which foster care is almost always viewed as the first option, even when there are doubts about the suitability of a particular placement. The general lack of commitment towards residential care is demonstrated in various ways, for example in the continuing shortage of training (or of locally available and appropriate training) for residential staff.

There have, of course, long been highly specialised and well respected therapeutic residential environments, such as those run by the Charterhouse Group. These facilities have been referred to as 'well kept secrets' where there is structure and a willingness to work with very damaged children (Kraemer 1998). However, such facilities are perceived to be expensive, coming as they do on top of the cost of running local services. Recent years have seen the closure of many such facilities, for example the well-known Peper Harrow Foundation. A relatively recent study of the Caldecott Community has drawn attention to the importance of stability and emotional warmth and the significance for all looked after children of the period between their fifteenth and sixteenth birthdays. Caldecott is reported to be relatively good at giving young people a start in life compared with other residential settings. For example, leavers from Caldecott were reported to be four times more likely to find employment in comparison with children in other residential settings (Little and Kelly 1995).

As we and other authors have noted (Berridge and Brodie 1998), many of the residents of residential care are now more volatile and difficult to manage, yet they are usually living in ordinary residential areas and *should* be attending local schools. However, the behaviour of some of these young people in mainstream schools is often not understood or tolerated and a combination of non-attendance and exclusion can compound any existing educational difficulties. It would appear (comparative data is not available on a reliable scale) that this situation may have got worse for looked after children in recent years (Berridge and Brodie 1998; Rollinson 1998). Part of the explanation for the apparent worsening in the educational provision for looked after children may lie with the increasing pressure on schools to 'perform', through local management of schools and central government emphasis on academic achievements and targets. Another factor has been the reduction in specialist and small group provision for this group of children (Hayden 1997b).

Overall, residential care continues to be perceived as a problem rather than a solution. We have already seen that residential child care does, indeed, have its problems. However, to see these problems as inherent in the practice of residential care would be defeatist and – in the context of the continued need for residential provision – counterproductive. Utting (1997) is rightly keen to portray residential care as a positive choice. So, too, are Frost *et al.* (1999), who mount a persuasive case that a model of residential care based on the empowerment of both staff and children can help to make such care a significant asset in an arsenal of strategies and resources for improving the lives of looked after children. Sinclair and Gibbs (1998), more prosaically, conclude that the case for residential care may in part be pragmatic; in some cases it would appear that residential care is the only provision which can hold certain individuals. Sinclair and Gibbs also found that many of the 'extremely difficult young people' in residential care preferred it to foster care (p.276). They do not, however, advise any increase in the sector, believing instead that there needs to be greater specialisation and a move away from locally based children's homes as the catch-all for a variety of care needs in a locality.

Foster care

Staff, carer and service perceptions of an increase in the percentage of young people in residential care with emotional and behavioural difficulties are echoed in foster care. Utting (1997) found that a substantial proportion (at least a quarter) of children in foster care have some form of disability, including emotional and behavioural difficulties, and reported that in one London borough as many as two-thirds of the children placed in foster care had been sexually abused (though only one-third had been known to be so at the time of placement). Dissatisfactions with residential care mean that we appear to have already made the decision that foster care is the better option in most cases, without effectively planning for it. This situation is fraught with difficulties and potential dangers. These are well illustrated in certain cases for children in foster care (and, indeed, their carers). In these cases things have gone badly wrong in foster placements: for example in the sexual abuse of a family's birth children by a teenage foster child in Essex (Inman 1998a); in the murder of Billie-Jo Jenkins for which her foster father (a deputy head teacher married to a social worker) was convicted (Rosser and Tweedie 1997); and in the abduction of their two foster children by the Bramleys, who had been refused in their application to adopt the children (Gerrard 1999; Veash and Thomas 1999). As Utting also highlights, the very nature of foster care means that children are more isolated and have fewer adults to turn to in comparison with their counterparts in residential care. Furthermore, as nearly half the children in foster care are under ten years old they are particularly vulnerable to abuse (Utting 1997). The effect of fostering on the children of carers is also receiving a little more attention than in recent years. For example, Pugh (1996) found that carers believed fostering exposed their children to the 'harsh realities' of life at an early age.

As we have seen, there is growing recognition that foster care must be improved in quality for its own sake, but also in order to recruit and retain a sufficient number of carers. The NFCA are supportive of a move towards the professionalisation of foster care in order to raise the standards of the care experience (Warren 1997a). An improved system would involve more support and training for carers, as well as the introduction of payment for care. International comparisons of foster care payments reveal that England comes tenth out of twelve European Union countries in relation to the level of foster care payments. Furthermore, it has been calculated that once children's special needs are taken into account, most foster carers are significantly subsidising the state (Berridge 1998). The use of a more professional approach to the task of foster care should mean that the roles and expectations of both parties (social services departments and carers) are more clearly defined. Providing greater remuneration and improving the status of carers would also mean that expectations and responsibilities can be greater and social workers should be able to involve carers more in the planning and organisation of services (Warren 1997a). As we have seen elsewhere in this volume, some local authorities are already operating systems which pay for the skill levels of foster carers, but the schemes in place are variable (Waterhouse 1997). On the other hand, there is also widespread resistance, in the UK and elsewhere, to the concept of professional foster care and the objections are not solely concerned with resources. Progress is halting and sporadic (Colton 1998, pp.18–20).

Leaving aside the debate about professionalisation, foster care in general remains popular. The ADSS give unqualified support to this form of care:

> ... without fully understanding why and how it works, the majority of us will say that the foster care service is the favoured choice when seeking placements for children needing our care. It is of note that there is an absence of any large scale definitive research about the effectiveness of foster care in relation to other forms of looked after services. We as professionals clearly **believe** it is. (ADSS 1997, p.4, their emphasis)

However, with the rise of independent fostering agencies (which many local authorities use and therefore promote), local authorities are faced with an increasing problem of recruiting and retaining sufficient carers to meet needs. The ADSS report (1997) found that 47 per cent of social service directors did not see independent fostering agencies as a serious threat at the time; however, over 35 per cent thought they may be in the future. Little is known at present about the quality of independent agencies or how many children are being cared for by carers from independent agencies. One study estimated that independent agencies were catering for four to five hundred children; however, this is now likely to have increased (DoH/SSI 1995a). This particular issue has remained an ongoing cause for concern (House of Commons 1998b, p.xxxiii; Utting 1997, pp.41–43) but should be at least partly resolved by government commitment to regulate in this field (DoH 1998b, p.75).

The professionalisation of foster care may become politically acceptable, in view of both its perceived cost relative to residential care and its ideological consonance with Labour's emphasis on the family. Demographic and social pressures are currently working against the recruitment and retention of foster carers. We have already seen that currently mainstream carers receive only expenses in many authorities. These payments do not include pension rights or sickness benefits, the training provided is patchy and support from social services is often weak. Furthermore, foster carers are currently not in a particularly favoured position to get access to resources necessary for dealing with the more pressing educational and health needs that some children in foster care have. The success of independent agencies is not just based on better payment for carers but also on their ability to respond to the support needs of carers, which often involve educational and therapeutic support. A major consultation exercise on the quality of foster care was undertaken during the summer of 1998 which produced a proposal for 25 National Standards. These standards are divided into three sections and include a mix of service and professional standards. This has since been followed by the publication of an agreed set of National Standards and a Code of Practice for Foster Care (UK Joint Working Party on Foster Care 1999). All of this suggests a foster care service at something of a crossroads (McAndrew 1998).

Care leavers

Our own research and that of others provides continuing evidence of the vulnerability of care leavers. A large number of reports confirm that the help that these young people can expect from local authorities is haphazard; by 1997, almost a quarter of local authorities had no leaving care policy in place (Broad 1997). The vulnerability of care leavers was illustrated in an extreme way by the West mass-murder case: seven of their ten victims had been in care (Davies 1996). The Bridge Report, which followed the West case by investigating Gloucestershire's records on children in care, found that out of 3000 files covering the period 1970–1994, 400 were missing. The whereabouts of 97 young people were not recorded or were recorded as 'unknown' when they left care (Valios 1996).

When we make comparisons between care leavers and the wider population of young people moving towards independence, the gap between the state as parent and birth parents quickly becomes apparent. Young people in the general population are moving into independence in their twenties, rather than their teens (Stein 1998), with 22 being the average age (DoH 1998j, p.24) and most of this group will have the option of going back home for some support (sometimes to live) in times of need. Indeed, Jones argues that the option of returning home to parents has been increasingly used by young people in recent years (Jones 1995, p.145). She goes on to argue that 'more recognition is needed that leaving home is a process and not necessarily a one-off event: returning home should be seen as part of the process' (Jones 1995, p.149). Biehal et al. (1994) in their study of care leavers found that the majority could not return to their families and conclude that expecting young people to move on to independent living between the ages of 16 and 18 years is unrealistic and unfair.

Although section 24 of the Children Act 1989 places a duty on councils to advise and befriend young people who leave care up to the age of 21, legislative power to provide real assistance has been limited to date. Moves to extend the statutory responsibility for looked after children to the age of 18 are to be welcomed, as indeed is the possibility that this responsibility might be extended to the age of 21. Likewise, the commitment to legislate to ensure that the last care authority retains parental responsibility for after-care assistance, regardless of the location of the young person – 'just like ordinary parents' (DoH 1998g, p.25) – is a step forward. It should help to prevent (and was perhaps in part prompted by) cases such as that of David Caddell. Caddell was an 18-year-old care leaver, originally from the London borough of Lambeth. The latter argued in the high court that because Caddell had spent the last five years in foster care in Kent, the borough was not required to pay his educational or living expenses beyond his eighteenth birthday. The judge in this case ruled that Lambeth had acted legally (George 1997).

Recent developments and future needs

There are signs of positive change in some aspects of the care system. More heads of homes are social work trained and specialist child care qualifications are available and being developed. There is a growing recognition of the need to better support foster carers with moves towards more realistic payment and training in some local authorities. There is also increasing understanding in child and adolescent mental health services about the need for a more accessible and appropriate service for young people with mental health problems and, within this group, looked after young people. The educational disadvantage of looked after children has developed a much higher profile since the mid-1990s and there is a growth in cross-departmental working in this area. The focus upon improving educational outcomes for looked after children is likely to continue with both SSDs and LEAs coming under greater pressure from a central government strongly committed to improving educational achievement.

The everyday experience of looked after children during the 1990s appears to have become more positive in many respects. Children often report forming good relationships with staff and carers and being consulted and involved in decision-making about their care in a range of ways (Berridge and Brodie 1998; Lynes and Goddard 1995).

As we have seen, very few people would currently claim that the state makes a good, even an adequate, parent. It is clear that the state child care system has long been in need of the policy attention that it is now receiving. The policy alternatives might be outlined as follows:

(a) a laissez-faire policy of non-intervention

(b) reform and improvement of the child-care system

(c) a renewed emphasis on prevention and family support

(d) extension of the possibilities and opportunities for permanent substitute care. (Baker and Townsend 1998)

Both reform and improvement of the child care system and an emphasis on prevention and family support underpin the current plans of the Blair administration. Extending the possibilities for permanent substitute care is an alternative approach. However, it is one that would move us away from the emphasis on family preservation as promoted by the Children Act 1989 and the family rights perspective which has become more dominant in the 1990s.

Since the Children Act 1989 there has been a further move away from adoption. There has been a dramatic drop in the number of children adopted over a thirty year period: from around 25,000 in 1968 to 6000 a year in 1998 (Dodd 1999). Whilst the majority (71%) of children spend less than a year looked after (in their last period of being looked after), it follows that 29 per cent spend more than a year in this situation. A minority (7%) spend more than five years looked after by the local authority in any one episode of care (DoH 1998i). Whilst there has been a reduction in the proportion of children being looked after for these longer periods during the 1990s, there remains room for a more open-minded look at what adoption might have offered some of these children (if indeed it was not considered).

Such an approach has its supporters. A report by Morgan (1998) for the Institute of Economic Affairs seeks to revive the fortunes of adoption and criticises the emphasis within social work practice of maintaining parental contact. Morgan regards the best approach for the most disadvantaged children to be adoption, rather than a number of episodes of fostering and/or residential care. She focuses upon the positive effects of permanency in a child's life. However, adoption may not be a permanent solution for a substantial minority of children. Baker and Townsend (1998) query the successes claimed in adoption studies on a number of counts; for example they raise the issue of social class and the extent to which children moving from 'poor' to 'rich' homes have their life chances enhanced by this factor as much as adoption *per se*; they also raise concerns about the possible hidden

effects of adoption and note that long-term effects are insufficiently understood (p.741). Furthermore, the evidence that adoption is necessarily better
for children than fostering is not clear. Gibbons *et al.* (1995), in a ten-year
follow-up study of physically abused children, did not find that adopted
children had particularly better outcomes in terms of behaviour. They also
emphasise the importance of maintaining contact with birth parents for the
well-being of children.

Understanding children's behaviour

Many adults in Britain experience difficulties in understanding and
interpreting children's behaviour and children do not have a tradition of
access to adolescent counsellors, as for example in the United States school
system. There is growing recognition that young people Europe-wide are
increasingly likely to suffer from 'psycho-social disorders' and that the
reasons for this are complex (Rutter and Smith 1995). Government
acceptance of the need for earlier intervention in child mental health has led
to a number of pilot projects in this field, all of which involve joint funding
and working between social services and health. In certain areas the focus is
very much on looked after children (Wellard 1998). More broadly, in the
everyday environments of school and home, Behaviour Support Plans and
the focus on 'Supporting Families' will begin to provide more systematic
support for schools and families in the field of managing behaviour. The
relationship between some forms of special educational need and very
difficult to manage behaviour, as well as adverse social and family
circumstances and these forms of behaviour, is recognised at government
level, as is the increased risk of criminal activity amongst such children and
young people (DfEE 1999). There is thus both more pressure for a better
understanding of children's behaviour at the same time as there is a desire to
control it. This is expressed at an official level, as it has been since at least
1908, by the linking of child care policy with juvenile justice issues (DoH
1998d; 1998j).

Education

There are few more important means of improving the life chances of looked
after children than education. Educational achievement is so central to the
future opportunities of most children that it is an issue about which most
birth parents have strong views. Most parents avoid unnecessary changes of
school, knowing that their children want to be with their friends. They also

appreciate the disadvantages created by time out of school, take pride in their children's achievements and are keen to let others know about them. In contrast, many looked after children, particularly those in residential care, lack such interested adults in their lives. We have seen from earlier chapters that social workers may have little or no knowledge about a child's examination passes and other educational achievements or even their longer term plans for education and training. Residential and foster carers will know more, but may not always be supportive and may, in any case, often lack continuity of knowledge due to changes of placement. The provision of additional support to ease the transition of children into new schools or maintain an existing educational placement at a time of crisis may be a crucial part of a strategy aimed at ensuring that looked after children are able to benefit from the education system. A range of educational support services and special partnerships between LEAs and SSDs, focusing on the educational needs of looked after children, already exist (Vernon and Sinclair 1998). In adopting approaches which target looked after children in particular, a great deal of care must be taken not to stigmatise recipients but to offer the additional, specific help at a time and in the way that it is needed. Guidance from the DfEE (1999) advises that 'social services departments should inform head teachers or another senior member of staff at the earliest opportunity that a child is looked after, and about any significant changes in the pupil's home circumstances' (p.13). At the same time, the guidance notes that information about children's home circumstances must be treated sensitively and shared amongst school staff on a 'need to know' basis.

Jackson's work on those who were high achievers from the care system is instructive in providing specific indicators of positive factors for educational achievement. Those factors most strongly associated with later educational success include: stability and continuity; learning to read early and fluently; having a parent or carer who valued education; having friends who did well at school; developing out-of-school interests; meeting a significant adult who offered consistent support and encouragement; and attending school regularly (Jackson and Martin 1998). Jackson's recommendations are very much in keeping with the kinds of objectives being set within the Quality Protects initiative. Many of the protective factors noted above can occur by chance, as they did in most of her sample. In other words, these young people generally felt that they achieved *despite* the care system, rather than because of it. On the other hand, many of these positive factors can also be actively enhanced and promoted, through training programmes which build upon this knowledge for those in charge of the everyday care of looked after children.

Training

As much of this book has illustrated, staff and carers looking after children, in both residential and foster care environments, need considerable personal skills and are often in need of more specialist training than they get. Although there has been some improvement in the training available in both sectors, there are still many staff who have had little or no relevant training. In relation to residential care in particular, the DoH review concludes that: 'It seems clear that continually tinkering with conventional social work training in an attempt to meet the special requirements of residential care is unlikely to achieve very much' (DoH 1998c, p.36). Rather, it suggests the need for clarity about the nature of the modern residential social work task before appropriate training is designed. Indeed, an appropriate starting point might be to ask whether residential child care really is a form of social work: the majority of other European countries have adopted social pedagogue or educateur models, in which the professional identity of residential workers is based on a larger grouping of people who work directly with children and young people. Such a move would entail a change of mind-set as well as of training systems. Residential workers would need to see themselves as child care workers. The diminished size of the sector now means that it is debated whether there is a sufficient 'critical mass' of residential child care workers to support such a development (Utting 1997). However, this argument seems questionable and is not used for other specialist forms of child care training in the health and education sectors, such as the training of child psychiatrists or educational psychologists. Both groups are less numerous than social services' residential child care workers. Furthermore, there are a range of other organisations which employ residential child care workers, such as residential education and the voluntary and independent sectors, to add to the volume of social services' staff in this type of work. It is also possible that elements of the same training programme could be taken by foster carers in line with moves to professionalise foster care.

The development of S/NVQs (Scottish/National Vocational Qualifications) for foster carers offers the opportunity for carers to gain a recognised qualification in foster care. If these courses are made use of by carers they will also represent a move towards a more standardised fostering service. Significant funds have been set aside by the DoH for the training of foster carers. Also important is increasing the profile of foster care as a topic within social work training, in order that social workers will have a fuller understanding of the role of foster carers in looking after children. The NFCA advocate joint training of foster carers, residential child care workers, family placement social workers and children's social workers, perceiving one further benefit of this in the increased awareness that each would have of the role of the other (Warren 1997a).

Inter-agency cooperation

Inter-agency cooperation and partnership (or, rather, the lack of it) underpins some of the difficulties of looking after children in the care system. The Audit Commission (1994) highlighted the need for social services and education departments to address the issues of the education of looked after children and also found a disappointing lack of collaboration between social services and health authorities in strategic planning for children. On the other hand, where cooperation is mandatory or strongly recommended, as in child protection, greater progress has been made. Subsequently, the requirement of services to take the lead in a number of areas which require multi-agency input via the production, for example, of Children's Services Plans has at least created a situation in which communication is positively promoted across agencies.

Whilst much is written about different professional cultures, about the lack of understanding across professions and services and about issues of confidentiality, the central issue of resources and statutory responsibilities has often been neglected. Whilst looked after children are a central part of child care work in social services departments, they are not a major issue for schools and health services when viewed against the very large population for which these services are responsible. Looked after children make up only 0.4 per cent of all school age children at any one time, thus even a large comprehensive school may have only a handful of children in this category, whilst some primary schools may have no such children. Similarly, looked after children as a definable group are a small fraction of the patients registered with the National Health Service. In this context, it is likely that the relevant needs of looked after children will be neglected without adequate structures and priority-setting determined by central government.

However, it is at the level of national legislation for different services, and historically the problems of lack of cooperation between the DoH and DfEE, that some of the greatest barriers to cooperation have existed. For example, throughout the 1990s the marketisation of the education system and the focus on academic achievement has sat uneasily with the concept of local authorities as corporate bodies being responsible for the welfare of children in need (Hayden 1997b). The growing official realisation that this relatively small group of young people have made, and are likely to continue to make, significant economic demands on a range of services both whilst they are looked after and on leaving care is leading to change. Government documents which concern themselves with vulnerable children and families are attempting to develop the concept of 'joined-up government' (Walker 1998) in combating social exclusion. This multi-agency perspective is evident in the 'Supporting Families' document (Ministerial Group on the Family 1998) and DfEE draft guidance on 'Social Inclusion: Pupil Support' (DfEE 1999).

Moving forward? New Labour, social policy and looked after children

Intimations that Labour might act differently from the Conservatives with regard to personal social services were detectable long before the 1997 general election. Tentative Conservative discussion in 1996 of the possibility of increasing privatisation of social care services was strongly opposed by Labour, which saw a renewed role for the centre in partnership with local government. Despite these different approaches, social services proved to be a non-issue in the election itself, largely because the potential financial implications of such a strategy were either ignored or not publicly addressed (Balloch 1998). Nonetheless, Labour's commitment to tackling 'social exclusion' has been repeated many times since their election victory. In this context, the contemporary policy agenda with regard to looked after children should come as no surprise: looked after children and care leavers are the social group to which the most significant and numerous features associated with this 'exclusion' attach themselves, including youth unemployment, truancy, school exclusions and homelessness (DSS 1998, pp.9–10).

This context helps to explain why there have been a number of policy initiatives relating to children and families emanating from the Blair government which together are likely to have a significant impact on the quality of provision for looked after children and those at risk of this status. Some initiatives, such as Sure Start with pre-school children, have more relevance to the long-term prevention of difficulties within birth families and thus the likelihood of reception into care. Other initiatives, such as Health Action Zones, Education Action Zones and Employment Action Zones, are targeted upon more vulnerable and relatively deprived communities, communities which house children at greater risk of being looked after. Programmes such as New Start (for disaffected 14–17-year-olds) and New Deal (for the long-term unemployed, lone parents and people with disabilities, especially 18–24-year-olds) are attempts to address the education and training deficits of individuals who are disaffected with compulsory education or have been unemployed for some time.

The links between all of these issues and the broader concern about social exclusion are clear. As we have emphasised, the desire to prevent and reduce social exclusion has been made central to a range of policy objectives. As we noted in Chapter 6, several of the recommendations of the first report from the Social Exclusion Unit refer to educational targets for looked after children and the expectation that educational achievement should be of concern to children's social workers (Social Exclusion Unit 1998). All of this work fits within the broader framework provided in the consultative document 'Supporting Families' (Ministerial Group on the Family 1998). Within this document, the issues highlighted as 'serious family problems' – problems with children's learning, youth offending, teenage pregnancy and domestic violence – are again all issues which are likely to disproportionately affect looked after children. In sum, a framework is being developed which sets out to improve the lot of vulnerable children and families, including those likely to be looked after or, indeed, being looked after by, local authorities.

Quality Protects

SSI reports and Joint Reviews in recent years have repeatedly demonstrated that the quality of children's services is inconsistent, both within and between authorities. Such reports and reviews have shown poor assessment, planning and case recording which has led to poorly focused work with families and young people. They have also shown that decisions about who receives services are often made on a haphazard basis and that poor planning for looked after children has resulted in unnecessary delays and inappropriate placements.

To attempt to address these and a wide range of other problems that we have already discussed, the Quality Protects initiative was announced in September 1998. It was no coincidence that the initiative was launched at the same time as a critical report from the Social Services Inspectorate of the inconsistencies in planning, decision-making and protection of looked after children (SSI 1998b). Frank Dobson, Secretary of State at the Department of Health, identified Quality Protects as a major extension of central control through targeting and standard-setting, with the pill sweetened for local authorities by the promise of extra resources:

> Children have the right to expect the best possible care. And, despite all the good work that is being done, this is not happening. Children's services need reform – the system isn't working – and nowhere is the transformation more needed than in the case of children in care.

> We are determined that we will have a system in place that first sets standards and then meets the standards that have been set. And there will be extra funds to bring about these much needed improvements. (DoH 1998k)

The substance of Quality Protects is that it is a three year programme, begun in 1999, that aims to significantly improve the management and delivery of social services for children. It focuses on improving the well-being of children for whom local authorities have taken on direct responsibilities – looked after children, children in the child protection system and other children in need requiring active support from social services. The five key areas where tasks have been set in order to improve service quality are as follows:

> *Children* – knowledge of which children need help in a locality (needs assessment); provision of a mechanism for hearing the views of children and young people;

> *Aspirations* – local authorities should set objectives for services which will benefit children, publicise them and measure achievement;

> *Services* – local authorities need to put in place an inter-agency strategy for commissioning services; expand placement choice; improve the quality of management of adoption services; enhance support for care leavers; collaboratively commission specialist services, where necessary with neighbouring authorities; provide quality assurance mechanisms; and have a financial and human resource strategy (including staff knowledge base and skills);

Management – this requires effective information systems; good assessment and care planning processes; effective record keeping; routine internal audits; and that managers are up-to-date on 'best practice';

Governance – political structures need to be compatible with members and officers working together; there should be the provision of a strategic policy framework; and performance review mechanisms should be in place. (DoH 1998a)

The Quality Protects initiative is essentially a strategic management tool which sets out to put systems in place which should ensure improvements in the quality of service delivered. The main elements of the programme are:

New national government objectives for children's services which for the first time set out clear outcomes for children, and in some instances give precise targets which local authorities are expected to achieve.

An important role for local councillors in delivering the programme, set out in new guidance sent from the Secretary of State to all councillors.

A new special grant of £375 million for children's services to be paid from April 1999 and for a three-year period.

A Quality Protects Management Action Plan (MAP), submitted to the DoH by local authorities by 31 January 1999.

The initial impact of Quality Protects has meant that all councils have had to audit their entire children's services in order to determine which services need addressing to hit the key objectives (Thompson 1998). The production of the local authority action plan by 31 January 1999 produced much frenetic activity within local authorities across England and Wales in the winter months of 1998/99.

The important role of elected councillors is identified in the Quality Protects documentation (DoH 1998b) as that of coordination of services across the range available – such as social services, housing, education and leisure – in order to operationalise the concept of 'corporate parenting'. While the concept of 'corporate parenting' is an ugly one and does not conjure up reassuring images of conventional family life, it does serve to make an important political point. Traditionally, social services departments have taken the sole responsibility for acting *in loco parentis*, but this is changing. More councils are beginning to look at the merits of corporate parenting, which starts from the idea that it is the responsibility of all local authority departments, not just social services, to look after children in care.

Examples of how this might work include, for example, the housing department providing low rent secure council tenancies for young people leaving care. Also, arts and leisure services might offer reduced price activities for foster carers and children in their care and local authorities may decide to earmark work placements and apprenticeships for looked after children (Miller 1998).

The Special Children's Grant is designed to help local authorities improve their children's services and the life chances of looked after children, specifically their educational attainment, health and levels of offending. Priority areas for spending are very much in keeping with the issues requiring urgent action outlined above and include:

Increasing the *choice* of foster and residential care placements;

Increasing the *support provided for care leavers,* including steps to prevent inappropriate discharge of young people at 16 and 17;

Improving the *management* of children's personal social services, including more and better management *information systems;*

Improving *assessment, care planning and record-keeping;*

Improving *quality assurance systems* to enable services to be delivered according to requirements and meeting local and national objectives;

Listening to the views and wishes of children and young people.
(DoH 1998a)

Local authorities will have to meet targets such as reducing to no more than 16 per cent by 2001 the number of children looked after who have three or more placements in one year. They need to show how they will improve the educational attainment of looked after children, by increasing to at least 50 per cent by 2001 the proportion of children leaving care at 16 with a GCSE or GNVQ qualification (75% by 2003). Authorities must prove that the level of employment, training or education among care leavers aged 19 in 2001/02 is at least 60 per cent of the level of all young people of the same age in the area. Every child or young person entering the care system should receive a health assessment (DoH 1998b).

Having properly monitored baseline data about looked after children is essential to this initiative and the expectation that improvements should be made in that area are welcome. As we have seen in a number of earlier chapters, there is a lack of good quality monitoring data in some areas. One could, however, question whether in fact the targets for looked after children are set too low, particularly in relation to educational attainment. For example, available evidence to date has suggested that between 50 and 75 per cent of care leavers have no qualifications; if the lower figure is correct then the 50 per cent overall target proposed is already being met (Inman 1998b).

Of concern to local authorities is, as ever, the issue of resources. The government is committed to pump-priming Quality Protects in its first year. For the second and third years resources are dependent on local authorities hitting the objectives that have been set. The government has made no secret of its intention to be more interventionist with social services departments providing poor services. Regional offices of the Social Services Inspectorate are being strengthened to enable active monitoring. Penalties are planned for failure and rewards for successes. Berridge (1998) assesses the Quality Protects document as 'impressive and ambitious'; we would agree that it is consistent with what professionals themselves and researchers would want to see achieved for children.

Wider changes in state child care

Apart from Quality Protects – which is focused on steering the activities of local government in child care provision – there have been a number of other recent initiatives at national level. These are intended to provide a new national framework within which local child care services will operate. Some of these initiatives affect child care specifically while others affect personal social services more generally. These latter include the creation of a General Social Care Council, in part to replace CCETSW. This initiative was publicised before the 1997 election and is designed to provide greater central regulation of a range of social services staff (Balloch 1998, pp.115–116). A further development is the creation of regional Commissions for Care Standards. Describing present regulatory protection as 'incomplete and patchy' due to regulation being either non-existent or spread across a range of agencies (DoH 1998d, pp.64–66), the government's solution is to introduce such commissions. These will both unify regulation and spread it to areas where it does not currently apply (such as domiciliary care and small children's homes). These and other developments are spelt out in detail in the *Modernising Social Services* White Paper and in the government's response to the Utting Report (DoH 1998d; 1998j). The most important of these developments are summarised in Table 10.1.

Table 10.1 Developments in policy for looked after children

Issue/area affected	Policy development
Foster care	National Standards for Foster Care, via NFCA. Quality Protects: funding for recruitment, retention and training of foster carers. Code of Practice on Recruitment, Assessment, Approval, Training, Management and Support. Targets: 2001; no more than 16 per cent of looked after children to have more than three moves per year.
Residential care	Targets: 2001; no more than 16 per cent of looked after children to have more than three moves per year. Development of specific child care qualifications. Increased funding for training residential workers.
Education	Targets: 1. 50 per cent of care leavers at 16 to have GCSE or GNVQ qualification by 2001 (75% by 2003). 2. 60 per cent of local figure for all young people, for post-17 care leavers to be in employment, training or education by age 19 in 2001/02. Future legislation to improve HE support up to age 24.
Leaving care	Legislation to extend duty of local authority care from 16 to 18 (possibly 21) and to ensure continuity of care. 'Pathway to independence' plans for 16–18-year-olds. Care leavers over 18 exempted from qualifying period for New Deal. Guidance to housing departments and SSDs on housing support. Children Act s. 24 'power to assist' to be replaced by 'duty to assess and meet needs' for 16–18-year-olds.
Training	National Training Organisation for social care staff. Training Support Programme: 7000 child care social workers to achieve new post-qualifying award, 9500 residential child care workers to attain NVQ level 3, three-year programme of increased foster care training. Quality Protects: three-year funding to train senior social services managers.
Inspections and monitoring	New regulatory oversight of small children's homes (fewer than four residents), state sector boarding schools, residential family centres and independent fostering agencies. Strengthened role for local councillors in local monitoring.
Standard-setting	General Social Care Council to set practice standards and register child care workers. Regional Commissions for Care Standards to regulate services. Quality Protects: 1999–2002; £375m extra funding, partly tied to local authorities achieving child care objectives.
Involving young people	Three-year funding for national child care users group. User representation on Commissions for Care Standards. Regional Childrens Rights Officers (as part of CCS). Quality Protects: local authorities to develop a 'mechanism for hearing the views of children and young people' on services.

(DoH 1998d; 1998j)

Dissident voices: the return of user group politics

One particular feature of the above developments deserves highlighting separately. Apart from the commitment to involve user views as part of the Quality Protects initiative, one of the most welcome developments in the current reform process is the willingness to support an independent voice for child care service users. Since the collapse of the National Association of Young People in Care (NAYPIC) in the mid-1990s, there has been an unhealthy gap in the plethora of voices arguing for state child care reforms. Pre-figured in the *Modernising Social Services* White Paper as a commitment to provide 'funding for a group to provide a national voice for children in care and those formerly in care, and to promote their interests' (DoH 1998d, p.48), the full package was revealed in the government's response to the Utting Report. This announced the allocation of £450,000 over three years for such a group, under the umbrella of the leaving care voluntary organisation, First Key (DoH 1998j, p.15). This followed a comprehensive and detailed feasibility study funded by the Department of Health and conducted by First Key, involving many ex-NAYPIC members (First Key 1997) and drawing on the lessons of the successes and failures of NAYPIC.

As well as this initiative, other developments give some cause for optimism regarding the higher profile of the voice of looked after young people and care leavers. A separate organisation, the National Association of Care Leavers, has already been established. Also, a recently established parliamentary group formed by former social worker and now MP Hilton Dawson, the Associate Parliamentary Group for Children and Young People In and Leaving Care, is significantly influenced by, and acts as a conduit for, the views of child care service users. All of these initiatives give room for hope. Agenda-setting, in child care as elsewhere, is primarily a political act. If young people have a seat at the table, then that agenda may at least reflect their concerns rather than interpretations of their needs developed by others.

Amidst the optimism, however, remains a good deal of uncertainty. It remains to be seen how Quality Protects and the other initiatives discussed above will work in practice in coming years. One of the repeated criticisms of the use of targets and standard-setting in other areas of the public sector has been of the ways in which they can distort professional behaviour in unhelpful directions. Child care professionals and managers may become overly concerned with meeting explicit performance-measurement criteria, particularly if money follows such performance, than with the less measurable needs of clients. Against this, it can be argued convincingly that past policy approaches to the needs of looked after children have had poor results. Given the policy emphasis on monitoring performance and outcomes, we should at least have a better basis for assessing success or failure than at present.

Outlines of the Four Research Projects

1 Issues of Care and Control in Children's Residential Care – The Use of Physical Restraint

Carol Hayden

The field research for this project was conducted during 1996 and 1997; the research was commissioned from the Social Services Research and Information Unit (SSRIU) at the University of Portsmouth by the local authorities in which it was conducted. An extensive programme of dissemination was undertaken with the authorities during 1997 and 1998, during which front line staff were able to respond and add to the research findings. The research is based on three social services departments (one county council and two unitary authorities). The focus for the research arose out of departmental concern about records of violent incidents towards staff in children's residential care, coupled with a desire to look at staff training in and use of physical restraint. The research was funded by the social services departments in which it was undertaken. In total the local authorities had 31 children's residential units during the period of research, including a secure unit, units for children with severe learning difficulties and/or respite care units. The great majority of the units were locally based children's homes, with some differentiation according to age in certain parts of the local authorities. Most units looked after around eight children/young people at any one time. Whilst the local authorities encompass a range of environments – inner city, county town, rural areas – the overall rate for the population of children looked after, at 3.1 per 1000 children, was considerably lower than the national average of 4.5 per 1000 children (CSO 1997).

The overall aim of the research was:

- to inform training and policy development in social services departments' residential child care sector, in respect of the appropriate use and recording of physical restraint procedures.

The research conducted was flexible in approach and responsive to the concerns and interests of the steering group for the project. The focus of successive parts of the research was informed by earlier findings, presented to and considered by the steering group for the project. Thus, although the research started out with the relatively narrow focus of violent incidents and physical restraint in residential care it moved out to investigate how children came to be looked after and the life events which might help explain their behaviour. In-depth case studies of individuals who experienced particularly problematic periods whilst in residential care were undertaken in order to illustrate the complexity of needs which some children bring to the residential environment.

Investigation into 'staff cultures' across eight homes with differing levels of records of violent incidents was also undertaken, in order to look at any possible relationship between attitudes and values towards the caring role in the context of a residential environment and recorded experiences of violent incidents.

Stages of the research and types of data collected

STAGE 1 THE WIDER PICTURE

- *Participant observation* – four-day staff training course in behaviour management with use of physical restraint.
- *Documentary analysis* – all records of violent incidents in two three-month periods in 1995 and 1996 (456 records in all).
- *Postal questionnaire* to all residential care staff – 113 responses: 81 per cent of unit managers; 36 per cent of care staff.
- *Semi-structured interviews* with staff and young people in 6 homes – 36 care staff; 5 unit managers; 6 young people.

- *Comparison of staff cultures in 8 residential units* (4 low recording; 4 medium/high recording with respect to violent incidents). Lickert scales completed by 59 staff (31 in low recording and 28 in medium/high recording homes) and discussions held with groups of staff.

- *Individual children* (11 in all) – individuals selected on the basis of having more than one record of involvement in a violent incident, during a three-month period of monitoring. Interviews with social services staff (unit manager(s), key worker(s), field social workers), parents/carers and some of the young people.

Availability of research report

Hayden, C. (1997) *Physical Restraint in Children's Residential Care.* Report no. 37. University of Portsmouth: SSRIU.

2 The View From the Front: The User View of Child Care in Norfolk

Dee Lynes and Jim Goddard

The field research for this project was carried out between June and August 1994 and data analysed during the subsequent year. It was mainly funded by Norfolk social services department. Its intention was to provide an independent analysis of the user view of services provided for looked after children in the county. Its conclusions were based on the questionnaire responses of 186 young people with substantial experience of life in care: 121 young people, aged between 10 and 18 years, answered a wide range of questions about their life in care; and 65 young people, who had left care between 1988 and 1994, answered questions about their leaving care experiences.

The overall aim of the research was:

- To provide for the authority concerned a range of user views on the services provided, with a view to the development of more responsive and more appropriate services.

Stages of the research and types of data collected

STAGE 1 RESEARCH DESIGN

The design of the questionnaire for looked after children owed much to that used by Fletcher (1993) in her national survey for the Who Cares? Trust. The design of the questionnaire for care leavers was solely the work of the authors. Both were piloted on the members of the in-care group of which both authors were members at the time. The relevant assistant director of social services was also consulted with regard to content, with a view to information gained being relevant and useful in the development of policy.

STAGE 2 QUESTIONNAIRE DISTRIBUTION

Questionnaires were distributed in two ways. The questionnaire for looked after children was distributed to all those in the county known to be looked after on 28 June 1994, to be between the ages of 10 and 18 (we judged 10 to be an appropriate cut-off age in terms of ability to fill in the questionnaire) and whose care episode had lasted for longer than six months. Names and addresses were derived from the SSD computer database. Carers were written to a few weeks prior, to inform them of the imminence of the survey, its nature and that it had the backing of senior management.

For the questionnaire going to care leavers, we first gained last contact addresses for those who were 16 and over and who had left care since October 1991, since these would be easier to track down. We restricted our sample to those whose last care episode had been for more than six months, in view of our questions concerning leaving care preparation. Where they had left care some time previously, we used foster carers and social workers to try to establish existing addresses. We sought to trace current addresses for all 222 care leavers identified in this way. However, we also various known post-care destinations: YMCA, YWCA, local drop-in centres and leaving care centres and workers.

STAGE 3 ANALYSIS

This was conducted in two ways. The data was analysed using SPSS. Where responses were ticking boxes or responding to yes/no questions, this was straightforward. Where responses were longer, more discursive answers, the judgement of the two researchers was used to develop categories and locate responses within them. These, too, could then be analysed using SPSS. However, we also sought to use these answers to add illustration and meaning to the analysis in the subsequent report.

Availability of research report

Lynes, D. and Goddard, J. (1995) *The View From the Front: The User View of Child Care in Norfolk*. Norwich: Norfolk County Council.

3 The Role of Foster Care in Services for Looked After Children

Sarah Gorin

Background to the research

This project was undertaken as a studentship jointly funded by the Social Services Research and Information Unit (SSRIU) at Portsmouth University and by the social services departments in which it was conducted. The three local authorities in this study are the same as for Hayden's study (section 1). The research was used as material for a PhD thesis and to inform the local authorities about the state of their service and the views of users. The project was undertaken over a three-year period, from February 1996 to February 1999 and the primary data collection took place in 1997 and 1998.

The aims of the project were:

- to examine the challenges faced by foster carers and the impact of caring for a foster child on their own family.

- to contribute an understanding of the support required by foster carers, particularly in respect of managing the emotional needs and behaviour of children in their care.

- to examine the process of placement of children with foster carers with particular regard to examining the choice of placement offered to children and the extent to which placements are meeting the needs of foster children and foster families.

- to assess the impact of foster placements on the emotional well-being and behaviour of the child and to assess the ability of foster care to make a difference to children's lives.

- to inform the positive development of foster care policy with the aim of sustaining existing foster carers and maintaining a high quality child care service.

Stages of the research and types of data collected

STAGE 1 SURVEY OF FOSTER CARERS AND THEIR CHILDREN

This was a survey to all foster carers (including family link) and their own children in the three authorities. The development of the questionnaire for foster carers was informed by interviews and consultation with key family placement personnel, a pilot study with a range of foster carers, attendance at foster carer meetings and meetings of family placement social workers. The postal questionnaire was sent to 872 carers (376 responses or a response rate of 43%) and 211 responses were received from the sons and daughters of foster carers.

STAGE 2 CASE STUDIES OF NEW PLACEMENTS

This stage of the research involved in-depth case studies of 10 placements, which included 13 children with a mainstream foster carer (5 placements) or a project carer (5 placements). New placements of children with foster carers in a specified time period were identified. Case file data was collated on each placement and interviews were conducted within two months of the beginning of a placement and followed up six months later. Interviews were carried out with foster carers, family placement social workers, the children's social worker and the foster child, where appropriate. Behaviour rating scales were used as a tool to identify and discuss children's behaviour. The process of placement was examined, as was the child's progress over the six months. The experience of caring from the point of view of the foster family was also included.

Availability of research report

For research report on stage 1 of the research see Gorin, S. (1997) *Time to Listen? Views and Experiences of Family Placement.* Report no. 36. University of Portsmouth: SSRIU.

4 The Post-Sixteen Educational Participation and Performance of Looked After Children

Niki Van Der Spek

In 1995 the Training and Enterprise Council in the geographical area of this research expressed an interest in examining post-sixteen educational participation and performance, particularly in relation to those young people who would be most vulnerable to leaving the education system early, with few qualifications and reduced life chances. Their response to the recognition of this problem was to undertake funding, with the University of Portsmouth, for a doctoral studentship that would incorporate a locally based research project. The data that was collected over the period October 1995 to June 1997 has been used as part of the requirements for a doctoral thesis. The findings have also been used to inform developing SSD policy whilst the department was undergoing structural change and to raise awareness of the experiences and needs of this group of young people in the local area within those agencies involved in the project.

More practically, data from the project was also used to substantiate successful bid submissions to central government from a multi-agency partnership coordinated via the Training and Enterprise Council concerned.

The aims of the project were:

- to establish baseline data concerning the educational attainment of looked after young people leaving compulsory education and their participation in post-compulsory education.

- to establish baseline data concerning the post-sixteen destinations of looked after young people.

- to access the views of care managers, carers and young people on barriers to further educational participation.

- to examine the role of the careers service and its interactions with looked after young people.

Stages of the research and types of data collected

STAGE 1 RESEARCH DESIGN

It was proposed that a combined data set would be formulated of all looked after children in the county area born between 1 September 1979 and 31 August 1981 and who had been looked after for six months or longer on 1 April 1996. The six-month minimum was chosen to limit those who had been looked after on a temporary basis and who had since returned home and also those who had only recently become looked after. The cohort would thus be of school leaving age in July 1996 or July 1997. By taking the entire population of looked after young people of this age into the research sample (n=143), a robust data set could be achieved that made comparison between the sample and their peers possible. It was intended to identify and establish reliable data held by social services for looked after young people in the geographical area with regard to their post-sixteen education and subsequent careers. Fieldwork, policy documents, observation and discussions with key personnel were undertaken to facilitate an evaluation of practices in relation to policy. It was also the intention to identify and review the information held by other agencies, notably secondary data analysis of careers service data, policy documents, and interviewing key personnel to establish whether looked after young people in the County area reflect the national trend of

poor educational participation and performance. The use of both quantitative and qualitative strategies was seen as appropriate for this purpose.
Quantitative methods allowed for statistical comparison with other quantitative research and for ease of replicability. However, they were limited in
providing only a 'snapshot' in time, and certainly where data has been
collected some time previously its accuracy cannot be taken for granted. In
the study, therefore, quantitative data was triangulated further by the use of
several different sources of quantitative data, notably: secondary data analysis of social services records; home and hospital teaching service records;
career services records; and the development of an original data set from
survey questionnaires and personal verification.

STAGE 2 BASELINE QUANTITATIVE DATA

Details were derived from existing computer records, notably the social
services computer database, and from a survey questionnaire (which was
piloted in one locality) of case-holding social service staff. The database held
quantifiable information about the population of all 'looked after' children in
the county providing details about age, gender, care history, etc. Like all
databases, its reliability was dependent on the information being updated
regularly. The survey questionnaire provided a useful triangulation technique
to double-check the records as well as provide more depth.

STAGE 3 INTERVIEWS AND QUESTIONNAIRES

Semi-structured and in-depth interviews were conducted with 21 young
people as well as carers and various members of staff from different agencies.
Informal interviews with young people and staff were also held at drop-in
centres, residential homes and semi-independent units. 83 care managers
also gave an individual response to open-ended questions about the barriers
to education faced by young people. The data set was updated on several
occasions and at the end of the academic year to include the latest careers
information and exam results. This combined data set was analysed using
computer software SPSS. The combined data set includes anonymised survey
questionnaire information about the nature and number of contacts between
agencies identified and 'looked after' children over the period of the study.

The research was overseen by a steering group with representatives from
the various agencies involved and the methodology was discussed at various
project steering group meetings to establish its practical implementation and
its strengths and limitations.

Availability of research report (summarised)

Van Der Spek, N. and Goddard, J. 'The post-sixteen educational participation and performance of looked after children: a case study'. Paper presented to the Social Policy Association Annual Conference, University of Lincolnshire and Humberside, Lincoln, 14–16 July 1998. Contact Niki Van Der Spek for further details.

References

Action on Aftercare Consortium (1996) *Too Much. Too Young. The Failure of Social Policy in Meeting the Needs of Care Leavers*. Ilford: Barnardos.

ADSS (1997) *The Foster Carer Market: A National Perspective*. Children and Families Committee Report. Bury St. Edmonds: Communique.

Aldgate, J., Colton, M., Ghate, D. and Heath, A. (1992) 'Educational attainment and stability in long-term foster care'. *Children and Society 6*, 2, 91–103.

Aldgate, J. and Hawley, D. (1986a) 'Helping foster families through disruption'. *Adoption and Fostering 10*, 2, 44–49.

Aldgate, J. and Hawley, D. (1986b) 'Preventing disruption in long-term foster care'. *Adoption and Fostering 10*, 3, 23–31.

Ames Reed, J. (1993) *We Have Learned a Lot From Them: Foster Care for Young People with Learning Difficulties*. London: NCB and Barnados.

Ames Reed, J. (1994) 'We live here too: Birth children's perspectives on fostering someone with learning disabilities'. *Children and Society 8*, 2, 164–173.

Ames Reed, J. (1997) 'Fostering children and young people with learning disabilities: The perspectives of birth children and carers'. *Adoption and Fostering 20*, 4, 36–41.

Aries, P. (1962) *Centuries of Childhood*. London: Jonathan Cape.

Audit Commission (1994) *Seen But Not Heard*. London: HMSO.

Audit Commission (1996) *Misspent Youth: Young People and Crime*. Abingdon: Audit Commission Publications.

Baker, A. and Townsend, P. (1998) 'Children in care – are there any arguments for an adoption revival?' *Justice of the Peace 162*, 740–742.

Baldry, S. and Kemmis, J. (1998) 'What is it like to be looked after by a local authority?' *British Journal of Social Work 28*, 129–136.

Baldwin, D., Coles, B. and Mitchell, W. (1997) 'The formation of an underclass or disparate groupings of "vulnerable youth"'. In R. MacDonald (ed) *Youth, the 'Underclass' and Social Exclusion*. London: Routledge.

Balloch, S. (1998) 'New partnerships for social services'. In H. Jones and S. MacGregor (eds) *Social Issues and Party Politics*. London: Routledge.

Bamford, F. and Wolkind, S.N. (1988) *The Physical and Mental Health of Children in Care: Research Needs*. Swindon: Economic and Social Research Council.

Bax, M., Hart, H. and Jenkins, S. (1983) 'The behaviour, development and health of the young child: Implications for care'. *British Medical Journal 286*, 1793–1796.

Baxter, S. (1989) *Fostering Breakdown: An Internal Study*. Belfast: Department of Health and Social Services, Northern Ireland.

Bebbington, A. and Miles, J. (1989) 'The background of children who enter local authority care'. *British Journal of Social Work 19*, 5, 349–368.

Bebbington, A. and Miles, J. (1990) 'The supply of foster families for children in care'. *British Journal of Social Work 20*, 283–307.

Berridge, D. (1985) *Children's Homes*. Oxford: Blackwell.

Berridge, D. (1994) 'Foster and residential care reassessed: A research perspective'. *Children and Society 8*, 2, 132–150.

Berridge, D. (1996) 'Foster care'. *NCB Highlight 141, 142*. London: NCB.

Berridge, D. (1997) *Foster Care: A Research Review*. London: HMSO.

Berridge, D. (1998) 'Acting on their own initiative'. *Community Care 1245*, 22–28 October, 24.

Berridge, D. and Brodie, I. (1996) 'Residential child care in England and Wales: The enquiries and after'. In M. Hill and J. Aldgate (eds) *Child Welfare Services: Developments in Law, Policy, Practice and Research*. London: Jessica Kingsley Publishers.

Berridge, D. and Brodie, I. (1998) *Children's Homes Revisited*. London: Jessica Kingsley Publishers.

Berridge, D., Brodie, I., Ayre, P., Barrett, D., Henderson, B. and Wenman, H. (1997) *Hello – Is Anybody Listening? The Education of Young People in Residential Care*. Warwick: University of Warwick/Social Care Association.

Berridge, D. and Cleaver, H. (1987) *Foster Home Breakdown*. Oxford: Blackwell.

Biehal, N., Clayden, J. and Stein, M. (1994) 'Leaving care in England – a research perspective'. *Children and Youth Services Review 6*, 3/4, 231–254.

Biehal, N., Clayden, J., Stein, M. and Wade, J. (1992) *Prepared for Living? A Survey of Young People Leaving the Care of Three Local Authorities*. London: NCB.

Biehal, N., Clayden, J., Stein, M. and Wade, J. (1995) *Moving On – Young People and Leaving Care Schemes*. London: HMSO.

Blau, G.M. and Gullotta, T.P. (eds) (1996) *Adolescent Dysfunctional Behaviour. Causes, Interventions and Prevention. Volume 3: Issues in Children's and Families' Lives*. London: Sage Publications.

Blyth, E. and Milner, J. (1997) *Social Work with Children: The Educational Perspective*. Harlow: Addison Wesley Longman.

Brandon, M., Schofield, J. and Trinder, L. (1998) *Social Work with Children*. Basingstoke: Macmillan Press.

Broad, B. (1994) *Leaving Care in the 1990s*. London: Royal Philanthropic Society.

Broad, B. (1997) *Young People Leaving Care*. London: Jessica Kingsley Publishers.

Bullock, R., Little, M. and Millham, S. (1993) *Residential Care for Children*. London: HMSO.

Butler, I. and Payne, H. (1997) 'The health of children looked after by the local authority'. *Adoption and Fostering 21*, 2, 28–35.

Cambridgeshire County Council (1990) *Consumer Survey: Foster Carers*. Cambridge: Cambridgeshire County Council.

Chaplain, R. and Freeman, A. (1994) *Caring Under Pressure*. London: D. Fulton.

Chartered Institute of Public Finance and Accountancy (1996) *Personal Social Services Statistics 1994/95*. London: CIPFA.

Clark, S. (1997) 'Immune systems?' *Community Care*, 22–28 May, 10–11.

Cleaver, H. (1996) *Focus on Teenagers*. London: HMSO.

Cleaver, H. (1997) 'New research on teenagers. Key findings and the implications for policy and practice'. *Adoption and Fostering 21*, 1, 37–43.

Cliffe, D. and Berridge, D. (1991) *Closing Residential Homes: An End to Residential Childcare?* London: NCB.

Coles, B. (1995) *Youth and Social Policy: Youth, Citizenship and Young Careers*. London: UCL Press.

Collins, S. and Grant, J. (1994) *Fostering Recruitment – A Study of Existing Hampshire Carers*. Winchester: Hampshire County Council Quality Service Unit.

Colton, M. (1988) *Dimensions of Substitute Care: A Comparative Study of Foster and Residential Care Practice.* Aldershot: Avebury.

Colton, M. (1992) 'Carers of children: A comparative study of the practices of residential and foster carers'. *Children and Society 6,* 1, 25–37.

Colton, M. (1998) 'Foster care in Europe: An overview'. In *Exchanging Visions: Papers on Best Practice in Europe for Children Separated from Their Birth Parents.* London: BAAF.

Cooper, J.D. (1993) 'The origins of the National Children's Bureau'. *Children and Society 1,* 5–19.

CSO (1997) *Social Trends 27.* London: HMSO.

Dando, I. and Minty, B. (1987) 'What makes good foster parents'. *British Journal of Social Work 17,* 383–400.

Daniel, P. and Ivatts, J. (1998) *Children and Social Policy.* London: Macmillan Press.

Dartington SRU (1995) *Child Protection: Messages From Research.* London: HMSO.

Davie, R., Butler, N. and Goldstein, H. (1972) *From Birth to Seven. The Second Report of the National Child Development Study (1958 Cohort).* London: Longman in association with the NCB.

Davies, W.R. (1996) 'From care to where?' *Local Government Chronicle,* 2 February, 10–11.

Davin, A. (1990) 'When is a child not a child?' In H. Corr and L. Jamieson (eds) *Politics of Everyday Life: Continuity and Change in Work and the Family.* London: Macmillan.

de Cruz, P. (1998) 'Child abuse and child protection in residential care'. *NCB Highlight 159.* London: NCB/Barnardos.

DfE (1994) *Pupils with Problems.* Circular 13/94, DH LAC, 9411, The Education of Children being Looked After by Local Authorities. London: DfE.

DfEE (1998a) *Statistical Bulletin 2/98.* London: DfEE.

DfEE (1998b) Permanent exclusions from schools in England 1996/97 and exclusion appeals lodged by parents in England 1996/97. *DfEE News,* 451/98, 30 September.

DfEE (1998c) *Absence Tables 1998.* DfEE Home Page: DfEE.gov.uk/absence98.

DfEE (1999) *Social Inclusion: Pupil Support.* The Secretary of States Guidance on Pupil Attendance, Behaviour, Exclusion, and Reintegration. 10/99, July. London: DfEE.

Dickens, C. (1838) *Oliver Twist.* Reprinted 1992. London: Tiger Books.

Dodd, V. (1999) 'Adoption row over teenage mothers'. *Guardian,* 26 January, 3.

DoH (1988) *Health and Personal Social Services Statistics for England.* London: HMSO.

DoH (1989) *An Introduction to The Children Act 1989.* London: HMSO.

DoH (1991a) *The Children Act 1989. Guidance and Regulations, Volume 4, Residential Care.* London: HMSO.

DoH (1991b) *Living Away from Home – Your Rights: A Guide for Children and Young People* (Leaflet CAG7). London: DoH.

DoH (1991c) *Patterns and Outcomes in Child Placement.* London: HMSO.

DoH (1992) *Choosing With Care: The Report of the Committee of Inquiry in the Selection, Development and Management of Staff in Children's Homes.* London: HMSO.

DoH (1994) *Health and Personal Social Services Statistics for England.* London: HMSO.

DoH (1995a) *Support Force for Children's Residential Care. Contracting for Children's Residential Care. Part 1: An Overview.* London: DoH.

DoH (1995b) *Looking After Children: Good Parenting and Good Outcomes.* London: HMSO.

DoH (1998a) *Objectives for Social Services for Children.* Wetherby: DoH.

DoH (1998b) *Quality Protects: Framework for Action.* Wetherby: DoH.

DoH (1998c) *Caring for Children Away from Home: Messages from Research.* Chichester: John Wiley.

DoH (1998d) *Modernising Social Services.* London: The Stationery Office.

DoH (1998e) *Health and Personal Social Services Statistics for England: 1998 Edition*. London: The Stationery Office.

DoH (1998f) *Statistical Bulletin*, 8 October. London: The Stationery Office.

DoH (1998g) *Quality Protects: Objectives for Social Services for Children*. Social Care Group DoH. London: Department of Health.

DoH (1998h) *Modernising Social Services. National Priorities Guidance 1999/2000–2001/ 2002*. London: The Stationery Office.

DoH (1998i) *Statistical Bulletin 1998/33. Children Looked After in England: 1997/98*. 8 October. London: Government Statistical Service.

DoH (1998j) *The Government's Response to the Children's Safeguards Review*. London: The Stationery Office.

DoH (1998k) Press Release: 'Health Secretary Pledges to Transform Children's Services', 21 September. London: DoH.

DoH/SSI (1995a) *Independent Fostering Agencies: A Study Conducted by the Social Services Inspectorate of the Department of Health*. London: DoH.

DoH/SSI (1995b) *Inspection of Local Authority Fostering 1994–95 National Summary Report*. London: HMSO.

DoH/SSI (1996) *Inspection of Local Authority Fostering 1995–96 National Summary Report*. London: HMSO.

DoH/SSI (1997) *The Control of Children in the Public Care: Interpretation of the Children Act 1989*. London: DoH/SSI.

Donnison, D., Jay, P. and Stewart, M. (1962) *The Ingleby Report: Three Critical Essays*. London: Fabian Society.

Donnison, D. and Stewart, M. (1958) *The Child and Social Services*. London: Fabian Society.

Doorbar, P. (1995) *We're Here Too. The Views of the Natural Children of Foster Parents*. Overton: Pat Doorbar and Associates.

Douglas, J.W.B. (1967) *The Home and the School*. London: MacGibbon & Kee.

DSS (1998) *New Ambitions for Our Country: A New Contract for Welfare – A Summary*. London: DSS.

Essen, J., Lambert, L. and Head, J. (1976) 'School attainment of children who have been in care'. *Child Care Health and Development 2*, 339–351.

First Key (1997) *Draft Report to the Department of Health: A National Voice Feasibility Study*. Leeds: First Key.

Firth, H. (1995) *Annual Review of the Education Support Service, 1995*. Social Services Library. Winchester: Hampshire County Council.

Firth, H. and Horrocks, C. (1996) 'No home, no school, no future: Exclusions and children who are "looked after"'. In E. Blyth and J. Milner (eds) *Exclusion from School. Inter-Professional Issues for Policy and Practice*. London: Routledge.

Fletcher, B. (1993) *Not Just a Name*. London: Who Cares? Trust/National Consumer Council.

Fletcher-Campbell, F. (1997) *The Education of Children Who are Looked After*. London: NFER.

Fletcher-Campbell, F. and Hall, C. (1990) *Changing Schools? Changing People? The Education of Children in Care*. London: NFER.

Foucault, M. (1979) *Discipline and Punish: The Birth of the Prison*. Harmondsworth: Penguin.

Fox Harding, L. (1997) *Perspectives in Child Care Policy*. London: Longman.

Franklin, A. and Franklin, B. (1996) 'Growing pains: The developing children's rights movement in the UK'. In J. Pilcher and S. Wagg (eds) *Thatcher's Children?: Politics, Childhood and Society in the 1980s and 1990s*. London: Falmer Press.

Franklin, B. (1989) 'Children's rights: Developments and prospects'. *Children and Society 3,* 1, 50–66.

Franklin, B. (1995) 'The case for children's rights: An overview'. In B. Franklin (ed) *The Handbook of Children's Rights: Comparative Policy and Practice.* London: Routledge.

Freeman, M. (1996) 'The convention: An English perspective'. In M. Freeman (ed) *Children's Rights: A Comparative Perspective.* Aldershot: Dartmouth.

Frost, N., Mills, S. and Stein, M. (1999) *Understanding Residential Child Care.* Aldershot: Ashgate Publishing.

Frost, N. and Stein, M. (1989) *The Politics of Child Welfare: Inequality, Power and Change.* London: Harvester Wheatsheaf.

Gardner, P. and Cunningham, P. (1997) 'Oral history and teachers' professional practice: A wartime turning point?' *Cambridge Journal of Education 27,* 3, 331–342.

Garnett, L. (1992) *Leaving Care and After.* London: NCB.

George, M. (1997) 'He's leaving home'. *Community Care,* 26 June–2 July, 29.

Gerrard, N. (1999) 'Hostages to a desperate need'. *Observer,* 17 January, 7.

Gibbons, J., Gallagher, B., Bell, C. and Gordon, D. (1995) *Development after Physical Abuse in Early Childhood; A Follow-Up Study of Children on Child Protection Registers.* London: HMSO.

Gibson, A. and Asthana, S. (1998) 'School performance, school effectiveness and the 1997 White Paper'. *Oxford Review of Education 24,* 2, 195–210.

Gil, E. (1982) 'Institutional abuse of children in out-of-home care'. *Child and Youth Services 4,* 7–13.

Goldson, B. (1997) 'Children, crime, policy and practice: Neither welfare nor justice'. *Children and Society 11,* 77–88.

Goldstein, S. (1994) 'Understanding and assessing ADHD and related educational and behavioural disorders'. *Therapeutic Care and Education 3,* 2, 111–129.

Gorin, S. (1997) *Time to Listen? Views and Experiences of Family Placement.* Report no. 36. University of Portsmouth: SSRIU.

Graham, P.J. (1986) 'Behavioural and intellectual development in childhood epidemiology'. *British Medical Bulletin 42,* 2, 155–162.

Hallett, C. (1995) *Inter-Agency Coordination in Child Protection.* London: HMSO.

Harrison, S. and Mort, M. (1996) 'Constructing User Group Legitimacy: A Case Study of Officials in Mental Health Care'. Paper presented at the Political Studies Association Annual Conference, Glasgow, 11 April.

Hayden, C. (1997a) *Physical Restraint in Children's Residential Care.* Report no. 37, University of Portsmouth: SSRIU.

Hayden, C. (1997b) *Children Excluded from Primary School. Debates, Evidence and Responses.* Buckingham: Open University Press.

Hayden, C. (1997c) 'Children excluded from school: Children "in need" and children with "special educational need"'. *Emotional and Behavioural Difficulties 2,* 3, 36–45.

Hayden, C. and Gorin, S. (1998) 'Care and control of looked after children in England'. *International Journal of Child and Family Welfare 3,* 3, 242–258.

Hayden, C. and Martin, T. (1999) *The Needs of Children in Out of Area Placements.* University of Portsmouth: SSRIU.

Hazelhurst, M. and Tijani, B. (1998) *Partners in Care.* London: Centrepoint.

Heath, A., Colton, M. and Aldgate, J. (1994) 'Failure to escape: A longitudinal study of foster children's educational attainment'. *British Journal of Social Work 24,* 241–260.

Hendrick, H. (1994) *Child Welfare: England 1872–1989.* London: Routledge.

Hersov, L. (1986) 'Child psychiatry in Britain – the last thirty years'. *Journal of Child Psychology and Psychiatry in Britain and Allied Disciplines 27*, 781–801.

Hester, M. (1994) 'Violence against social services staff: A gendered issue,'. In C. Lupton and T. Gillespie (eds) *Working with Violence.* Basingstoke: Macmillan.

Heywood, J. (1978) *Children in Care.* London: Routledge and Kegan Paul.

Hill, M. and Tisdall, K. (1997) *Children and Society.* Harlow: Addison Wesley Longman.

Hodgkin, R. (1994) 'Cultural relativism and the U.N. Convention on the Rights of the Child'. *Children and Society 8,* 4, 296–299.

Holman, B. (1996) 'Fifty years ago: The Curtis and Clyde reports'. *Children and Society 10,* 197–209.

Home Department (1946) *Report of the Care of Children Committee.* Cmd.6922. London: HMSO.

House of Commons (1977) *First Report from the Select Committee on Violence in the Family: Violence to Children.* London: HMSO.

House of Commons (1984) *Report of the Social Services Select Committee: Children in Care.* London: HMSO.

House of Commons (1998a) *Fifth Report of the Education and Employment Select Committee: Disaffected Children* (HC 498–1). London: The Stationery Office.

House of Commons (1998b) *Second Report of the Health Select Committee – Children Looked After by Local Authorities* (HC 319–1). London: The Stationery Office.

Howe, E. (1992) *The Quality of Care: Report of the Residential Staffs Inquiry.* London: Local Government Management Board.

Hudson, J.R. (1998) 'Marching in step'. *Children's Residential Care Newsletter 8,* Spring, 5.

Inman, K. (1998a) 'Social work opened to challenge'. *Community Care 1219,* 23–29 April, 8–9.

Inman, K. (1998b) 'Thou shalt meet thy new targets'. *Community Care 1244,* 15–21 October, 8–9.

Jackson, S. (1987) *The Education of Children in Care.* Bristol Papers. Bristol: School of Advanced Urban Studies.

Jackson, S. (1989) 'Residential care and education'. *Children and Society 4,* 335–350.

Jackson, S. (1998a) 'Looking after children: A new approach or just an exercise in form filling? A response to Knight and Caveney'. *British Journal of Social Work 28,* 1, 45–56.

Jackson, S. (1998b) 'High achievers: A study of young people who have been in residential or foster care'. University of Wales, Swansea: Final Report to the Leverhulme Trust.

Jackson, S. and Martin, P.Y. (1998) 'Surviving the care system: Education and resilience'. *Journal of Adolescence 21,* 569–583.

Jesson, D. and Gray, J. (1990) *England and Wales Youth Cohort Study: Access, Entry and Potential Demand for Higher Education Amongst 18–19 Year Olds in England and Wales.* London: Department of Employment Training Agency.

Jones, G. (1995) *Leaving Home.* Buckingham: Open University Press.

Jones, K. (1994) *The Making of Social Policy in Britain: 1830–1990.* London: Athlone Press.

Kahan, B. (1989) *Child Care Research, Policy and Practice.* London: Hodder and Stoughton in association with the Open University Press.

Kahan, B. (1995) *Growing Up in Groups.* London: HMSO.

Keane, A. (1983) 'Behaviour problems among long-term foster children'. *Adoption and Fostering 7,* 3, 53–62.

Kelly, G. (1995) 'Foster parents and long-term placements: Key findings from a Northern Ireland study'. *Children and Society 9,* 2, 19–29.

Kelly, J. (1995) 'Blissful ignorance'. *Community Care 1073*, 22 June, 26–27.

Kendrick, A. (1995) *Residential Care in the Integration of Child Care Services*. Edinburgh: Scottish Office Central Research Unit.

Kendrick, A. (1998) 'In their best interests? Protecting children from abuse in residential and foster care'. *International Journal of Child and Family Welfare 3*, 2, 169–185.

Kent, P., Pierson, J. and Thornton, B. (1990) *Guide to the Children Act 1989*. Wallington: Community Care.

Kirkwood, A. (1993) *The Leicestershire Inquiry 1992*. Leicester: Leicestershire County Council.

Knapp, M., Baines, B. and Gerrard, B. (1990) 'Performance measurement in child care: When a falling boarding out rate should attract congratulation not castigation'. *Policy and Politics 18*, 1, 39–42.

Knight, T. and Caveney, S. (1998) 'Assessment and action records: Will they promote good parenting?' *British Journal of Social Work 28*, 1, 29–43.

Kraemer, S. (1998) 'Aimless, expensive and lost'. Paper presented at: Who is Responsible for Me? 50th anniversary of the Mulberry Bush School Conference, 14 September, Royal College of Physicians, London.

Labour Party (1964) *Crime – A Challenge To Us All* (Chair: Lord Longford). London: Labour Party.

Leadbetter, D. (1993) 'Trends in assaults on social work staff: The experience of one Scottish department'. *British Journal of Social Work 23*, 613–628.

Levy, A. and Kahan, B. (1991) *The Pindown Experience and the Protection of Children*. Stafford: Staffordshire County Council.

Lindsay, M. (1991) 'Complaints procedures and their limitations in the light of the "Pindown" Inquiry'. *Journal of Social Welfare and Family Law 1*, 432–441.

Little, M. and Kelly, S. (1995) *A Life Without Problems? The Achievements of a Therapeutic Community*. Aldershot: Arena.

Lowe, K. (1990) *Teenagers in Foster Care: A Survey by the National Foster Care Association*. London: NFCA.

Lowe, M. (1989) *The Challenge of Partnership: A National Foster Care Charter*. London: NFCA.

Lupton, C. and Gillespie, T. (eds) (1994) *Working With Violence*. Practical Social Work, BASW. Basingstoke: Macmillan.

Lynes, D. and Goddard, J. (1995) *The View from the Front: The User View of Child Care in Norfolk*. Norwich: Norfolk County Council SSD.

Lyon, C. and Parton, N. (1995) 'Children's Rights and the Children Act 1989'. In B. Franklin (ed) *The Handbook of Children's Rights: Comparative Policy and Practice*. London: Routledge.

Maginnis, E. (1993) 'An Interagency Response to Children with Special Needs – the Lothian Experience'. Paper presented to National Children's Bureau Conference: Exclusions from School – Bridging the Gap between Policy and Practice, 13 July, London.

Mather, M., Humphrey, J. and Robson, J. (1997) 'The statutory medical and health needs of looked after children. Time for a radical review?' *Adoption and Fostering 21*, 2, 36–39.

McAndrew, G. (1998) 'The voice of the people'. *Community Care. Inside Adoption and Fostering*, 27 August–2 September, 6–7.

McCann, J., James, A., Wilson, S. and Dunn, G. (1996) 'Prevalence of psychiatric disorders in young people in the care system'. *British Medical Journal 1313*, 1529–1530.

McCaughan, N. (1992) 'Speaking out: Setting up a forum of young users'. *Children and Society 6*, 3, 241–249.

McMillen, J.C. (1997) 'Independent living services: The views of former foster youth'. *Families in Society*, September/October, 471–479.

Meegan, F. (1997) *Business Support for Young People Leaving Care: A Very Positive Response*. London: Who Cares? Trust, The Prince's Trust and Business in the Community.

Miedema, B. and Nason-Clark, N. (1997) 'Foster care redesign: The dilemma contemporary foster families face'. *Community Alternatives 9*, 2, 15–27.

Mill, J.S. (1972) *Utilitarianism, On Liberty, and Considerations on Representative Government*. London: JM Dent and Sons Ltd.

Miller, A. (1998) 'Bringing up baby'. *Community Care 1235*, 13–19 August, 21.

Ministerial Group on the Family (1998) *Supporting Families*. London: The Stationery Office.

Moore, S.T. and Kelly, M.J. (1996) 'Quality now: Moving human services towards a consumer orientation to service quality'. *Social Work 41*, 1, 33–40.

Morgan, P. (1998) *Adoption and the Care of Children*. London: Institute of Economic Affairs.

Morris, S., Wheatley, H. and Lees, B. (1994) *Time to Listen. The Experiences of Children and Young People in Foster and Residential Care*. London: ChildLine.

Morris, T. (1989) *Crime and Criminal Justice Since 1945*. Oxford: Blackwell/ICBH.

Newsome, M. (1992) 'The impact of the past on the care and education of deprived children'. *Children and Society 6*, 151–162.

NFCA (no date) *Managing Behaviour: A National Foster Care Handout*. London: NFCA.

NFCA (1997) *Foster Care Finance/Minimum Allowances 1998*. Part Three, 10. London: NFCA.

NHS/HAS (1995) *Child and Adolescent Mental Health Services: Together We Stand*. London: HMSO.

Nixon, S. (1997) 'The limits of support in foster care'. *British Journal of Social Work 27*, 913–930.

NSPCC (1976) *At Risk: An Account of the Work of the Battered Baby Child Research Department, NSPCC*. London: Routledge and Kegan Paul.

O'Neill, T. (1981) *A Place Called Hope*. Oxford: Blackwell.

Osborn, A. and Sinclair, L. (1987) 'The ability and behaviour of children who have been in care or separated from their parents'. *Early Child Development and Care 28*, 3, 187–354.

Owen, S. (1989) 'The unobjectionable service: A legislative history of childminding'. *Children and Society 2*, 367–382.

Packman, J. (1968) *Child Care: Needs and Numbers*. London: Allen & Unwin.

Packman, J. and Hall, C. (1996) *Draft Report on the Implementation of Section 20 of the Children Act 1989*. Totnes: Dartington SRU.

Packman, J. and Hall, C. (1998) *From Care to Accommodation: Support, Protection and Control in Child Care Services*. London: The Stationery Office.

Packman, J. and Jordan, B. (1991) 'The Children Act: Looking forward, looking back'. *Children and Society 21*, 4, 315–327.

Parker, R.A. (1988) 'Residential care for children'. In I. Sinclair (ed) *Residential Care: The Research Reviewed*. London: HMSO.

Parker, R., Ward, H., Jackson, S., Aldgate, J. and Wedge, P. (1991) (eds) *Assessing Outcomes in Child Care*. London: HMSO.

Part, D. (1993) 'Fostering as seen by the carers' children'. *Adoption and Fostering 17*, 1, 26–31.

Parton, N. (1985) *The Politics of Child Abuse*. London: Macmillan.

Pearce, N. and Hillman, J. (1998) *Wasted Youth. Raising Achievement and Tackling Social Exclusion Amongst 14–19 year olds.* London: Institute of Public Policy Research.

Philpot, T. (1994) 'History of hope'. *Community Care,* 3–9 November, 28–29.

Pinchbeck, I. and Hewitt, M. (1969) *Children in English Society, Volume One: From Tudor Times to the Eighteenth Century.* London: Routledge and Kegan Paul.

Pinchbeck, I. and Hewitt, M. (1973) *Children in English Society, Volume Two: From the Eighteenth Century to the Children Act 1948.* London: Routledge and Kegan Paul.

Prins, H. (1975) 'A danger to themselves and others'. *British Journal of Social Work 5,* 297–309.

Pugh, G. (1996) 'Seen but not heard? Addressing the needs of children who foster'. *Adoption and Fostering 20,* 1, 35–41.

Quine, L. and Pahl, J. (1986) 'Parents with severely handicapped children: Marriage and the stress of caring'. In R. Chester and P. Divall (eds) *Mental Health, Illness and Handicap in Marriage.* Rugby: NMGC Research Group, Report 5.

RAPP (1998) *Which Way Now? Young People's Experiences of Leaving Care.* London: Save the Children.

Redding, D. (1989) 'The little slavies'. *Community Care,* 4 May, 19–20.

Rhodes, P. (1993) 'Like any other job: Paying for foster carers'. *Foster Care 75,* October, 6–7.

Roberts, N. and Morey, P. (1992) *Survey of Local Authority Provision for Young People Leaving Care.* Leeds: First Key/DoH.

Robinson, P. (1998) 'Education, training and the youth market'. In P. Greg and J. Wadsworth (eds) *The State of Working Britain.* London: Centre for Economic Performance, London School of Economics.

Rollinson, R. (1998) '50 years of helping troubled children'. Paper presented at: Who is Responsible for Me? 50th Anniversary of the Mulberry Bush School Conference, 14 September, Royal College of Physicians, London.

Rosser, N. and Tweedie, N. (1997) 'Billie-Jo: Foster father arrested'. *Evening Standard,* 24 February, 1.

Rowe, J., Caine, M., Hundleby, M. and Keane, A. (1984) *Long-Term Foster Care.* London: Batsford.

Rowe, J. and Lambert, L. (1973) *Children Who Wait.* London: ABAA.

Rutter, M. (1985) 'Family and school influences: meanings, mechanisms and implications'. In A.R. Nichol (ed) *Longitudinal Studies in Child Psychology and Psychiatry.* New York: John Wiley and Son.

Rutter, M. (1997) 'An update on resilience: Conceptual considerations and empirical findings'. In S.J. Meisels and J.T. Shonkoff (eds) *Handbook of Early Childhood Intervention.* New York: Cambridge University Press.

Rutter, M., Maughan, B., Mortimore, P. and Custon, J. (1979) *Fifteen Thousand Hours: Secondary Schools and their Effects on Pupils.* London: Open Books.

Rutter, M., Quinton, P. and Liddle, C. (1983) 'Parenting in two generations: Looking back and looking forwards'. In N. Madge (ed) *Families at Risk.* London: Heinemann.

Rutter, M. and Smith, D. (1995) *Psychosocial Disorders in Young People. Time Trends and their Causes.* Published for Academis Europaea. Chichester: Wiley.

Ryan, M. (1999) *The Children Act 1989: Putting It Into Practice.* Aldershot: Ashgate Publishing.

Sammons, P., Hillman, J. and Mortimore, P. (1995) *Key Characteristics of Effective Schools.* London: Institute of Education/OFSTED.

Saunders, L. and Broad, B. (1997) *The Health Needs of Young People Leaving Care.* Leicester: De Montford University, Centre for Social Action.

Saunders, L. and Broad, B. (1998) 'Involving young people leaving care as peer researchers in a health research project: A learning experience'. *Research, Policy and Planning 16*, 1, 1–9.

Sellick, C. (1996) 'Short term foster care'. In M. Hill and J. Aldgate (eds) *Child Welfare Services*. London: Jessica Kingsley Publishers.

Shaw, M. and Hipgrave, T. (1989) 'Specialist fostering – 1988. A research study'. *Adoption and Fostering 13*, 3, 17–21.

Sime, N., Pattie, C. and Gray, J. (1990) *What Now? The Transition from School to the Labour Market amongst 16 to 19 Year Olds*. England and Wales Youth Cohort Study 62. Sheffield: Training Agency Research and Development.

Sinclair, I. and Gibbs, I. (1996) *Quality of Care in Children's Homes. Report to the Department of Health*. York: University of York.

Sinclair, I. and Gibbs, I. (1998) *Childrens' Homes: A study in Diversity*. Chichester: John Wiley and Sons.

Sinclair, R. (1997) *The Education of Children in Need*. London: National Children's Bureau/ Dartington Research in Practice.

Sinclair, R., Garnett, L. and Berridge, D. (1995) *Social Work and Assessments with Adolescents*. London: NCB.

Smith, C. (ed) (1998) *Leaving Care: Messages From Young People*. London: RPS Rainer.

Social Exclusion Unit (1998) *Truancy and School Exclusion*. London: SRU.

Sone, K. (1997) 'Moving stories'. *Community Care 1156*, 30 January, 20–21.

SSI (1997) '... *When Leaving Home is Also Leaving Care* ...': *An Inspection of Services for Young People Leaving Care*. Wetherby: DoH.

SSI (1998a) *Social Services Facing the Future: The Seventh Annual Report of the Social Services Inspectorate, 1997/98*. London: The Stationery Office.

SSI (1998b) *Someone Else's Children: Inspections of Planning and Decision Making for Children Looked After and The Safety of Children Looked After*. Wetherby: DoH.

SSI/OFSTED (1995) *The Education of Children Who are Looked After by Local Authorities*. London: HMSO.

Stein, M. (1994) 'Leaving care, education and career trajectories'. *Oxford Review of Education 20*, 3, 348–360.

Stein, M. (1998) *Leaving Care. Fact Sheet*. London: The Prince's Trust.

Stein, M. and Carey, K. (1986) *Leaving Care*. Oxford: Blackwell.

Stewart, J. (1995) 'Children, parents and the state: The Children Act 1908'. *Children and Society 9*, 1, 90–99.

Stone, M. (1990) *Young People Leaving Care*. London: Royal Philanthropic Society.

Thompson, A. (1996) 'Nurturing danger'. *Community Care 1144*, 31 October–6 November.

Thompson, A. (1998) 'Protect and survive'. *Community Care 1245*, 22–28 October, 22–25.

Triseliotis, J. (1989) 'Foster care outcomes: A review of key research findings'. *Adoption and Fostering 13*, 3, 5–16.

Triseliotis, J., Borland, M. and Hill, M. (1998) *Fostering Good Relations: A Study of Foster Care and Foster Carers in Scotland*. The Scottish Office Central Unit. Edinburgh: The Stationery Office.

Triseliotis, J., Sellick, C. and Short, R. (1995) *Foster Care: Theory and Practice*. London: B.T. Batsford in association with BAAF.

UK Joint Working Party on Foster Care (1999) *Report and Recommendations on Foster Care*. London: National Foster Care Association.

Utting, W. (1991) *Children in the Public Care.* London: HMSO.

Utting, W. (1997) *People Like Us: The Report of the Review of Safeguards for Children Living Away From Home.* Department of Health/Welsh Office. London: The Stationery Office.

Valios, N. (1996) 'Report reveals scale of missing runaways'. *Community Care 1146,* 14–20 November, 1.

Van Der Spek, N. (1998) *The Post-Sixteen Educational Participation and Performance of 'Looked After' Children.* Research report prepared for Thames Valley Enterprise Ltd.

Veash, N. and Thomas, R. (1999) 'Dramatic end to runaway saga'. *Observer,* 17 January, 6–7.

Vernon, J. and Sinclair, R. (1998) *Maintaining Children in Schools. The Contribution of Social Services Departments.* London: NCB/Joseph Rowntree Foundation.

von Gontard, A. (1988) 'The development of child psychiatry in 19th century Britain'. *Journal of Child Psychology and Psychiatry in Britain and Allied Disciplines 29,* 569–588.

Wagner, G. (Chair) (1988) *Residential Care – Positive Answers.* Final Report of the Wagner Development Group. London: HMSO.

Walker, T. (1998) 'Educating looked after children'. *Young Minds Magazine 37,* 10–11.

Walvin, J. (1972) *A Child's World: A Social History of English Childhood, 1800–1914.* Harmondsworth: Penguin Books.

Ward, A. (1998) Responses to the Utting Report: People Like Us. Training needs and the Utting Report. *Children's Residential Care Newsletter 8,* Spring, 4–5.

Ward, H. (ed) (1995) *Looking After Children: Research into Practice.* London: HMSO.

Ward, H. (1996) 'Constructing and implementing measures to assess the outcomes of looking after children away from home'. In M. Hill and J. Aldgate (eds) *Child Welfare Services: Developments in Law, Policy, Practice and Research.* London: Jessica Kingsley Publishers.

Ward, H., Jackson, S., Aldgate, J. and Wedge, P. (1991) *Looking After Children: Assessing Outcomes in Child Care.* London: HMSO.

Warnock, H.M. (Chair) (1978) Special Educational Needs. *Report of the Committee of Inquiry into the Education of Handicapped Children and Young People.* London: HMSO.

Warren, D. (1997a) *Foster Care in Crisis.* London: NFCA.

Warren, D. (1997b) Serious failings in the 'Cinderella' service. *Children UK,* Summer, 4–5.

Waterhouse, S. (1992) 'How foster carers view contact'. *Adoption and Fostering 16,* 2, 42–47.

Waterhouse, S. (1997) *The Organisation of Fostering Services: A Study of the Arrangements for Delivery of Fostering Services in England.* London: NFCA.

Wellard, S. (1998) 'Out of mind'. *Community Care 1248,* 12–18 November, 22–23.

West, A. (1995) *You're on Your Own: Young People's Research on Leaving Care.* London: Save the Children.

West, A. (1996) 'You're on your own now'. *Young People Now,* pp.30–31.

Wilding, P. (1994) *Welfare and Ideology.* London: Harvester Wheatsheaf.

Williamson, H. (1997) 'Status zero youth and the "underclass": Some considerations'. In R. MacDonald (ed) *Youth, the "Underclass" and Social Exclusion.* London: Routledge.

Wilson, P. (1993) 'A Crisis in Residential Childcare and Therapy'. *Young Minds 13,* 2–4.

Winter, K. and Connolly, P. (1996) '"Keeping it in the family": Thatcherism and the Children Act 1989'. In J. Pilcher and S. Wagg (eds) *Thatcher's Children?: Politics, Childhood and Society in the 1980s and 1990s.* London: Falmer Press.

Wolkind, S.N. (1977) 'Women who have been "in care": Psychological and social status in pregnancy'. *Journal of Child Psychology and Psychiatry 18,* 179–182.

Subject Index

abuse 63
  by a fostered child 55
  in foster families 89
  of looked after children 94
  within the child care
    system 9, 40–41
  see also child abuse
accommodation, for children
  in need 32–3
Action and Assessment
  Records 48, 173
adoption 199–200
After-Care Policy 148
Area Review Committees 26
Assessing Outcomes in Child Care
  49

'baby farming' 19–20
'battered baby syndrome' 25
Beckford Inquiry 26–7
behaviour
  attention seeking
    behaviour, and foster
    children 103
  and entry into care 53
  of looked after children
    41–2, 91–2, 200
  range of problem
    behaviours 101–3
  threatening behaviour
    experienced by foster
    carers 100–101
  experienced by residential
    staff 97–100
  types and reasons for 93–4
behavioural difficulties 93–6
  and foster care 92–3
biological theories of
  behaviour 93
boarding-out system 16, 18,
  22
Bridge Report 197

British Association of Social
  Workers (BASW) 24, 75
bullying 95–6
Caldecott Community 193
care
  and control 41–3
  entry into 53–4
care experience, children's
  views 170–71
care leavers see leaving care
care managers' perspectives,
  education 127–9
care order 10, 24
careers, and leaving care 148
careers advice, and leaving
  care 149–52
Caring for Children and Young
  People (Open University)
  157
Catholic Children's Society
  20
Central Council for the
  Education and Training
  of Social Workers
  (CCETSW),
  establishment 24
The Challenge of Foster Care
  (NFCA) 157
Charterhouse Group 193
child abuse 26–7, 34, 176
  in the nineteen seventies
    25–6
  in the nineteenth century
    19–20
child care, before 1834
  15–16
child guidance clinics 21
child protection 19–20, 34
Child Protection: Messages from
  Research 34, 35
child welfare 34
child-centredness 161
childhood, definition 15–16,
  17, 18
Childline 95
children, in the welfare state
  (1945–89) 21–5
Children Act (1908) 17, 20

Children Act (1948) 23
Children Act (1975) 25
Children Act (1989) 9–10,
  13, 27–9, 113, 134,
  135, 193, 199
  themes and issues 31–5
Children and Young Persons
  Act (1933) 20
Children and Young Persons
  Act (1963) 23
children's homes, and external
  consultancy 108
Children's Legal Centre 26
children's rights 47
  and consultation 32
children's rights approach
  175–6
Church of England Waifs and
  Strays Society 20
Cleveland case 27, 31
Clyde Report 23
Colwell enquiry 25
'coming into care' 53–4
Commissions for Care
  Standards 209
Community Homes with
  Education (CHEs) 115
complaints procedures 187
consultation, and children's
  rights 32
consultation and information
  files 181–6
  moving home 183
contiuum of services 193
control, and care 41–3
corporate parenting 112,
  129, 173
Crime – A Challenge to Us All
  23
Crime and Disorder Act
  (1998), impact on
  families 35
crises, and looked after
  children 172
Curtis Committee 22–3
decision-making
  at reviews and case
    conferences 179–81

everyday decision-making, and young people 177–9
involvement of young people 177, 183–6
deprivation 23
links with delinquancy 29
Dr Barnardo's 20
and emigration 19
'drift', and looked after young people 34–5
education
before 1834 16
care managers' perspectives 127–9
of looked after children 13, 43–5, 111–32, 118–19, 200–2
post-sixteen education, and looked after children 119, 122–3, 125–7, 131–2
Education Act (1870) 18
Education Act (1997) 149
educational achievement, of looked after children 116–17
educational support services 201
Emergency Protection Orders 27
emigration 18–19
emotional and behavioural difficulties 93–6
ethnicity
and foster care 52
and race 39–40
evacuation 22
evaluation, of child care 173–4
exclusion from school 108, 114–16, 123–4
expectations, of looked after children 116
external consultancy, and children's homes 108
families 24, 25
family breakdown 52, 63

family circumstances, and entry into care 51–2
Family Law Act (1996) 27
family link social workers (FLSWs) 165, 166
family placement 11
family placement social workers (FPSWs) 165, 166
family preservation 199
Family Rights Group 26, 27
family support 34
family-based care, and institutional care 29
Fifteen Thousand Hours 112
files, consultation and information 181–6
First Key 142, 211
foster care 13, 73, 194–7
and behavioural problems 92–3, 103
expense 75
how children come into 65–8
impact on foster families 77–8, 84–5, 89
impact on young people looked after 85–7
and leaving care experience 144–5
National Standards 74
overview of literature 51–8
planning of placements 60–63
problems 195
professionalisation 75–6, 87, 88–9, 90, 155–6, 196–7
quality 161–2
and race 52
and residential care 35–8
reviews 74–5
role in services for looked after children, research project 217–18
and violent behaviour 106–7
foster carers

experience of threatening behaviour 100–101
feeling valued 166
level of acceptable fee 83
money and motivation 81–4
motivation 77, 78–81, 87
perception of role 79
support for 158, 159–60, 165–8
training 155, 157–8, 164–5, 202–3
value of support 167
foster families, abuse in 89

GCSE results, of looked after young people 124–5
General Social Care Council 209

health
of looked after children 42–3
mental health problems of looked after young people 198
The Health Needs of Young People Leaving Care 47
high achievers, from the care system 201
Home and Hospital Teaching Service (HHTS) 123–4
home tuition 115
Houghton Report 25
Housing Act (1996) 134
Howe inquiry 47

'in care', definition 14
Industrial Schools 20
Industrial Schools Act (1861) 18
Infant Life Protection Acts (1872 and 1897) 20
Ingleby Report 23
institutional care, and family-based care 29
inter-agency cooperation 135–6, 148, 191, 203–4
intervention, by social service departments 29

'joined-up government' 204
juvenile court 20

Labour government 9, 205
laissez-faire approach 31
leaving care 13, 45–6,
    133–54, 197–8
    and careers 148
    and careers advice 149–52
    experience 139–40
    first six months 142–5
    grants 142
    life after 145–8
    preparation 140–42
    study 12
    vulnerability 197
Local Authority Social
    Services Act (1970) 24
looked after children
    abuse of 94
    Action and Assessment
        Records 48
    aspirations 138–9
    behaviour 41–2, 91–2,
        200
        range of problem
            behaviours 101–3
    and crises 172
    definition 10, 14
    education 13, 43–5,
        111–32, 200–2
    post-sixteen education
        119, 122–3,
        125–7, 131–2
    post-sixteen educational
        participation and
        performance,
        research project
        218–21
    educational achievement
        116–17
    experience of school
        120–22
    health 42–3
    placement, changes in
        number and type 36
    policy developments for
        210
    see also young people

looked after young people
    and 'drift' 34–5
    GCSE results 124–5
    "Looking After Children" 50

Modern Apprenticeships 136
Modernising Social Services
    White Paper 10, 50, 74,
    209, 211
Monckton Inquiry 22
motivation, in foster care 77,
    78–81
moving home, consultation
    and information 183
multiple placements, and
    placement breakdown
    56–8

National Association of Care
    Leavers 211
National Association of
    Young People in Care
    (NAYPIC) 185, 211
National Children's Bureau
    24, 26
National Children's Home 20
National Foster Care
    Association (NFCA) 38,
    76, 157, 195
neglect 63
NSPCC 20, 25

O'Neill case 22
out of school provision
    223–4

'paramountcy principle' 28
Patterns and Outcomes in Child
    Placement 49
Peper Harrow Foundation
    193
permanency 24–5
physical restraint 58–9, 99,
    104–5
    research project 213–15
'pindown' 40, 47
placement breakdown 54, 70,
    81
    defined 57
    and multiple placements
        56–8
placement(s)

availability and choice
    38–9
    changes in number and
        type 36
    choice and availability
        54–6
    inappropriate 55, 68, 108
    policy developments, for
        looked after children
        210
Poor Law Act (1601) 16
Poor Law Amendment Act
    (1834), and state child
    care 17–21
post-sixteen educational
    participation and
    performance of looked
    after children, research
    project 218–21
Prevention of Cruelty to
    Children Act (1889) 20
professionalisation, of foster
    care 75–6, 90
programme abuse 40
psychological approach to
    child care 21
psychological theories of
    behaviour 93
Pupil Referral Units (PRUs)
    115
Pupils with Problems 44, 113

Quality Protects initiative 10,
    35, 54, 74, 114, 160,
    205–9

race
    and ethnicity 39–40
    and foster care 52
residential care 156, 192–4
    case studies, placement and
        care issues 64
    cost 37
    and foster care 35–8
    how children come into
        63–5
    overview of literature 51–8
    planning of placements
        58–60
    quality 160–61

staff training 162–3
study 10–11
support for staff 164–5
and violent behaviour 104–6
Residential Child Care Initiative (RCCI) 157
residential staff
experience of threatening behaviour 97–100
training 157
rights-based approach 26

school attendance 114–16
Seebohm Report 24
self-esteem 117
service quality 47–8, 160–62
significant harm 31
and state intervention 33
social democratic approach, to child care policy 23
social exclusion 204–5
social policy for children, origins 16
Social Security Act (1986) 134
social workers
and foster carers 80, 88, 159
views of looked after children 168–9, 171
social-psychological theories of behaviour 93
socio-cultural theories of behaviour 93
Special Children's Grant 208
special educational needs 117–18
specialist provision, move away from 108
state child care
after Poor Law Amendment Act (1834) 17–21
policy alternatives 198–9
shortcomings 192
state intervention 28
and significant harm 33
state paternalism 31

'Status ZerO' 137
stigma, of care background 146
support, for carers 158–60
support groups, for foster carers 159
system abuse 41, 129

The Child, the Family and the Young Offender 23
therapeutic residential environments 193
Total Quality Management (TQM) 47–8
training 155, 157–8, 171
of staff and carers 202–3

user group politics 211–12
user view of child care in Norfolk, research project 215–16
user view of child care services, study 11
user views, of the child care system 46–7
Utting Report 38, 41

verbal abuse, in residential care 101–2
Violence to Children 26
violent behaviour
and foster care 106–7
and residential care 104–6
Voice of the Child in Care 32
'voluntary care' 32–3
voluntary child care organisations 20–21

Warner Report 157
'Waters case' (1872) 20
welfare checklist 34–5
welfare state (1945–89), and children 21–5
West case 197
Who Cares? Trust 178, 179, 182

young offenders 23–4
young people
and everyday decision-making 177–9
involvement in decision-making 175–7, 183–6
see also looked after children
You're On Your Own: Young People's Research on Leaving Care 47
Youth Training Guarantee scheme 136
youth transitions 136–7

Author Index

Action on Aftercare
    Consortium 133
ADSS 52, 68, 74, 75, 82, 88,
    107, 161, 196
Aldgate, J. 43, 57, 92, 118,
    131
Ames Reed, J. 77
Aries, P. 15
Asthana, S. 112
Audit Commission 111, 115,
    135, 148, 203

Baines, B. 48
Baker, A. 199
Baldry, S. 74
Baldwin, D. 134
Balloch, S. 204, 209
Bamford, F.N. 42, 93
Bax, M. 42
Baxter, S. 81
Bebbington, A. 51, 52, 75,
    157
Beckford, Jasmin 26
Berridge, D. 37, 38, 39, 40,
    42, 49, 50, 52, 53, 55,
    57, 58, 73, 76, 81, 88,
    91, 94, 107, 116, 118,
    156, 158, 159, 160,
    164, 172, 173, 174,
    188, 193, 194, 195,
    198, 209
Biehal, N. 43, 44, 117, 118,
    133, 148, 197
Blau, G.M. 41, 93
Blyth, E. 120
Borland, M. 77
Brandon, M. 15
Broad, B. 44, 47, 119, 197
Brodie, I. 37, 40, 49, 53, 58,
    91, 94, 107, 116, 156,
    160, 164, 172, 173,
    174, 188, 193, 194,
    198
Bullock, R. 51
Butler, I. 42
Butler, N. 111

Cambridgeshire County
    Council 160
Carey, K. 45, 47, 133
Caveney, S. 173
Chaplain, R. 156, 161
CIPFA 37
Clark, S. 78
Clayden, J. 44
Cleaver, H. 42, 43, 57, 81,
    92, 96, 158
Cliffe, D. 39, 52, 55, 159
Coles, B. 134, 136
Collins, S. 78
Colton, M. 38, 43, 161, 196
Connolly, P. 28, 29
Cooper, J.D. 24
CSO 37, 213
Cunningham, P. 22

Dando, I. 78
Daniel, P. 24, 25
Dartington SRU 34
Davie, R. 111
Davies, W.R. 197
Davin, A. 17
de Cruz, P. 40
DfEE 115, 117, 200, 201,
    204
Dickens, Charles 19
Dodd, V. 199
DoH 9, 10, 28, 31, 35, 37,
    39, 41, 45, 49, 50, 52,
    53, 54, 55, 74, 113,
    119, 133, 135, 154,
    155, 157, 173, 183,
    185, 191, 192, 193,
    196, 197, 198, 199,
    200, 202, 206, 207,
    208, 209, 211
DOH/SSI 37, 43, 56, 74,
    88, 91, 156, 161, 196
Donnison, D. 23
Doorbar, P. 77
Douglas, J.W.B. 111

DSS 204
Essen, J. 117
First Key 14, 211
Firth, H. 116, 118
Fletcher, B. 14, 87, 121, 177,
    178, 179, 182, 183,
    186
Fletcher-Campbell, F. 43,
    112, 118, 119, 131
Foucault, M. 18
Fox Harding, L. 21, 23, 31,
    175
Franklin, A. 26
Franklin, B. 26, 176
Freeman, A. 156, 161
Freeman, M. 176
Frost, N. 14, 16, 17, 33, 48,
    49, 101, 194

Gardner, P. 22
Garnett, L. 118
Garnett, L. 42
George, M. 198
Gerrard, B. 48
Gerrard, N. 195
Gibbons, J. 199
Gibbs, I. 69, 76, 91, 95, 161,
    194
Gibson, A. 112
Gil, E. 40
Gillespie, T. 97
Goddard, J. 11, 47, 78, 87,
    119, 129, 137, 138,
    162, 168, 198, 216,
    221
Goldson, B. 24
Goldstein, H. 111
Goldstein, S. 93
Gorin, S. 11, 58, 63, 76, 77,
    78, 88, 94, 157, 162,
    217, 218
Graham, P.J. 95
Grant, J. 78
Gray, J. 45
Gullotta, T.P. 41, 93

Hall, C. 33, 41, 43, 91, 95,
    118
Hallett, C. 135
Harrison, S. 175

Hart, H. 42
Hawley, D. 57, 92
Hayden, C. 10, 42, 58, 63, 76, 108, 115, 116, 162, 172, 194, 204
Hazelhurst, M. 45, 133
Head, J. 117
Heath, A. 43, 114, 116
Hendrick, H. 17, 18, 19, 26
Hersov, L. 21
Hester, M. 97
Hewitt, M. 16, 18
Heywood, J. 16
Hill, M. 14, 77, 114, 186
Hillman, J. 112, 136, 137
Hipgrave, T. 159
Hodgkin, R. 176
Holman, B. 23
Home Department 22
Horrocks, C. 116
House of Commons 26, 49, 50, 75, 76, 90, 111, 115, 117, 135, 175, 176
Howe, E. 32, 47, 175
Hudson, J.R. 158
Humphrey, J. 42

Inman, K. 55, 195, 209
Ivatts, J. 24, 25

Jackson, S. 42, 43, 51, 52, 113, 114, 116, 117, 118, 123, 140, 201
Jay, P. 23
Jenkins, S. 42
Jesson, D. 45
Jones, G. 197
Jones, K. 16, 17, 18, 24
Jordon, B. 28

Kahan, B. 9, 38, 39, 42, 47, 56, 91, 92, 156, 173
Keane, A. 92
Kelly, G. 92
Kelly, J. 55
Kelly, M.J. 48
Kelly, S. 193
Kemmis, J. 74
Kendrick, A. 40, 54, 56, 74, 118

Kent, P. 32
Kirkwood, A. 9, 41
Knapp, M. 48
Knight, T. 173
Kraemer, S. 193

Lambert, L. 117
Lambert, M. 39
Lees, B. 40
Levy, A. 9, 47
Liddle, C. 92
Lindsay, M. 187
Little, M. 51, 193
Lowe, K. 159
Lowe, M. 76
Lupton, C. 97
Lynes, D. 11, 13, 47, 78, 87, 119, 129, 137, 138, 162, 168, 198, 216
Lyon, C. 176

McAndrew, G. 197
McCann, J. 95, 101
McCaughan, N. 175
McMillen, J.C. 77
Maginnis, E. 115
Martin, P.Y. 42, 201
Martin, T. 116
Mather, M. 42
Mather, N. 43
Meegan, F. 135
Miedema, B. 77
Miles, J. 51, 52, 75, 157
Mill, J.S. 19
Miller, A. 208
Millham, S. 51
Mills, S. 17
Milner, J. 120
Ministerial Group on the Family 204, 205
Minty, B. 78
Mitchell, W. 134
Moore, S.T. 48
Morey, P. 142
Morgan, P. 199
Morris, S. 29, 40, 95, 96
Mort, M. 175
Mortimore, P. 112

Nason-Clark, N. 77
Newsome, M. 30

NHS/HAS 95
Nixon, S. 89, 158
NSPCC 25

O'Neill, T. 22
Osborn, A. 51, 117
Owen, S. 20

Packman, J. 28, 33, 41, 52, 91, 95
Pahl, J. 52
Parker, R. 42
Parker, R.A. 57, 58
Part, D. 77
Parton, N. 25, 176
Pattie, C. 45
Payne, H. 42
Pearce, N. 136, 137
Philpot, T. 22
Pierson, J. 32
Pinchbeck, I. 16, 18
Prins, H. 97
Pugh, G. 78, 195

Quine, L. 52
Quinton, P. 92

RAPP 47
Redding, D. 19
Rhodes, P. 77
Roberts, N. 142
Robinson, P. 137
Robson, J. 42
Rollinson, R. 194
Rosser, N. 195
Rowe, J. 39, 77
Rutter, M. 42, 52, 92, 95, 112, 200
Ryan, M. 27, 29, 38

Sammons, P. 112
Saunders, L. 47
Schofield, J. 15
Sellick, C. 75, 159
Shaw, M. 159
Short, R. 75
Sime, N. 45
Sinclair, I. 69, 76, 91, 95, 161, 194
Sinclair, L. 51, 117
Sinclair, R. 42, 116
Smith, C. 47

Smith, D. 95, 200
Social Exclusion Unit 111,
    114, 191, 205
Social Services Research and
    Information Unit
    (SSRIU) 213
Sone, K. 56, 57
SSI (Social Services
    Inspectorate) 9, 34, 35,
    37, 39, 47, 115, 134,
    160, 187, 205
SSI/OFSTED 43, 44, 114,
    116, 117, 119, 131,
    161
Stein, M. 16, 17, 44, 45, 47,
    93, 117, 133, 197
Stewart, M. 23
Stone, M. 45, 47

Thomas, R. 195
Thompson, A. 78, 207
Thornton, B. 32
Tijani, B. 45, 133
Tisdall, K. 14, 114, 186
Townsend, P. 199
Trinder, L. 15
Triseliotis, J. 57, 75, 77, 88,
    157, 158, 159
Tweedie, N. 195

Utting, W. 9, 38, 39, 40, 41,
    43, 45, 46, 47, 53, 54,
    56, 68, 73, 74, 76, 78,
    104, 113, 133, 135,
    156, 157, 171, 175,
    192, 194, 195, 202

Valios, N. 197
Van Der Spek, N. 12, 119,
    122, 129, 137, 148,
    2221
Veash, N. 195
von Gontard, A. 21

Wagner, G. 113
Walvin, J. 20, 21
Ward, A. 158
Ward, H. 49
Warnock, H.M. 95
Warren, D. 68, 73, 76, 88,
    107, 156, 195, 203

Waterhouse, S. 37, 52, 54,
    74, 82, 87, 88, 196
Wellard, S. 200
West, A. 45, 47, 142, 177
Wheatley, H. 40
Wilding, P. 48
Williamson, H. 136, 137
Wilson, P. 175
Winter, K. 28, 29
Wolkind, S.N. 42, 92, 93